Organizational and Work Psychology

Organizational and Work Psychology

Topics in Applied Psychology

Ian Rothmann
Cary Cooper

HODDER
EDUCATION
PART OF HACHETTE LIVRE UK

First published in Great Britain in 2008 by
Hodder Education, part of Hachette Livre UK, 338 Euston Road, London NW1 3BH

www.hoddereducation.com

© 2008 **Ian Rothmann and Cary Cooper**

The advice and information in this book are believed to be true and
accurate at the date of going to press, but neither the authors nor the publisher
can accept any legal responsibility or liability for any errors or omissions.

Every effort has been made to trace and acknowledge the owners of copyright.
The publishers will be glad to make suitable arrangements with any
copyright holders whom it has not been possible to contact.

British Library Cataloguing in Publication Data
A catalogue record for this book is available from the British Library

Library of Congress Cataloging-in-Publication Data
A catalog record for this book is available from the Library of Congress

ISBN 978 0 340 92891 2

1 2 3 4 5 6 7 8 9 10

Cover & section opener © James Steidl/IStockphoto.com
Typeset in 10pt Berling Roman by Servis Filmsetting Ltd., Manchester
Printed and bound in Malta

What do you think about this book? Or any other Hodder
Education title? Please send your comments to the
feedback section on www.hoddereducation.com.

Contents

Series preface

Psychology is still one of the most popular subjects for study at undergraduate degree level. As well as providing the student with a range of academic and applied skills that are valued by a broad range of employers, a psychology degree also serves as the basis for subsequent training and a career in professional psychology. A substantial proportion of students entering a degree programme in Psychology do so with a subsequent career in applied psychology firmly in mind, and as a result, the number of applied psychology courses available at undergraduate level has significantly increased over recent years. In some cases, these courses supplement core academic areas and in others, they provide the student with a flavour of what they might experience as a professional psychologist.

Topics in Applied Psychology represents a series of six textbooks designed to provide a comprehensive academic and professional insight into specific areas of professional psychology. The texts cover the areas of **Clinical Psychology, Criminal Psychology, Educational Psychology, Health Psychology, Sports and Exercise Psychology**, and **Organizational and Work Psychology**, and each text is written and edited by the foremost professional and academic figures in each of these areas.

Each textbook is based on a similar academic formula which combines a comprehensive review of cutting-edge research and professional knowledge with accessible teaching and learning features. The books are also structured to be used as an integrated teaching support for a one-term or one-semester course in each of their relevant areas of applied psychology. Given the increasing importance of applying psychological knowledge across a growing range of areas of practice, we feel this series is timely and comprehensive. We hope you find each book in the series readable, enlightening, accessible and instructive.

Graham Davey
University of Sussex, Brighton, UK
September 2007

Preface

Organizational and Work Psychology is an academic subject and a profession which focuses on human behaviour related to organizations, work and productivity. It applies psychological principles to the workplace. The purpose of this book is to introduce the undergraduate psychology student to both academic and professional aspects of organizational and work psychology. The book begins with a chapter to give the reader an insight into the domain of organizational and work psychology, the development of the field of organizational and work psychology, tasks and competencies of organizational and work psychologists, and careers in organizational and work psychology. The rest of the book is then divided into thirteen chapters which address the fields of organizational psychology and work psychology. Organizational psychology includes individual differences and diversity (Chapter 2), motivation (Chapter 3), group behaviour (Chapter 4), communication (Chapter 5), leadership (Chapter 6), well-being and dysfunctional behaviour at work (Chapter 13), and organizational design, development and culture (Chapter 14). Work psychology includes human resource planning and job analysis (Chapter 7), recruitment and selection (Chapter 8), induction, training and development (Chapter 9), compensation management (Chapter 10), performance appraisal (Chapter 11), and career development (Chapter 12).

As with all the books in the *Topics in Applied Psychology* series, this text is written as a support for a one-term or one-semester course in Organizational and Work Psychology, and contains all the teaching and learning features appropriate to the series, including focus boxes on research methods in organizational and work psychology and issues of theoretical, ethical or contemporary interest, and activity boxes that provide the student with the opportunity to engage in active learning. Each chapter also ends with extensive support for further reading, including relevant journal articles, books and websites, and this should enable the interested student to engage with a topic in some depth.

Ian Rothmann
Cary Cooper
September 2007

1 Introduction to organizational and work psychology

This first chapter introduces the reader to the field and history of **organizational** and **work psychology**, and the tasks and competencies of organizational and work psychologists. The first section describes the field of organizational and work psychology in terms of its two major sub-fields, namely **work psychology** (often referred to as **'human resource management'**), and organizational psychology (often referred to as **'organizational behaviour'**). We then look at how the various schools of thought about human **behaviour in** work and organizational context developed since the early 1900s, including **scientific management,** classical organizational theory, the Hawthorne studies, the human relations approach, **the socio-technical systems approach,** contingency theories, theories about **organizational transformation, organizational culture,** the learning organization, teamwork, **total quality management** and **positive psychology**. The chapter then proceeds to the tasks of organizational and work psychologists. Finally, we look at the competencies of organizational and work psychologists.

Learning outcomes

When you have completed this chapter you should be able to:

1. Define organizational and work psychology.
2. Describe the tasks of the organizational and work psychologist.
3. Summarize the activities of the organizational and work psychologist.
4. Explain the challenges for organizational and work psychologists.
5. Discuss the competencies of a organizational and work psychologist.
6. Identify the attractions and drawbacks of careers in organizational and work psychologists.

Definition of organizational and work psychology

Organizational and work psychology is defined as an applied division of psychology concerned with the study of human behaviour related to work, organizations and productivity (Cascio, 2001). Organizational and work psychologists are involved in research on employees and the application of psychological principles of that research to the workplace to help to optimize an organization's success. The term **'behaviour'** is defined as the sum of the responses, reactions and/or movements made by an organism in any situation.

Organizational and work psychologists help people to do their jobs and organizations to reach their objectives in the following ways:

1. Help employers to treat employees fairly, by ensuring fair treatment of people from diverse backgrounds, selecting people for jobs, providing training, rewarding promotions/raises, addressing harassment and assessing performance accurately.
2. Ensure interesting and satisfying jobs by creating rewarding work and safe, efficient work areas, motivating employees to perform, and creating teams that work well together by combining diverse talents and perspectives.
3. Help employees to be productive by designing work patterns that enhance **effectiveness** and **efficiency,** providing **skills** training and development, helping to meet the challenges of competition.

Organizational and work psychology is comprised of two branches, namely **Work Psychology** (also referred to as Industrial Psychology), and **Organizational Psychology**. Work Psychology is primarily concerned with issues that are more molecular in nature, while Organizational Psychology takes a molar approach. A molecular approach implies a focus on small units, while a molar approach refers to a focus on large units.

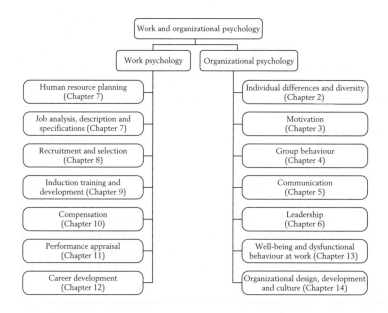

Figure 1.1 Fields of organizational and work psychology.

Organizational Psychology is directed at the behaviour of individuals, groups and organizations in the work situation. It focuses on the following topics (see Figure 1.1 for the chapters in which these sub-fields are discussed):

■ **Individual differences and diversity management**. Individual differences refer to differences between people regarding any characteristic, such as a personality trait, through which an individual could be distinguished from others. **Diversity** includes the mixture of many dimensions which makes people unique and different from each other.

■ **Motivation**. The term motivation refers to the factors which determine or regulate behaviour.

■ **Communication**. Communication is defined as the process by which a person, group or organization transmits information to another person.

■ **Leadership**. Leadership is the process whereby one individual influences other group members towards the attainment of defined group or organizational goals.

■ **Group dynamics**. Group dynamics refers to the dynamics of interaction in social groups.

■ **Health, safety and well-being**. A safe work environment is defined as one in which all the physical, electrical and mechanical conditions are of a sound nature. A healthy work environment is one in which no diseases occur. Wellness is a way of life oriented towards optimal well-being in which body, mind and spirit are integrated by the individual to live more fully.

■ **Organizational design and organizational development**. Organizational design is defined as the formal **system** of communication, authority and responsibility adopted by an organization which constitutes its internal structure. Organization development is defined as a long-range effort to improve an organization's ability to cope with change and its problem solving and renewal processes through effective management of the organizational culture.

Figure 1.1 shows that Work Psychology focuses on topics which are often covered in textbooks on human resource management, including:

■ **Human resource planning**. Human resource planning is a planned analysis of the present and future human resource needs of an organization and the implementation of action plans in order to ensure the adequate supply of human resources.

■ **Job analysis, description and job specifications**. Job analysis is defined as the process of gathering job information by breaking the job down into its components. A job description is a written summary of the key performance areas of a specific job. A job specification is a written explanation of the minimum requirements needed for effective performance on a given job.

■ **Recruitment and selection**. Recruitment is defined as the process of attracting suitable candidates to apply for vacancies that exist in an organization. Selection involves the sorting out of applicants for a vacant job and the elimination of those applicants who do not fit the requirements of the job and/or the organization.

■ **Induction and training**. Induction is defined as the introduction of new employees to the organization, work unit and job. Training is a form of job-specific education directed at improving the **knowledge,** skills and attitudes of employees.

- **Career development**. Career development is the process of guiding the placement, movement and the growth of employees through assessment, planned training activities and planned job assignments. It includes personal career planning and organizational career management.

- **Job evaluation and compensation**. Job evaluation involves rating of jobs through the use of a job evaluation plan, and conversion of relative job values to a definite wage rate. The total remuneration employees receive from work is called compensation. Compensation means the provision of a suitable return for services.

- **Performance appraisal**. Performance appraisal is the process by which the organization determines how effectively the employee is performing the job.

The development of the field of organizational and work psychology

Various approaches and theories contributed to the field of organizational and work psychology and contributed to its identity. Early contributions (including the scientific management approach) stressed efficient performance according to economic principles. **Classical organization theory** was concerned with the effective organization of people. The Hawthorne studies, in turn, stressed the social nature of human beings. This was followed by the **human relations movement,** which paid attention to aspects such as human needs, attitudes, motives and relationships. In contrast to an emphasis primarily on structure or the human side of organizations, organizational thought in the past few decades has emphasized the integration of these two perspectives. More recent development in the field of organization development (including the systems approach and **contingency theory**) also contributed to the field of organizational and work psychology. Lastly, the developments in positive psychology also impacted on the field of organizational and work psychology. Next, these developments will be reviewed in more detail.

Early contributions

Since the Industrial Revolution of the nineteenth century relatively large numbers of people started working together voluntarily in manager–subordinate relationships. The Industrial Revolution brought much technological change to the workplace. During this era, the emphasis was on the job being performed, not the person performing the job. Engineers focused on the development of efficient machines. They argued that if the machines which were used for the production of goods could be improved, greater efficiency would follow. Efficiency problems led engineers to start considering the people who were operating the machines. This, in turn, led to the implementation of time and motion studies. Through these studies attempts were made to design jobs so that they could be performed in the most efficient manner (Baron and Greenberg, 1990).

Scientific management

Scientific management is the name of the approach to organizational and work psychology initiated by Frederick Winslow Taylor. Scientific management was concerned with maximizing efficiency and getting the highest possible production out of employees. As an industrial engineer, he was concerned with inefficiencies in manual labour jobs and believed that by scientifically studying the specific motions that made up the total job, a more rational, objective and effective method of performing the job could be determined. This approach emphasized the design of jobs, so as to ensure that work tasks were planned in a systematic manner. Scientific management had two features. The first feature was that employees were to be carefully selected and trained for their jobs. Taylor also realized that motivation in work settings was very important. During this period, managers saw their job as increasing efficiency and were less interested in the well-being of workers (Furnham, 1997).

Taylor's ideas had a profound influence on the management practices and business thinking of his time, because it facilitated job specialization and mass production. However, labour unions opposed his ideas, because the goal of scientific management was to get more output from employees. Some government members thought that the implementation of his ideas would lead to the dehumanization of the workplace and to workers becoming robots.

Classical organization theory

Classical organization theory was concerned with the question as to how large numbers of workers and managers could be effectively organized into an overall organizational structure (Moorhead and Griffin, 1989). Max Weber was one of the most prominent contributors to the thinking concerning classical organization theory. He was of the opinion that a bureaucratic form of organization structure would work for all types of organizations.

Early in the 1900s, Hugo Munsterberg, a German psychologist who subsequently emigrated to the USA and who is regarded by some as one of the 'founding fathers' of organizational and work psychology, argued that the field of psychology could provide important insights into areas such as the selection of new employees and the motivation of employees. At the same time a vocational guidance expert by the name of Mary Parker Follett argued that organizations should strive harder to meet their employees' human needs and that management should become more democratic in its dealings with employees (Moorhead and Griffin, 1989).

The Hawthorne studies

The Hawthorne studies were carried out between 1924 and 1932 at Western Electric's Hawthorne plant in Chicago, USA. Two staff members of Harvard University, namely Elton Mayo and Fritz Roethlisberger, were, from 1927, involved in the Hawthorne studies.

Research methods 1.1

The Hawthorne studies

The first of the Hawthorne studies were designed by industrial engineers who wanted to study the effects of different levels of lighting on productivity. They used an experimental group and a control group of women workers for this experiment. The control group worked in a control room in which the lighting was kept constant. The experimental group worked in a test room in which the lighting level was systematically manipulated. At first, the lighting in the test room was systematically increased. As has been expected, the productivity in the test room increased. However, the unexpected happened in the sense that the productivity in the control room also increased. What was surprising was the fact that when the lighting in the test room was subsequently decreased, the productivity in both rooms continued to increase. It was obvious that something else beside the lighting levels (e.g. the human factor) was playing a role (Luthans, 1992).

Elton Mayo started a series of studies which got the name of the Relay Room studies. The subjects in these experiments were again female employees who worked in a special test room. In these studies, the impact of 13 different factors on productivity was examined. These factors included the length of rest pauses, length of the work-day, length of the work-week, method of payment, place of work and a free mid-morning lunch. The results showed that the productivity of the group increased with almost every change in work conditions. Even when the initial standard conditions were again instituted, productivity continued to increase (Baron and Greenberg, 1990).

The next series of experiments were known as the Bank Wiring Room study. Unlike the Relay Room experiments, the Bank Wiring Room involved no experimental changes once the study had started. Instead, an observer and an interviewer gathered objective data for study (Luthans, 1992). As the experimenters wanted to keep the situation as realistic as possible, they used the department's regular supervisors. These supervisors' main function was to maintain order and control. The group they had to supervise included nine males who had to assemble terminal banks for telephone exchanges. A piecework incentive payment system was introduced at the start of the experiment. Because of this payment system, it was expected that each man would work as hard as he could to maximize his own personal income. Much to their surprise, the researchers instead found that the group as a whole established an acceptable level of output for its members. In the Bank Wiring Room Study, industrial engineers determined that employees could make 7312 terminal connections per day (which represented 2½ equipments). However, employees decided that 2 equipments were a 'proper' day's work. Workers who failed to meet this output of 2 equipments were dubbed 'chiselers', while those who exceed it by too much were branded 'rate busters'. The men in the Bank Wiring Room used social ostracism, ridicule and name-calling as major sanctions to enforce the restriction of 2 equipments per day. Social ostracism was more effective in gaining compliance to the informal group norm than money and security was in attaining the scientifically derived management norm (Luthans, 1992). The Bank Wiring Room experiments were carried out during a period of great economic depression. Even while there was the possibility that these men in the Bank Wiring Room could lose their jobs, they still restricted their output.

The question arises why employees in the Bank Wiring Room restricted their output while those in the Relay Room experiments did not. Mayo and his colleagues arrived at the conclusion that it is necessary to understand factors such as worker attitudes, and communication between workers. Women in the Relay Room might have reacted favourably to the experimental conditions because they knew they were being studied, because of the novelty of the situation and because of the attention they received. These three factors are associated with the so-called 'Hawthorne effect', and it remains a real problem when doing research with humans. However, the impact of the small group, the type of supervision and the earnings were more important than the attention that employees received (Luthans, 1992).

The human relations movement

The human relations movement paid attention to aspects such as human needs, attitudes, motives and relationships. According to this approach, people respond primarily to their social environment, motivation depends more on social needs than on economic needs, and satisfied employees work harder than dissatisfied workers (Moorhead and Griffin, 1989). The values of the human relations movement are, to a certain extent, best mirrored by Theory Y of Douglas McGregor (1960) that he set out in his book called *The Human Side of Enterprise*. In this book he identified two opposing perspectives which he believed typified managerial views of employees. Theory Y represents an optimistic and a positive view of human nature. McGregor also refers to Theory X, which represents a much more negative and pessimistic view of human nature.

The human relations movement has also been criticized. For instance, a happy (satisfied) worker is not necessarily a productive worker. In some instances it might turn out that because a worker is being able to be productive, he or she might be satisfied. The human relations movement in some instances led managers to believe that workers wanted them to act as mothers/fathers towards the workers. This practice is known as paternalism. Workers often resent a paternalistic manager. Many of the assumptions of the human relations movement were also rather simplistic and situation specific.

Integrative perspectives

In contrast to an emphasis primarily on structure or the human side of organizations, organizational thought in the past few decades has emphasized the integration of these two perspectives.

The socio-technical systems approach

Trist and Bamforth (1951) described a change in technology in a British coal mine. In the mine, workers were used to working independently in small, self-contained units in which they organized the work themselves. However, the technology for mining coal improved in a way that required management to increase job specialization and decrease the workers' participation in job assignments. The coal miners hated the specialization, because they preferred working closely with each other and performing a variety of tasks. The researchers compared the performance of work groups, the jobs of which had become specialized by the new technology, to work groups which had kept their former social structure. They found that absenteeism in the specialized group was several times greater and productivity much lower than in the groups that had maintained their group organization. The socio-technical systems researchers concluded that neither technology, nor human relations, could be excluded when trying to understand a work system.

Systems theory

Systems theory offers an integrated and comprehensive view of organizational functioning. The general systems model (Katz and Kahn, 1978) represents an organization as an open system, one that interacts with environmental forces and factors. A system has four characteristics, namely:

1. It comprises a number of interdependent and interrelated subsystems (e.g. individual employees, work teams, departments).
2. It is open and dynamic. The organization continually receives new energy in the form of new resources (people, materials and money) or information (concerning strategy, environment and history) from the environment. These inputs are then transformed into outputs. The transformation of inputs creates changes in individual, group and organization behaviour and attitudes (e.g. performance, morale, satisfaction, turnover and absenteeism).
3. It strives for equilibrium. When organizations become unbalanced or experience disequilibrium, such as when changes in the environment make current staffing inadequate, organizations attempt to return to a steady state, which may differ from the original state of equilibrium.
4. It has multiple purposes, objectives and functions, some of which are in conflict. Organizations which survive adapt to a particular situation. They respond to changes in the environment with appropriate changes in the system (Clegg et al, 2005).

Contingency theory

In organizations, contingency theory emphasizes the fit between organizational processes and the characteristics of the situation. Therefore there is no best way to manage people or situations. The best way to manage people or situations depends on the situation in which the organization finds itself. Early contingency research looked at the fit between an organization's structure and its environment. Burns and Stalker (1961) described two different types of management systems: mechanistic and organic. Mechanistic systems have characteristics such as those described in the scientific and classical management traditions. Organic systems are much more flexible and loosely structured, and allow more employee influence over decisions than do mechanistic systems. Mechanistic systems are appropriate to stable environmental conditions, while organic systems are appropriate to changing organizations. Mintzberg (1983) emphasized the importance of fitting organization structure to various contingencies. Thus contingency theory has also extended to leadership, group dynamics, power relations and work design. Fiedler (1967) developed a contingency theory of leadership, which states that leadership effectiveness depends on the situation in which the leader finds himself or herself (including the characteristics of followers).

New developments

The following developments in the field of organization development have contributed to the field of organizational and work psychology:

- Interest in organizational transformation. Organizational transformation is a multi-dimensional, multi-level, qualitative, discontinuous and radical organization change.

- Interest in organizational culture. Efforts to define, measure and change organizational culture have become more sophisticated. Schein (1985) has done much work on organizational culture, and has devised interventions to help leaders and employees identify those cultural assumptions which will assist the organization in attaining its goals.

- Interest in the **learning organization.** Stimulated by the works of Argyris, Putnam and Smith (1985), Argyris and Schön (1978) and Senge (1990), there has been considerable interest in the conditions under which individuals, teams and organizations learn. It is clear that some organizations learn better than others. A learning organization is an organization which has developed the continuous capacity to adapt and change. Argyris (1990) has focused on the defensive routes of organization members. Senge (1990) writes about the learning disabilities which plague organizations. One learning disability is exclusively focusing on one's own job with little sense of responsibility for the collective product. Another is to do a lot of blaming of 'the enemy out there' for things which are wrong.

- Interest in teams. Although the study of teams was always important in organizational and work psychology, there is currently a deepened interest in self-managed or self-directed teams. This interest was caused by the pressure on organizations to improve quality, to become more flexible, to reduce layers of management and to enhance employee morale. Laboratory training methods have been found to be useful in training team members in effective membership and leadership behaviour, and in training supervisors and managers in delegation and empowerment.

- Total quality management. Total quality management is a company-wide effort seeking to install and make permanent a climate where employees continuously improve their ability to provide products and services, which customers will find of value, on demand.

Positive psychology

The prevailing values perspective in organizational and work psychology, emphasizing a utilitarian, cost-benefit approach, has strongly influenced research and practice (Wright and Wright, 2002). A consequence of the utilitarian perspective has been that applied research tends to focus unduly on the identification of financial costs to the organization of distressed, dissatisfied and unhappy employees. The cause of this employee dissatisfaction and unhappiness is typically seen as being deeply imbedded in the emotional maladjustment of the employee, as opposed to aspects of the job itself (Wright, 2003). As a result, the cure for this maladjustment usually involves some type of prevention-based employee therapy (Wright and Cropanzano, 2000).

Positive psychology is a movement in psychology which emphasizes what is right with people rather than what is wrong with them (Nelson and Cooper, 2007). According to Seligman (2002), the central objective of positive psychology is to understand and facilitate happiness and subjective well-being. The field of positive psychology at the subjective level is about valued subjective experiences: well-being, contentment and satisfaction; hope and optimism, and flow and happiness (Seligman and Csikszentmihalyi, 2000).

Luthans (2002a, 2002b) noted the need for a more relevant, proactive approach to organizational research. He termed this ***positive organizational behaviour***, defined as the study and application of positively oriented human resource strengths and psychological capabilities that can be measured, developed and effectively managed for performance improvement in today's workplace. Research has shown that work, and more specifically goal-directed,

Figure 1.2 Positive psychology studies the factors that contribute to human flourishing.

Source: Time & Life Pictures/Getty Images.

structured activity, translates directly into other mental health outcomes (Kelloway and Barling, 1991; Turner et al, 2002) and indirectly affects employees' life satisfaction (Judge and Watanabe, 1993; Hart, 1999). The field of positive psychology is rapidly gaining momentum in organizational and work psychology (Snyder and Lopez, 2002; Wright, 2003).

The tasks of organizational and work psychologists

The primary task of organizational and work psychologists is to apply psychological principles and research to workplace phenomena. Organizational and work psychologists use the scientific approach, characterized by qualitative observation as well as quantitative measurement and statistics to conduct research and intervene in the workplace (Brewerton and Millward, 2004). Furthermore, they are concerned about the effectiveness of the organization and the wellness of individuals. Lastly, organizational and work psychologists operate with an implicit multi-level model, i.e. they recognize that in addition to individual influences on individual behaviour and attitudes, higher-order units such as teams and the organizational context have influence (Ryan, 2003). The tasks of organizational and work psychologists are shown in Focus box 1.1.

Focus 1.1

Tasks of an organizational and work psychologist

Four broad tasks of the organizational and work psychologists are distinguished, namely:

1. Explaining individual, group and organizational behaviour.

2. Measuring behaviour and predicting potential.

3. Contributing to organization development.

4. Translating research findings and empowering potential users thereof.

Explaining individual, group and organizational behaviour

The first task of a organizational and work psychologist is to explain individual, group and organizational functioning based on theories and models. For example, the work and organizational psychologist can meet with clients or managers to discuss the nature of a problem (e.g. the turnover rate among employees is too high), conduct interviews or send out questionnaires to employees to determine the nature of their job tasks, conduct a study to determine what training is needed, survey employees to determine how they feel about their jobs, and identify solutions to an organization's problem (e.g. too much employee absence).

Measuring behaviour and predicting potential

Over the years psychological tests have become essential tools for implementing change. The term 'test' refers to group and individually administered standardized measures of aptitudes, achievement, intelligence, personality, social, language, perception and motor skills (Oakland, 2004). Strong evidence exists to support the merit of tests for providing policy-makers with information for decision making, aiding psychologists in the individual screening and diagnostic process, credentialing and licensing candidates in professions and specialties, and providing organizations with data for employee selection, promotion and evaluation of training (Hambleton and Oakland, 2004).

Various methodological questions should be raised when applying assessment tools (Cheung, 2004), namely:

1. Is paper-and-pencil testing familiar to people in a specific culture?
2. Are respondents proficient in reading English?
3. Is the translation done accurately?
4. Is the translated test equivalent to the original test?
5. Are there cross-cultural differences in the means and distributions of test scores?
6. How can cross-cultural differences in test scores be interpreted?

Organizational and work psychologists should ensure that assessment materials and measures are reliable, valid, equivalent and unbiased (Smith et al, 2001). Assessment materials and measures could be inequivalent or **biased** as a function of **culture** and other differences (Bryson and Hosken, 2005).

Contributing to organizational development

To contribute to organizational development, organizational and work psychologists need to conceptualize organizational effectiveness and develop measures thereof. Characteristics of effective organizations include profitability, return on investment, market share, growth, adaptability and innovation, and perhaps the ultimate objective: survival. An organization is effective when it offers its consumers the services and products desired with reasonable conditions of price, quality and delivery date. Effectiveness stems from both efficiency and **equity** (Milkovich and Boudreau, 1994: 3–4).

- **Efficiency**. Organizational and work psychologists help an organization manage its human resources efficiently. At one level, efficiency addresses the question, 'Are we doing things right?' Are we controlling labour costs, hiring the right number of people with the right skills, and doing these things in a timely manner? Answering these questions requires information on costs, quantity, quality and timeliness. At another level, efficiency addresses the question, 'Are we doing the right things?' How can we do things better? Efficiency can be increased by redesigning a form to make it easier to understand; efficiency can also be increased by eliminating the need for the form in the first place.

- **Equity.** Equity is the perceived fairness of both the procedures used to make human resource decisions and the actual decisions. An effective organization may look at whether the amount paid to employees is fair in comparison to what they do and fair in relation to what other employees are paid. An effective organization treats its employees fairly and with respect.

Efficiency and equity are interrelated. For example, many organizations believe that policies to foster employees' sense of fair treatment (such as grievance systems, open-door policies and employee assistance programmes) enable them to operate more efficiently. They reason that if employees believe they are being treated fairly, they will be more willing to do their best for the organization. On the other hand, efficiency and equity may sometimes be in conflict. For example, layoffs that retain younger employees who are more likely to accept change may seem unfair to older employees who believe their loyalty and years of service to the organization are being undervalued. Balancing efficiency and equity is a constant challenge as both are required for an effective organization.

Four dimensions of organizational results should be evaluated when measuring the effects of interventions, namely financial results, time and personnel resources, customer satisfaction and health and safety (Kompier and Cooper, 1999). Financial results are taken from an organization's profit and loss account and balance sheet. Time and personnel resources include hours worked, personnel statistics and personnel reports, which show the levels of staffing and **competency** that have been used to achieve the financial result. Measurement of customer satisfaction shows how effective an organization has been in satisfying customers' requirements. Health and safety include the physical and psychological working environment, stress, burnout, health, work engagement and job satisfaction.

Translating research findings and empowering potential users thereof

Although a large body of research findings exists, potential users often do not act on them. This might be attributed to a lack of knowledge of research findings, a lack of implementation skills, a lack of motivation and/or limitations created by the prevailing organizational culture. According to Watkins (2001), many industrial leaders uphold dysfunctional paradigms which may profoundly diminish the effectiveness of Organizational and Work teaching, practice and research. Reacting to the opinions of industrial leaders, without at least considering organizational success factors to support their reasoning, may potentially be devastating to the subject.

The competency profile of organizational and work psychologists

The competency profile of organizational and work psychologists is addressed on the websites of various psychological associations, including the American

Psychological Association (http://www.apa.org) and the Canadian Society for Industrial and Organizational Psychology (http://psychology.uwo.ca/csiop). A competency profile can be defined as a list of competencies required in a specific job or profession. Competencies are the work-related knowledge, skills, attitudes and behaviour needed to effectively perform in a role. Knowledge is the awareness and understanding of facts, truths or information gained through learning, experience and or introspection. A skill is the ability to perform a work-related activity which contributes to the effective work performance. An attitude involves beliefs, feelings, values and dispositions to act in certain ways. Behaviour is the manner of acting or controlling yourself.

The education and training of organizational and work psychologists are rooted in the various foundations, namely: a) psychological science (including biological bases of behaviour, cognitive-affective bases of behaviour, social bases of behaviour and individual differences); b) research methods; c) theory and methods of psychological and behavioural measurement; and d) **advanced** statistical theory. Based on these foundations, the competency areas of organizational and work psychologists are reported in Focus box 1.2.

In Figure 1.3, the competencies of organizational and work psychologists are classified based on three areas, namely knowledge of organizational and work psychology theory, research and statistical skills, and professional skills.

Knowledge of organizational and work psychology includes an understanding of theory and research (as described in Focus Box 1.2), the ability to assimilate new psychological knowledge, and knowledge of ethical considerations. Research and statistical skills include the ability to use research methods and statistics, an understanding of published research, and critical thinking. Professional skills include effective oral and written communication skills, an awareness of career options, and the ability to apply knowledge to real-life situations.

Careers in organizational and work psychology

Careers in organizational and work psychology are characterized by both rewarding and frustrating aspects (www.wcupa.edu): The attractions of careers in organizational and work psychology include the following:

- There are many career opportunities in organizational and work psychology. One can work in a human resource department in various types of private and public organizations, work in management, or work for consulting companies.

- Careers in organizational and work psychology are challenging because it is a new field and because the field presents opportunities for learning, variety and autonomy.

- Organizational and work psychologists are in demand because organizations realize that human potential management is the key to business success.

- Organizational and work psychologists could work for organizations or they may become entrepreneurs and initiate their own businesses.

Focus 1.2

Competencies of organizational and work psychologists

Knowledge of organizational and work psychology theory and research (The organizational and work psychologist should understand psychological theory and research, demonstrate the ability to assimilate new psychological knowledge, and demonstrate knowledge of ethical considerations)

- Individual differences
- Work motivation
- Attitude theory measurement and change
- Human resource planning, recruitment, selection and placement
- Career development
- Job analysis, description and evaluation
- Health, safety and well-being in organizations
- Human factors and performance in work
- Individual, group and organizational assessment methods
- Decision theory
- Training and development
- Performance appraisal and management
- Group and team behaviour
- Leadership
- Compensation and benefits
- Organizational theory
- Organizational development
- Ethical, legal, and professional contexts

Research and statistical skills (The organizational and work psychologist should demonstrate the ability to use research methods and statistics, understand published research, and show the ability to think critically)

- Research methodology
- Statistical analysis

Professional skills (The organizational and work psychologist should demonstrate the ability to apply knowledge to real-life situations, demonstrate effective oral and written communication skills, and show an awareness of career options)

- Consulting and business skills
- Knowledge of careers
- Oral and written communication skills

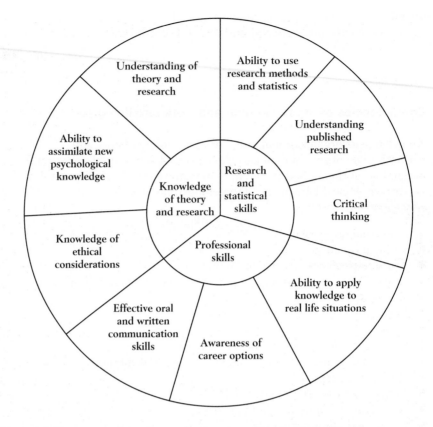

Figure 1.3 Competencies of organizational and work psychologists.

The drawbacks of careers in organizational and work psychology include the following:

- Many jobs in organizational and work psychology require a master's or a doctorate in organizational and work psychology.

- Organizational and work psychologists are at risk for developing burnout because of the nature of people work they do.

- Organizational and work psychologists often become intensely involved with people and those who do not like dealing with people might find the careers in the field frustrating.

- Organizations and employees often depend on organizational and work psychologists to help them and they might experience intense frustration if people do not want to change.

Some useful websites to obtain more information about the field of organizational and work psychology are given in Focus box 1.3.

Ethics

Ethical conduct

Ethics are the basic rules or first principles that have been proposed to ensure a 'good' society, i.e. one in which people are willing to cooperate for the benefit of all. Ethics is the discipline which deals with what is good or bad and with moral duty and obligations. Ethical Behaviour conforms to accepted standards of conduct. Ethical Reasoning involves the sorting out of principles that help determine what is right in the face of a human dilemma. An ethical dilemma is a situation or problem facing an individual where complex and often conflicting principles of behaviour are in play. The question: 'Is abortion good or bad?' is one example of an ethical dilemma.

Minimum ethical guidelines for organizational and work psychologists

A professional must always:

- Support, promote and apply the *principles of human rights, equity, dignity and respect* in the workplace, i.e. must respect people as individuals and inherently of equal worth regardless of race, origin, gender, sexual orientation or any of the grounds enunciated under the relevant human rights code.
- Hold in *strict confidence all confidential information* acquired in the course of the performance of their duties and not divulge confidential information unless required by law and/or where serious harm is imminent.
- Strive to *balance organizational and employee needs and interests* in the practice of their profession, i.e. a professional must support and represent the best interest of their employer or client (employee), and acknowledge and respect their fiduciary duty in this relationship with the highest standards of honesty and integrity.
- Question pending individual, group and organizational actions when necessary to ensure that *decisions are ethical and are implemented in an ethical manner.*
- Either avoid or disclose a potential *conflict of interest* that might influence or might be perceived to influence personal actions or judgements. A professional is in a conflict of interest situation when he or she tend to favour, for reasons that are extraneous to the interests of the organization, a client (employee) that he or she is currently representing, or a course of action not in the best interest of the organization or the client.

Focus 1.3

Useful websites about organizational and work psychology

www.siop.org (Website of the Society of Industrial and Organizational Psychology (SIOP) in the USA. Contains information about organizational and work psychology and publications.)

www.wcupa.edu (Contains information about careers in organizational and work psychology.)

www.apa.org (Website of the American Psychological Association. Contains valuable resources and publications for organizational and work psychologists.)

www.aomonline.org (Website of the Academy of Management, a leading professional association for management research and education in the USA.)

www.ucm.es/info/Psyap/enop (Website of the European Association of Work and Organizational Psychologists.)

www.iaapsy.org (Website of the International Association of Applied Psychology.)

www.see.ed.ac.uk/~gerard/MENG/ME96 (Contains information about the role of leadership in the management of small teams and small projects.)

www.leadership.com (Contains interesting material on leadership.)

www.ccl.org/leadership (Website of the Center for Creative Leadership, a non-profit institution dedicated exclusively to leadership.)

www.odnetwork.org (Contains information about the activities of the Organizational Development Network.)

Activity 1.1

Challenges for and competencies of organizational and work psychologists

Study the websites in Focus box 1.3. Identify the major challenges for organizational and work psychologists in the next 10 years. List the competencies needed by organizational and work psychologists. Compare your competencies with those required of organizational and work psychologists and identify the most important gaps between your competency profile and the profile as specified.

Summary

- Organizational and work psychology is defined as an applied division of psychology concerned with the study of human behaviour related to work, organizations and productivity.

- Organizational and work psychology is comprised of two branches, namely Organizational Psychology and Work Psychology. Organizational Psychology focuses on individual differences and diversity management, motivation, communication, leadership, group behaviour, health and well-being, organizational design and organization development. Work Psychology focuses on human resource management, including human resource planning, job analysis, description and job specifications, recruitment and selection, induction and training, career development, job evaluation and compensation, and performance appraisal.

- Various approaches and theories contributed to the field of work and organizational psychology. Early contributions stressed efficient performance according to economic principles. Classical organization theory was concerned with the effective organization of people. The Hawthorne studies, in turn, stressed the social nature of human beings. This was followed by the human relations movement, which paid attention to aspects such as human needs, attitudes, motives and relationships. In contrast to an emphasis primarily on structure or the human side of organizations, organizational thought in the past few decades has emphasized the integration of these two perspectives. More recent developments in the field of organization development and the positive psychology movement also contributed to the field of organizational and work psychology.

- Four tasks of the organizational and work psychologists are distinguished, namely explaining individual, group and organizational behaviour, measuring behaviour and predicting potential, contributing to organization development, and translating research findings and empowering potential users thereof.

- The competencies of work and organizational psychologists are classified based on three areas, namely knowledge of work and organizational psychology theory, research and statistical skills, and professional skills.

- Careers in organizational and work psychology are characterized by both rewarding and frustrating aspects.

Key concepts and terms

Attitude	Learning organization
Bias	Organizational behaviour
Behaviour	Organizational culture
Classical organization theory	Organizational psychology
Competency	Organizational transformation
Contingency theory	Positive organizational behaviour
Culture	Positive psychology
Diversity	Scientific management
Effectiveness	Skill
Efficiency	Socio-technical systems approach
Equity	System
Human relations movement	Total quality management
Human resource management	Work psychology
Knowledge	

Sample essay titles

- What is the relevance of positive psychology for organizational and work psychologists?
- What are the main tasks and competencies of organizational and work psychologists?

Further reading

Books

Arnold, J., Silvester, J., Patterson, F., Robertson, I., Cooper C.L., and Burnes, B. (2005). *Work Psychology: Understanding Human Behavior in the Workplace* (4th Ed.). Harlow, Essex: Pearson Education.

Journal articles

Luthans, F. (2002a). Positive organizational behavior: Developing and maintaining psychological strengths. *Academy of Management Executive*, 16, 57–72.

Luthans, F. (2002b). The need for and meaning of positive organizational behavior. *Journal of Organizational Behavior*, 23, 695–706.

Wright, T.A. (2003). Positive organizational behavior: An idea whose time has truly come. *Journal of Organizational Behavior*, 24, 437–442.

1 | Organizational psychology

2 Individual differences and diversity management

This chapter focuses on individual-level variables that may affect individuals, groups and organizations. The first section describes **personality,** taking into account a cross-cultural perspective. More specifically, the **'Big Five' personality model** (which distinguishes between five personality dimensions, namely **extraversion, emotional stability, conscientiousness, agreeableness** and **openness to experience**) is introduced. Furthermore, the salutogenic approach, which is consistent with the assumptions of the positive psychological paradigm, is explained. We then look at **values** and the implications thereof for organizations. The chapter then proceeds to **attitudes** and how they can be measured and managed in organizations. This is followed by a discussion of mental abilities. Finally, we focus on diversity in the workplace.

Learning outcomes

When you have completed this chapter you should be able to:

1. Know what is meant by 'personality' and evaluate the elements of the most commonly accepted model of personality – the Five-Factor Model.
2. Describe how personality affects job performance and other work-related outcomes.
3. Understand the relationship between attitudes and behaviour, especially regarding performance on the job.
4. Understand how work and organizational psychologists are helping companies to assess and manage job attitudes and their impact on organizational performance.
5. Know what job attitudes are, and be familiar with the assumptions that underlie them.
6. Understand why diversity in the workplace matters, know the different types of diversity, and identify how work and organizational psychologists could help organizations to manage diversity.

Personality

Definition of personality

The word *personality* is derived from the word **'persona'**, which has Greek and Latin roots and refers to the theatrical masks worn by Greek actors (Pervin and

John, 2001). Personality has been defined in many different ways (Pervin and Cooper, 1999). In the broadest sense, the term refers to the enduring, inner characteristics of individuals that organize their behaviour (Derlega et al, 2005). Most uses of the term can be summarized in terms of two major themes. The first meaning of the term originates from the perspective of an observer and involves an individual's public presence and social reputation. The second meaning refers to the inner self or being of an individual: one's private, vital and essential nature. With time, personality in this sense has come to mean the deep and enduring structures of an individual that form the central core of the self (Derlega et al, 2005). The measurement of personality becomes complicated by the fact that these two perspectives are not easily integrated, and require quite different measurement strategies, since one emphasizes the outer visible aspects, while the other focuses on the inner, dynamic whole for the outer perspective on personality.

History of personality theory and research

Trait theorists are concerned with the measurement of psychological characteristics (Arnold et al, 1995) and this approach forms the basis of the psychometric approach to personality analysis, as portrayed by the use of factor analysis, where the factors are conceptualized as measurements of traits.

Within the framework of the trait theories, human behaviour is characterized by consistent patterns of behaviour known as traits, factors, dimensions or types. The trait approach can be divided into two paradigms, namely ideographic and nomothetic. Ideographic theorists (e.g. Allport, 1961) believe that every human being has their own unique set of traits that are fundamental to their personality. Nomothetic theorists (e.g. Cattell, 1965), on the other hand, believe that the exact same set of traits exists within each individual, but they differ from each other in the way and intensity to which each trait is manifested.

Cattell (1965) considered **language** a valuable tool to gather information regarding personality. He used a lexical approach to generate an original list of trait names. By means of factor analysis he identified 16 core personality traits and developed the well-known personality assessment questionnaire, the *Sixteen Personality Questionnaire* (16PF). The development of the 16PF has played an important role in the development of the Big Five factor model.

An etic or emic approach to the conceptualization of personality may be employed. The **etic approach** emphasizes 'universals' or 'core similarities' in all human beings. The **emic** approach, on the other hand, supposes a culture-specific orientation (Berry, 1989). The cross-cultural generalizeability of personality characteristics has most often been investigated by means of an imposed etic approach, which implies that assessment instruments developed in western countries were adopted in other cultural contexts, assuming that the underlying theories and constructs are universal. According to Church and Lonner (1998: 36), an etic strategy may increase the chances of finding cross-cultural comparability and exclude culture-specific dimensions. However, an imposed etic strategy may be biased towards the discovery of universals and may miss personality dimensions that are specific to particular cultures. Moreover, the specific values and tendencies of the western culture may unknowingly lead to the de-emphasis or omission of some universal constructs. The emic approach seeks to identify an optimal way of structuring personality variables reflecting the indigenous patterns of each culture (Saucier, 2003).

Conceptualization of personality

The Big Five personality model

Since the mid 1980s research has focused on the use of the five-factor model (FFM) or some variant to classify personality (Barrick et al, 2001). The FFM of personality represents a structure of traits, developed and elaborated over the last five decades (McCrae and Costa, 1997). The FFM originated in the works by Fiske (1949) and Norman (1963), who reproduced a highly stable structure with five factors (John, 1990). Researchers agree that almost all personality measures could be categorized according to the FFM of personality (also referred to as the 'Big Five' personality dimensions) (Goldberg, 1990). Research also showed that the five personality factors have a genetic basis (Digman, 1989) and that they are probably inherited (Jang et al, 1996).

According to the FFM, five basic personality dimensions underlie all others (see Focus box 2.1).

Focus 2.1

The Big Five personality dimensions

- **Extraversion**: a personality dimension describing someone who is sociable, talkative and assertive.
- **Agreeableness**: a personality dimension describing someone who is good-natured, cooperative and trusting.
- **Conscientiousness**: a personality dimension describing someone who is responsible, dependable, persistent and achievement oriented.
- **Emotional stability**: a personality dimension which characterizes someone who is calm, enthusiastic, secure (positive) to tense, nervous, depressed and insecure (negative).
- **Openness to experience**: a personality characteristic which characterizes someone who is imaginative, sensitive and intellectual.

Theory and research show that Big Five factors impact on motivation, which in turn affects performance. Personality is something that is expressed in attitudes and behaviours. A conscientious person does not perform high because of the property of conscientiousness. Usually it is assumed that personality is a 'distal' predictor of performance, operating through the more 'proximal' processes of motivation. **Self-efficacy** (Bandura, 1977) and goals (Locke and Latham, 2002) are important motivational constructs in organizational and work psychology. Self-efficacy impacts both on goals and performance. Research shows the effects of both conscientiousness and emotional stability on self-efficacy and goals (Judge and Ilies, 2002).

It is necessary to acknowledge that the FFM is not unanimously accepted. According to Block (1995), factor analysis is not an appropriate and adequate base to decide the theoretical constructs of personality. Other researchers have criticized the model on the basis of the number of factors (Eysenck, 1992; Tellegen and Waller, 1995). However, Costa and McCrae (1995) and Barrick (2001) responded to this criticism by stating that the Big Five has been reproduced a great number of times, through different factor analysis methods, by different researchers, with different instruments and in different languages.

A fundamental question for work and organizational psychologists interested in the measurement of personality and culture is whether personality traits are universal or culture-specific. The results from several other studies indicated that the Big Five structure is less universal than supposed in the beginning of the 1990s (Digman, 1997; Goldberg, 1993). Systematic comparisons among the five-factor solutions of several lexical studies have also proven the instability of the Big Five across languages. Some researchers found quite different personality structures in different cultures (Church et al, 1996; Caprara et al, 2001).

Salutogenesis

The term 'salutogenesis' originates from the Latin *salus* (health) and the Greek *genesis* (origin), emphasizing the origins of health or wellness (Antonovsky, 1987). Salutogenesis focuses on the origins of health, rather than the origins of disease (Strümpfer, 1995).

Salutogenic constructs include the following:

- **Sense of coherence**. Sense of coherence is defined as a global orientation that expresses the extent to which an individual has a pervasive, enduring feeling of confidence that: a) the stimuli deriving from the internal and external environments in the course of living are structured, predictable and explicable (comprehensibility); b) the resources are available to the individual to meet the demands posed by these stimuli (manageability); and c) these demands are challenges, worthy of investment (meaningfulness) (Antonovsky, 1987). A strong sense of coherence was found to be moderately related ($r = 0.47$) to job satisfaction (Strümpfer et al, 1998).

- **Hardiness**. Hardiness is a personality style consisting of interrelated orientations of *commitment, control* and *challenge* (Kobasa, 1982). Persons high on hardiness involve themselves in whatever they are doing (commitment), believe and act as if they can influence the events forming their lives (control), and consider change to be not only normal but also a stimulus to development (challenge) (Beehr and Bowling, 2005).

- **Locus of control**. Locus of control refers to the attitude people develop regarding the extent to which they are in control of their own destiny (Rotter, 1966). An individual with an external locus of control believes that outside forces are the cause of the reinforcement. Research has shown that individuals with an external locus of control are less satisfied with their jobs, have higher absenteeism rates, are more alienated from the work setting and are less involved in their jobs than internals. Individuals with an internal locus of control search more actively for information before making a decision, are more motivated to achieve and make a greater attempt to control their environment. Spector (1986) found that high levels of perceived control were associated with high levels of job satisfaction, commitment and involvement, and low levels of stress, absenteeism and turnover.

- **Self-efficacy.** Self-efficacy refers to an individual's belief in their capacity to mobilize cognition resources and to take action to take control over task demands (Bandura, 1982). A high level of self-efficacy can be achieved in three ways, namely performance attainments, vicarious experiences and social influence. Performance attainments refer to doing something competently. This is a result of the availability of appropriate resources, and an absence of barriers to engage in a given activity. Vicarious experiences refer to seeing someone similar to oneself succeed by sustained effort. Self-efficacy is also promoted when a credible person persuades individuals about their capabilities of performing a task. According to Bandura (1989), employees with a low level of self-efficacy doubt their capabilities, shy away from difficult tasks and have low aspirations and weak commitment to the goals they choose to pursue.

Personality assessment as a tool in decision making

Personality predicts aspects of job performance that may not be strongly related to knowledge, skills or abilities. Personality traits predicts what a person *will do*, as opposed to what he or she *can do*. Borman and Motowidlo (1997) distinguish between two types of performance, namely **task performance** and **contextual performance.** a) Task performance refers to 'the effectiveness with which job incumbents perform activities that contribute to the organisation's technical core' (Borman and Motowidlo, 1997: 100). For a salesperson, task performance will include components such as product knowledge, time management and task knowledge. b) Contextual performance includes 'volunteering to carry out task activities that are not formally part of the job and helping and cooperating with others in the organization to get tasks accomplished' (Borman and Motowidlo, 1997: 100). Contextual performance includes the following aspects: a) persisting with enthusiasm and extra effort as necessary to complete own task activities; b) volunteering to carry out activities that are not formally part of the job; c) helping and cooperating with others; d) following organizational rules and procedures, and e) endorsing, supporting, and defending organizational objectives. **Organizational citizenship behaviours,** which indicate contextual performance, are defined as the willingness to 'go above and beyond' the call of duty. Unlike other selection tools, little or no evidence of adverse impact (different selection ratios between demographic groups) has been shown when personality traits are used to predict organizational citizenship behaviour.

There are various reasons why personality matters in the workplace (Barrick and Mount, 2005: 359). a) Managers care about personality – few managers will be willing to appoint a person who is anxious, unstable or irresponsible. b) Meta-analytic techniques assisted researchers to develop an understanding of the relationship between personality and performance. c) Personality contributes incremental validity in the prediction of job performance beyond that accounted for by other predictors. d) Meta-analytic derived estimates of the relation between a specific personality trait and performance is an underestimation. e) Small differences exist between racial and ethnic groups. f) Longitudinal data showed that personality traits predicted multiple facets of career success over a span of 50 years. g) Personality traits are significant predictors of organizational citizenship behaviour, turnover, absenteeism, safety and leadership effectiveness.

Activity 2.1

Use of personality tests for personnel selection

Study the following article and answer the questions which follow:

Meiring, D., Van de Vijver, F.J.R., Rothmann, S., and Barrick, M. (2005). Construct, item and method bias of cognitive and personality tests in South Africa. *South African Journal of Psychology*, 31, 1–8.

Questions:

1. What were the major findings of Meiring et al (2005) regarding the use of personality tests imported from Europe for use in South Africa?
2. Do you think that the South African Police Service could use the personality test described in the study for selection purposes? Motivate your answer.

Research methods 2.1

Meta-analytical studies of the relationship between personality and work outcomes

Early researchers believed the personality–job performance relationship was weak. The reasons for this were that weak analytic techniques were employed, inappropriate measures of personality were used, no theoretical framework existed on which research findings could be based, and it was believed that behaviour is determined more by situations than by traits. Some people have argued that situations drive behaviour. However, psychologists would now agree that behaviour is best understood by taking into consideration both the person and the situation. It seems that personality has a much larger effect on performance than previously supposed.

The results of various studies showed that various Big Five personality dimensions are related to job performance. In the USA Barrick and Mount (1991) found that Conscientiousness is a valid predictor across occupations and across criteria and that the other personality factors only generalize their validity for some occupations and some criteria. Barrick and Mount found that Extraversion is a valid predictor for managers; Emotional Stability is a valid predictor for police; and Agreeableness is a valid predictor for police and managers. Openness to Experience did not show validity for any occupational group. Extraversion is a valid predictor of training proficiency, as are Emotional Stability, Agreeableness and Openness to

Experience. The relative non-validity of Emotional Stability may have been due to a type of range restriction based on a 'selecting-out' process in the applicant pool, where the applicants low in Emotional Stability were already excluded from the applicant pool (Barrick and Mount, 1991).

Tett, Jackson and Rothstein (1991) found that all personality dimensions are valid predictors of job performance. However, Extraversion and Conscientiousness have lower validity coefficients, whereas Neuroticism, Openness to Experience and Agreeableness have higher validities. Salgado (1997) conducted a **meta-analysis** of the Big Five dimensions in relation to performance for three criteria (i.e. supervisory ratings, training ratings and personnel data) and for five occupational groups using 36 validity studies conducted in Europe. Results indicated that Conscientiousness and Emotional Stability were valid predictors for all performance criteria and for most occupational groups. Openness to Experience and Agreeableness showed validity for training criterion. Extraversion showed generalized validity for managers and police, although the validity for managers was very low.

Barrick et al (2001) summarized the results of 15 meta-analytic studies. They found that the validity of Conscientiousness in predicting job performance was the highest (of the personality traits studied) and that it generalized across all criterion types and all occupations studied. The validity of Emotional Stability was distinguishable from zero, but its overall relationship with performance was smaller than the effect for Conscientiousness. Barrick et al suggested that a reason for the relatively low validity of Emotional Stability is that it might be a considerably broader construct than previously considered, and that it should include aspects such as self-esteem, self-efficacy and locus of control. Extraversion, Agreeableness and Openness to Experience predicted some aspects of performance in some occupations.

Values

Definition of values

Values are among the most stable and enduring characteristics of individuals. They are the basis upon which attitudes and personal preferences are formed. An organization, too, has a value system, usually called its organizational culture.

Values are types of **beliefs,** centrally located within one's total belief system, about how one ought or ought not to behave, or about some end state of existence worth attaining (Rokeach, 1973). Values are general beliefs about desirable or undesirable ways of behaving and about desirable or undesirable goals or end states (Lonner and Malpass, 1994). Schwartz (1994a) defines values as constructs that determine what people will strive for in their lives and what they are prepared to sacrifice. Values are trans-situational criteria or goals ordered by importance as guiding principles in life.

Values and culture

Values can be seen as culturally bound. This becomes clear when one looks at the different values and attitudes of different culture groups (Schwartz, 1994b). According to Smith and Bond (1993), individuals who find themselves in a specific culture are also bound in a specific social environment. This social environment is home to their own unique norms, language, systems and values. This results in members of similar culture groups sharing many cultural and social values. Individual values and value priorities are, however, also formed by the individual's unique personal experience (Schwartz, 1999). This may result in individuals within a certain culture group having different and unique values and value priorities.

Recent studies have shown that values and value priorities are not displayed only by people, but that nations, countries and other social categories also display distinct value profiles or patterns (Roe and Ester, 1999). According to research, cultural dimensions of values reflect the basic issues or problems that societies must face in order to regulate human activities (Hofstede, 1980; Schwartz, 1999). Values are the foundation of cultural norms, and set the standard for appropriate behaviour in specific situations (Schwartz, 1999).

Cultural values manifest in two main areas, namely collectivism and individualism. Traditional western thinking tends to rate success and achievement very highly and is a good example of typical individualism (Duckitt and Foster, 1991). The opposite can be found in an African thinking pattern, where the emphasis falls on traditions and conformity. Collectivism is therefore more important. In these societies the needs of the group are more important than those of the individual (Smith and Bond, 1993; Triandis, 1994).

Models of values

Different value models have been developed by various researchers and all these models are evidence that values are part of culture. Kluckhohn and Strodtbeck (1961) were the first to develop a model on values. According to their model, different value systems can be found within different culture groups. They identified five main problems that can be found across all cultural groups, namely: a) What is the essence of being human?; b) What is the relationship between humans, nature and the supernatural?; c) What should the time focus of humans be?; d) What is acceptable for human activity?; e) What is the essence of human interpersonal relations? According to Kluckhohn and Strodtbeck (1961), these five problems are present within all cultures. Priorities may, however, vary within different groups.

Rokeach (1973) placed values in hierarchical order within every individual. He distinguished between two main sets of values, namely terminal values and instrumental values. Terminal values are values that people find important in order to live a meaningful life. In order to achieve one's terminal values, instrumental values must be applied. Instrumental values are the values individuals use to achieve the end state of their objectives. In all culture groups a total of 36 terminal and instrumental values are present, but the hierarchal order may vary (Hoag and Cooper, 2006).

Activity 2.2

Article on a theory of cultural values

Study the following article and answer the questions that follow below:

Schwartz, S.H. (1999). A theory of cultural values and some implications for work. *Applied Psychology: An International Review*, 48, 23–47.

Questions:

1. Which cultural values are distinguished by Schwartz?
2. What are the implications of these values for work contexts?

Outcomes of values in organizations

Employees who hold values which are congruent with their organization's values are more productive and satisfied. Holding values which are inconsistent with company values is a major source of conflict, frustration and non-productivity. People sometimes lose touch with their own values, behaving in ways which are inconsistent with those values. Not being aware of one's own value priorities can lead to misdirected decisions and frustration in the long term. Because values are seldom challenged, people forget value priorities and behave in ways that do not fit the values. Until people encounter a threat to their values, they seldom seek to clarify them. Becoming mature in value development requires that individuals develop a set of internalized principles by which they can govern their behaviour. The development of those principles is enhanced and value maturity is increased as value-based issues are confronted, discussed and thought about.

Attitudes

Definition of attitudes

An attitude represents a predisposition to respond in a favourable or unfavourable way to persons or objects in one's environment (Fishbein and Ajzen, 1975: 6; Steers and Porter, 1991). When we say we 'like' something or 'dislike' something, we are in effect expressing an attitude toward the person or object. Fishbein (1967) defines an attitude as follows: 'an attitude is characterized as a learned implicit response that varies in intensity and tends to guide (mediate) an individual's overt responses to an object'. In Fishbein's conceptualization, attitude refers only to the evaluation of a concept and there is a mediating evaluative response to every stimulus. Consequently, people have attitudes towards all objects which may be positive, negative, or neutral.

Research has shown that job attitudes of employees were very stable over a five-year period (Staw and Ross, 1985). Employees with negative job attitudes tended to remain negative, even those who changed jobs or occupations. In contrast, employees with positive job attitudes remained positive after five years.

Attitudes should not be confused with values. Values represent global beliefs that influence behaviour across situations, while attitudes relate only to behaviour directed towards specific objects, persons or situations. Values and attitudes are generally, but not always in harmony. Three important assumptions underlie the concept of attitudes, namely: a) An attitude is a hypothetical construct. We cannot actually see attitudes, although we can often see their consequences. Therefore, the existence of attitudes must be inferred from people's statements and behaviours. b) An attitude is a unidimensional construct. It can be measured along a continuum which ranges from very positive to very negative. c) Attitudes are believed to be somewhat related to subsequent behaviour.

Attitudes and behavioural intentions

An attitude is defined as an evaluation of a psychological object (Ajzen, 2001). The work of Ajzen and Fishbein (1977, 1980) is frequently cited as a theoretical framework concerned with attitude formation, behavioural intentions, and the prediction of overt behaviours. According to this work, beliefs about aspects of a job (e.g. 'I do not have sufficient advancement opportunities in my job') lead to an attitude (e.g. 'I am dissatisfied with my job'), which in turn results in behavioural intentions (e.g. 'I'm intending to quit my job'). Behavioural intentions are then often translated into actual behaviour, such as leaving the organization, assuming that the person is able to carry out the intention. The model of behavioural intention is given in Figure 2.1.

Figure 2.1 shows that behavioural intentions are influenced by one's attitude towards the behaviour as well as the perceived norms about exhibiting the behaviour. Attitudes and subjective norms are influenced by personal beliefs.

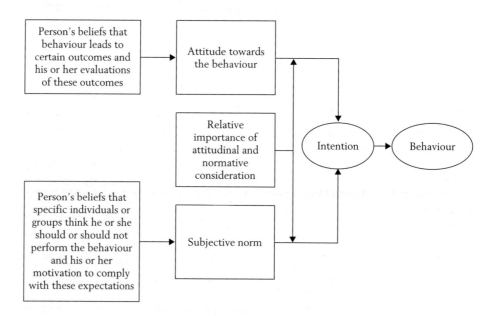

Figure 2.1 A model of behavioural intention.

Source: Ajzen, I., & Fishbein, M. (1980, p. 8). *Understanding attitudes and predicting social behaviour.* Upper Saddle River, NJ: Prentice Hall.

- **Beliefs influence attitudes**. Beliefs are the result of direct observation and inferences from previous learned relationships. Attitudes are based on salient or important beliefs that may change as relevant information is received. Figure 2.1 shows that an individual will have positive attitudes towards performing a behaviour when he or she believes that the behaviour is associated with positive outcomes. If the employee believes that quitting a job will lead to positive outcomes (e.g. better advancement opportunities), he or she will be more likely to quit.

- **Beliefs influence subjective norms**. Subjective norms are an outcome of beliefs that specific individuals or groups think that the individual should (or should not) perform the behaviour. Subjective norms can exert a powerful influence on the behavioural intentions of individuals who are sensitive to the opinions of role models.

According to Breckler (1984), who presented an alternative model of attitudes, attitudes have three different components: affective, behavioural and cognitive. The affective component consists of the feelings that a particular topic arouses. The behavioural component consists of a tendency to act in a particular way with respect to a particular topic. The cognitive component consists of a set of beliefs about a topic – beliefs that can be expressed in words. The affective components of attitudes can be very strong and pervasive. Like other emotional reactions, these feelings can be strongly influenced by direct or vicarious classical conditioning. The affective component of attitudes tends to be rather resistant to change. The cognitive components of attitudes can be acquired quite directly by reading a fact or opinion, or reinforcement by other people. Behavioural components of attitudes are not as clear cut as once believed. People do not always behave as their expressed attitudes and beliefs would lead us to expect.

Attitude change

Although one can regard attitudes as causes of behaviour, behaviour may also affect attitudes. Festinger's (1957) theory of cognitive dissonance attempts to explain the impact of behaviour on attitude formation and change. According to Festinger, when an individual perceives a discrepancy between their attitudes and our behaviour, between behaviour and self-image, or between one attitude and another, an unpleasant state of dissonance results, a state that people are motivated to eliminate. A person can achieve dissonance reduction by: a) reducing the importance of one of the dissonant elements; b) adding consonant elements; or c) changing one of the dissonant elements. For example, an employee believes that they are a good performer, but receives poor performance ratings. Because the obvious prediction is that good performers get good ratings, the discrepancy causes the employee to experience dissonance. To reduce dissonance, the employee may decide that performance ratings are not important and that performance is not closely related to ratings. They are using strategy 1, reducing the importance of one of the dissonant elements. Or the employee may believe that their supervisor was unfair or that they had difficult circumstances at home which affected their performance. In this case, they are using strategy 2, reducing dissonance by adding consonant elements. Finally, the employee can use strategy 3 to change one of the dissonant elements (by performing better or by revising their opinion of their performance).

Assessing and managing attitudes

Work and organizational psychologists can assist managers to appreciate the dynamic relationships between beliefs, attitudes, subjective norms and behavioural intentions when attempting to foster productive behaviour (Conner and Clawson, 2004). Although attitudes are often resistant to change, they might rest on incorrect beliefs, which could be indirectly influenced by education and training experiences. Subjective norms can also be redirected through clear and credible communication and role models.

Work and organizational psychologists can play the following roles in assessing and managing attitudes in organizations:

- **Attitude surveys**. The most obvious attitude-related activity of work and organizational psychologists is to develop, administer, analyse and report on the results of attitude surveys. Organizations use surveys to learn about employees' attitudes on employment issues such as compensation, quality of supervision, work/non-work balance. A weakness of attitude surveys is that management of organizations often fails to use the data and to implement recommended changes.

- **Job design**. Work and organizational psychologists assist organizations to design jobs in such a way that positive attitudes could be built.

- **Personnel selection**. Work and organizational psychologists are instrumental in developing reliable and valid prediction tools that incorporate attitudinal components.

- **Change management**. Work and organizational psychologists assist with change management in organizations by using attitude surveys to assess how employees view changes and their attitudes toward them.

Abilities

Definition of an ability

An **ability** is a broad and stable characteristic which is responsible for a person's maximum rather than typical performance on mental and physical tasks. An ability is the capacity to perform a physical or mental function.

Intelligence and cognitive abilities

Intelligence is regarded as a cognitive ability. Wechsler (1944) defined intelligence as '... the aggregate or global capacity of the individual to act purposefully, to think rationally and to deal effectively with his environment'. It is described as the general ability to perform cognitive tasks. Sternberg (1994) defined intelligence as the cognitive ability of an individual to learn from experience, to reason well, to remember important information and to cope with the demands of daily living. Intelligence is affected by the environment and more specifically schooling, socio-economic status, healthy nutrition and the technologically complex society (Azar, 1996).

According to Sternberg (1994), intelligence comprises three interrelated abilities, namely analytical ability, creative ability and practical ability. The analytical ability solves familiar problems by using strategies that manipulate the elements of a problem or the relationship among the elements (e.g. comparing, and analysing). The creative ability solves new kinds of problems that require thinking about the problem and its elements in a new way (e.g. inventing, and designing). The practical ability solves problems that apply what individuals know to everyday contexts (e.g. applying, and using).

Intelligence is considered as a set of skills which consists of behaviours that are modifiable. Three abilities are distinguished, namely a practical problem-solving ability, a verbal ability and social competence. Practical problem-solving ability includes behaviours such as good and logical reasoning, identifying connections among ideas, seeing all aspects of a problem, keeping an open mind and responding thoughtfully to others' ideas, and sizing up situations well. Verbal ability includes behaviours such as speaking clearly and articulating well, studying hard, reading widely with high comprehension, writing without difficulty, setting aside time for reading and displaying good vocabulary. Social competence includes behaviours such as accepting others for what they are, admitting mistakes, displaying interest in the world at large, being on time for appointments, thinking before speaking and doing, making fair judgements and assessing well the relevance of information to a problem at hand.

Dunette (1976) distinguished seven mental abilities that underlie performance of employees, namely verbal comprehension (i.e. the ability to understand the meaning of words and to comprehend verbal material), word fluency (i.e. the ability to produce specific words that fulfil certain requirements), numerical ability (i.e. the ability to make quick and accurate arithmetic computations), spatial ability (i.e. the ability to visualize how geometric shapes would look if transformed), memory (having a good memory for symbols, and words), perceptual speed (i.e. the ability to perceive similarities and differences) and inductive reasoning (i.e. the ability to reason from specifics to general conclusions).

Abilities and performance

Ability tests are valid predictors of job performance and can be used for employee selection (Schmidt and Hunter, 1981). In a later study it was found that general mental ability is one of the best predictors of job performance (Schmidt and Hunter, 1998).

Diversity

Diversity refers to the multitude of individual differences and similarities that exist among people. Diversity includes the mixture of many dimensions which make people unique and different from each other (Thomas, 1996).

Dimensions of diversity

Diversity has primary and secondary dimensions (Loden, 1996). These dimensions are described in Focus box 2.2.

Focus 2.2

Primary and secondary dimensions of diversity

Primary dimensions of diversity refer to human differences which affect the early socialization of individuals and have a powerful and sustained impact throughout their lives. Primary dimensions of diversity include gender, ethnicity, race, mental and physical abilities, sexual orientation and age.

Secondary dimensions of diversity refer to personal characteristics that include an element of personal choice. These dimensions are less visible to others, and their power to influence individuals' lives is less constant and more individualized. Secondary dimensions of diversity include education, language, religion, income, experience, geographic location, organizational role and communication style.

Figure 2.2 The workforce of organizations is increasingly becoming diverse.
Source: Jupiter images/Comstock Images/Alamy.

There is also a difference between valuing diversity and managing diversity. **Valuing diversity** refers to the awareness, recognition, understanding and appreciation of human differences (Thomas, 1996). It takes place through training and development of workers to improve interpersonal relationships among diverse groups (Nemetz and Christensen, 1996). In contrast, **managing diversity** entails enabling people to perform to their maximum potential by changing an organization's culture and infrastructure to allow people to be productive.

Managing diversity is different from **affirmative action**. Managing diversity focuses on maximizing the ability of all employees to contribute to organizational goals. Affirmative action focuses on specific groups because of historical discrimination, such as people of colour and women. Affirmative action is an artificial intervention which aims at giving organizations a chance to correct injustices, imbalances and mistakes of the past. Affirmative action emphasizes legal necessity and social responsibility; managing diversity emphasizes business necessity. While managing diversity is also concerned with under-representation of women and people of colour in the workforce, it is more inclusive and acknowledges that diversity must work for everyone.

Importance of diversity management

Diversity management is important because it enables organizations to grow and to be sustainable in an increasingly competitive marketplace (Agars and Kotke, 2005). The most important reasons for the management of diversity at work include:

- **A diverse workforce**. More women are entering the workforce, people of colour represent a growing share of the workforce, there is a mismatch between the educational attainment and occupational requirements of occupations, the workforce is ageing, more people with disabilities are entering the labour market, and sexual orientation and political views can also create tensions in the workplace.

- **The service economy**. In the USA it is estimated that 74 per cent of employees work in the service industry (McGammon and Griffin, 2000). The interpersonal nature of service transactions makes similarities between employee and customer more important. As the population in general becomes more diverse, employees who can communicate most efficiently with those clients become a business advantage.

- **Globalization**. Globalization has increased the contact with clients and co-workers from other countries. An understanding of cultural differences can not only facilitate communication but can also avoid potentially embarrassing or even insulting situations.

- **The changing labour market**. To deal with the changing labour market, employers are developing new recruiting strategies to target older employers, minorities and immigrants. They are developing more flexible benefits packages (more flexible hours, working from home, leaves of absence) to accommodate the new diversity they must manage.

The role of work and organizational psychologists in managing diversity

The most common intervention used by work and organizational psychologists to help organizations manage diversity is diversity training. Training for managers will focus on how to recruit and hire a more diverse workforce. This training often entails raising awareness of new sources or outlets that allow employers to find a greater pool of applicants. Manager training will also focus on how to manage the diversity of the newly hired workers. Specifically, training will focus on how to integrate the new employees into the existing workforce and how to raise the awareness of the current employees as to the benefits of greater diversity. This often requires a shift in the style of management. The focus of management shifts from treating everyone equally to treating everyone equitably, given the differences that each employee brings to the job. Training for all employees goes through several steps. The first step entails raising awareness that differences do exist. The second step focuses on how these differences influence working together to get the job done. The third step focuses on how these differences can be used to enhance productivity without treating people unfairly.

Activity 2.3

Individual differences and diversity management

Individual differences will influence a person's experience of the workplace. For example, introverts and extraverts might experience workplace challenges very differently.

1. Identify a person that functions in a team in a medium to large organization and who is regarded as an **introvert**. Schedule an interview with the person. What you want to learn from this interview is how the individual experiences their work environment. Several issues to explore include:

   - How does the individual prefer to interact with others in the team?
   - How does the individual prefer others to interact with him or her?
   - Does he or she feel appreciated by others in the workplace? Elaborate.
   - What challenges does he or she experience in the workplace because of his or her introversion?
   - What strategies does he or she apply to overcome these challenges?

2. Identify a person that functions in a team in a medium to large organization and who is regarded as an **extravert**. Schedule an interview with the person. What you want to learn from this interview is how the individual experiences their work environment. Several issues to explore include:

   - How does the individual prefer to interact with others in the team?
   - How does the individual prefer others to interact with him or her?
   - Does he or she feel appreciated by others in the workplace? Elaborate.
   - What challenges does he or she experience in the workplace because of his or her extraversion?
   - What strategies does he or she apply to overcome these challenges?

Present your findings to the class

Summary

- Personality has been defined as the enduring, inner characteristics of individuals that organize their behaviour. An etic or emic approach to the conceptualization of personality may be employed. The five-factor model of personality represents a structure of traits, including extroversion, agreeableness, conscientiousness, emotional stability and openness to experience. Personality predicts aspects of job performance that may not be strongly related to knowledge, skills or abilities. There are various reasons why personality matters in the workplace. The results of several studies showed that various Big Five personality dimensions are related to job performance.

- Values are constructs that determine what people will strive for in their lives and what they are prepared to sacrifice. Values can be seen as culturally bound. Values and value priorities are not displayed only by people; nations, countries and other social categories also display distinct value profiles or patterns. Cultural values manifest in two main areas, namely collectivism and individualism. Different value models have been developed by various researchers and all these models are evidence that values are part of culture. Employees who hold values that are congruent with their organization's values are more productive and satisfied.

- An attitude represents a predisposition to respond in a favourable or unfavourable way to persons or objects in one's environment. Research has shown that job attitudes of employees were very stable over years. Beliefs about aspects of a job lead to an attitude, which in turn results in behavioural intentions. Behavioural intentions are often translated into actual behaviour. Although attitudes are often resistance to change, they might rest on incorrect beliefs, which could be indirectly influenced by education and training experiences.

- An ability is a broad and stable characteristic that is responsible for a person's maximum rather than typical performance on mental and physical tasks. Intelligence is regarded as a cognitive ability. Seven abilities underlie performance of employees, namely verbal comprehension, word fluency, numerical ability, spatial ability, memory, perceptual speed and inductive reasoning. Ability tests are valid predictors of job performance.

- Diversity refers to the multitude of individual differences and similarities that exist among people. Diversity has primary and secondary dimensions. Diversity management is important because it enables organizations to grow and to be sustainable in an increasingly competitive marketplace. The most common intervention used to help organizations manage diversity is diversity training.

Key concepts and terms

Ability	Hardiness
Agreeableness	Intelligence
Attitude	Locus of control
Attitude change	Meta-analysis
Attitude survey	Openness to
Behavioural intention	experience
Beliefs	Organizational citizenship
'Big Five' personality model	behaviour
Conscientiousness	Personality
Contextual performance	Salutogenesis
Emic approach	Self-efficacy
Emotional stability	Sense of coherence
Etic approach	Task performance
Extraversion	Value

Sample essay titles

- Is personality a predictor of work-related outcomes? Motivate your answer.
- What are the contents and methodology of a diversity training programme?

Further reading

Books

Chamorro-Premuzic, T. (2007). *Personality and Individual Differences.* London: Blackwell.

Journal articles

Cheung, F.M., Leung, K., Zhang, J.X., Sun, H.F., Gun, Y.G., Song, W.Z., and Xie, D. (2001). Indigenous Chinese personality constructs: Is the five-factor model complete? *Journal of Cross-Cultural Psychology*, 32, 407–433.

McAdams, D.P., and Pals, J.L. (2006). A new big five: Fundamental principles for an integrative science of personality. *American Psychologist*, 61, 204–217.

Pendry, L.F., Driscoll, D.M., and Field, S.C.T. (2007). Diversity training: Putting theory into practice. *Journal of Occupational and Organizational Psychology*, 80, 27–50.

3 Motivation and satisfaction

This chapter focuses on **motivation** and **job satisfaction.** The first section describes motivation and theories thereof. Early theories of motivation are introduced, followed by the content and process theories of motivation. The content theories try to explain what motivates people, while the process theories try to explain the processes which play a role in motivated behaviour. The content theories are Maslow's theory of a need hierarchy, Herzberg's two-factor theory, Alderfer's needs theory, and McClelland's theory. Three process theories are discussed, namely equity theory, **expectancy theory** and **goal-setting theory.** The chapter then proceeds to motivation principles and the application thereof in organizations. Finally, we focus on job satisfaction.

Learning outcomes

When you have completed this chapter you should be able to:

1. Define motivation.
2. Compare and evaluate the different theories of motivation.
3. Explain how the different theories of motivation can be used to influence the behaviour of people in organizations.
4. Define job satisfaction and explain the factors which influence job satisfaction.
5. Give a description of the consequences of job satisfaction.
6. Explain the relationship between job satisfaction, motivation and performance.

Definition of motivation

Usually one or more of the following words are included in the definition: 'desires', 'wants', 'wishes', 'aims', **'goals'**, 'needs', 'drives', 'motives', and 'incentives'. The term 'motivation' can be traced to the Latin word *movere*, which means 'to move' (Luthans, 1992). Motivation is a set of energetic forces that originate both within and outside an individual to initiate work-related behaviour and to determine the direction, intensity and duration thereof (Latham and Pinder, 2005).

Theories of motivation

One way in which to 'classify' contemporary work motivation theories is by distinguishing between two broad types of motivation theories, namely the content theories and the process theories (Luthans, 1992).

Focus 3.1

Content and process theories of work motivation

Content theories of work motivation a) attempt to determine what it is that motivates people at work; b) are concerned with identifying needs/drives and how these needs/drives are prioritized; and c) are concerned with the types of incentives or goals that people strive to attain in order to be satisfied and perform well. Thus they focus on causes that motivate individuals.

Process theories of work motivation stresses the thought processes that individuals engage in when choosing between different courses of action that they can follow when trying to satisfy their needs.

Content theories of work motivation

The following theories can be described as being of the 'content' type: the **hierarchy of needs theory** of Maslow (1970), the two-factor theory of Herzberg, Mausner and Snyderman (1959), the **ERG theory** of Alderfer (1969), and the needs theory of McClelland (1987).

The hierarchy of needs theory of Maslow

Maslow (1971) proposed that the needs of a person are arranged in a hierarchical order of importance. The most important needs appear at the bottom of the hierarchy. Once a given level of need is satisfied, it no longer serves to motivate. The following needs are distinguished (Baron and Greenberg, 1990):

- **Physiological needs**. Physiological needs (e.g. hunger, thirst and sleep) are the most basic of all the needs.

- **Safety/security needs**. Safety/security needs involve the protection from physical danger and economic instability. The appropriate encouragement in this field is stable working conditions, the prospect of increasing cost of living being covered by an increase in salary, that provision shall be made for illness, disability and old age by contributing toward medical, insurance and pension schemes.

- **Social needs**. Social needs refer to the need to affiliate with other people. It refers to the need to have friends, to be loved by others and to be accepted by other people. The group of which the individual is a member plays a very important role in satisfying these needs.

- **Esteem/ego needs**. These needs can be divided into two groups, namely self-esteem needs and needs concerning (receiving) esteem from others. The first group is concerned with needs which are related to a person's self-value and self-respect (e.g. achievement, independence and freedom). The second group is concerned with needs that are related to reputation or prestige that others ascribe to the person (e.g. status, recognition and respect).

- **Self-actualization needs**. Self-actualization needs are found at the top of the hierarchy of needs. Self-actualization needs are associated with the desire to become all that one is capable of being.

Figure 3.1 Money can be used to satisfy various needs as distinguished by Maslow.
Source: Cut and Deal Ltd/Alamy.

Maslow's theory has not been subjected to much research. In cases where it has been researched in organizations, the data gathered do not seem to strongly support the theory. There seems to be an overlap between the different categories of needs. Some people are of the opinion that the physiological and the safety/security needs should be grouped together in one category, and that the higher order needs should be grouped together in another category. It is also possible that many of people's different needs may be partially satisfied and partially unsatisfied at the same time.

The two-factor theory of Herzberg

Frederick Herzberg proposed this theory, which is also known as the motivation–hygiene theory (Herzberg et al, 1959). Herzberg wanted to know the answer to the following question: What do people want from their jobs? Herzberg and his colleagues interviewed about 200 engineers and accountants. The participants were asked to describe occasions when they had felt particularly good about their jobs, and describe occasions when they had felt particularly bad about their jobs. Job factors which tended to be consistently related to job satisfaction were achievement, recognition, the work itself, responsibility, advancement and growth. Job factors that tended to be consistently related to job dissatisfaction were company policy and administration, supervision, interpersonal relations with supervisor, work conditions, salary, factors in personal life, status and job security.

Herzberg and his colleagues made a distinction between **motivators** and **hygiene** factors, because the factors which lead to satisfaction and thus to motivated behaviour (the motivators) (if they are present) are distinct from those that lead to dissatisfaction (the hygiene factors) (if they are absent). Also, based on the above findings, the researchers were led to believe that the opposite of satisfaction (when the motivators are present) is not dissatisfaction, but rather 'no satisfaction' (when the motivators are absent), and that the opposite of dissatisfaction (when the hygiene factors are absent) is not satisfaction, but rather 'no dissatisfaction' (when the hygiene factors are present). Once the hygiene factors are in order, they form a kind of a base or a platform on which to build the motivators.

Although the motivators appear to be distinct from the hygiene factors (81 per cent of the factors which contributed to job satisfaction were motivators, and 69 per cent of the factors which contributed to dissatisfaction were hygiene factors), hygiene factors sometimes lead to satisfaction (19 per cent of the factors which contributed to job satisfaction were hygiene factors), and motivators sometimes lead to dissatisfaction (31 per cent of the factors which contributed to dissatisfaction were motivators). Aspects like a good pay, good supervision and a pleasant work environment are important factors to prevent employees from becoming dissatisfied. If employees become dissatisfied, they will tend to become demotivated. On the other hand, employee motivation is a result of factors such as the nature of the work they perform, the recognition they receive for tasks well done, the responsibility they carry, the opportunity they have to achieve and the promotion they receive. In practice, then, one should attend to both the motivators and the hygiene factors.

Herzberg placed a lot of emphasis on personal growth as a motivating factor. There are, however, limits to what can be achieved in organizations regarding making use of the motivators (e.g. changing the nature of the jobs of employees). There might be employees who do not wish to have their jobs enriched or changed. Some employees do not have the skills needed to handle these enriched or changed jobs. Criticism directed at the theory is that the procedure which Herzberg used is limited by its methodology. When things are going well, people tend to take credit themselves. Contrarily, they blame failure on the external environment. Furthermore, the theory provides an explanation of job satisfaction rather than motivation (Robbins, 1996).

Alderfer's ERG theory

Alderfer's theory may be viewed as an extension of both Herzberg's and, especially, Maslow's theories. Alderfer (1969) identified three groups of important needs, namely existence (E), relatedness (R) and growth (G), hence the ERG. The existence needs are concerned with survival or physiological well-being of the individual, and they correspond to Maslow's physiological and safety/security needs. The relatedness needs are concerned with interpersonal and social relationships, and they correspond to Maslow's social needs. The growth needs are concerned with a person's desire for personal development, and they correspond to Maslow's **esteem needs** and self-actualization needs. According to the ERG theory, more than one need may be in operation at a given moment. This implies that a lower level need does not have to be substantially gratified in order for a higher level need to come into operation (Robbins, 1996: 219).

McClelland's theory of needs

McClelland (1955, 1984, 1987) did extensive research about the needs for power, affiliation and achievement. Let us now take a closer look at each of these needs.

- **The need for power**. This need for power is characterized by a desire to have impact, to be influential and to have control over one's environment. Individuals high in the need for power enjoy being in charge, strive for influence over others, prefer to be placed into competitive and status-oriented situations and tend to be more concerned with prestige and gaining influence over others than with effective performance.

- **The need for affiliation**. The need for affiliation has to do with the desire to form strong interpersonal ties and to get close (on a psychological basis) to other people. It thus is a need for human companionship, and to be liked and accepted by others. They strive for friendship, prefer cooperative situations rather than competitive ones and desire relationships involving a high degree of mutual understanding.

- **The need for achievement**. The need for achievement has to do with the desire to reach goals or to accomplish tasks more effectively than in the past. A person with a high need for achievement sets him or herself goals which are neither too easy (because then there is very little challenge involved) or too difficult (because then there is little chance that he or she will reach the goal). At the same time these goals should constitute a challenge to the person, so that he or she needs to make use of his or her abilities. Such a person also wants immediate and concrete feedback on his or her performance. A person with a high need for achievement tends to be preoccupied with his or her work, even when away from the work situation. The last principal characteristic of a person with a high need for achievement is the tendency for such a person to take personal responsibility for getting things done.

Activity 3.1

Similarities between need theories

If we call the theories of Maslow, Herzberg, Alderfer and McClelland 'need' theories, what are the similarities between these theories?

Process theories of motivation in organizations

Process theories of motivation are concerned with the processes which influence the way in which motivated behaviour is channelled. Three process theories of motivation, namely equity theory, expectancy theory and goal-setting theory, will be discussed next.

Equity theory

Equity theory was developed by J.S. Adams (1963). The essence of the theory is that perceived inequity is a motivating state, that is, when people believe that they have been inequitably treated in comparison to others, they will try to eliminate the discomfort and restore a sense of equity to the situation. Equity theory is based on the principle that people want to be treated fairly. Equity is defined as the belief that a person is being treated fairly in relation to others, and inequity as the belief that a person is being treated unfairly in relation to others (Moorhead and Griffin, 1989). When employees work for an organization, they basically exchange their services for pay and other benefits. Equity theory proposes that individuals attempt to reduce any inequity they may feel as a result of this exchange relationship.

Individuals compare themselves with other people/situations to decide whether they have been treated fairly. This comparison takes into consideration the input(s) the person makes in relation to the outcome(s) they receive from these inputs, and this ratio (outcomes to inputs) is compared to what the person sees as the ratio of outcomes to inputs of the person/people/situation(s) they compare themselves with. The inputs are the characteristics the person brings with him or her to the job, for example race, sex, age, education or experience. It is important to note that these characteristics are subjectively perceived by the person. The outcomes are those things the individual receives from the job, such as pay/salary, promotions and fringe benefits (Gray and Starke, 1980).

What is rather complicated about equity theory is the role of the specific person or situation which the individual chooses to compare him or herself to (this person/situation is called the referent). It thus implies that the referent who or which is chosen plays an important role in equity theory. An equity comparison typically occurs whenever organizations allocate extrinsic **rewards,** especially monetary incentives or pay increases. Inequity is perceived whenever people feel the rewards received for their work are unfair given the rewards other persons are getting. The comparison others may be co-workers in the group, workers elsewhere in the organization, and even persons employed by other organizations. According to Adams (1963), these comparisons can result in any of three states (see Focus box 3.2).

What happens when a person feels inequity? He or she is motivated to reduce this inequity (Gray and Starke, 1980). On the other hand, if a person feels equity, he or she tends to try and maintain the current situation. The first two methods of reducing inequity are rather straightforward. A person may increase/decrease his or her effort, depending on the type of inequity that is felt. A person might try to alter the outcomes. This may take on a demand for a higher pay/salary, seeking

Focus 3.2

States of inequity

Overpayment inequity occurs when a person's outcome/input ratio is greater than the corresponding ratio of the other person with whom that person compares him or herself. According to equity theory such a person will tend to feel guilty.

Underpayment inequity occurs when a person's outcome/input ratio is less than the corresponding ratio of the other person with whom that person compares him or herself. According to equity theory such a person will tend to feel angry.

Equitable payment occurs when a person's outcome/input ratio is equal to the corresponding ratio of the other person with whom that person compares him or herself. According to equity theory such a person will tend to feel satisfied.

other ways in which to develop and grow, or it might even go as far as stealing. In these two ways a person alters his or her own ratio. A more complex situation arises when a person wants to alter the perceptions of self and of others. This means that a person has to change his or her original view of the ratio between his or her own outcomes and inputs, or change his or her original view of the ratio of the comparison-other regarding the comparison-other's outcomes and inputs. Another way of reducing inequity is to exchange the current comparison-other for another comparison-other, who would provide a more valid basis for comparison. Of course, a person might, as a last resort, simply decide to leave the situation, by resigning or by asking for a transfer to another job or department (Moorhead and Griffin, 1989).

People who feel overpaid (positive inequity) have been found to increase the quantity or quality of their work. Those who feel underpaid (negative inequity) reduce their work efforts to compensate for the missing rewards, which means they are less motivated to work hard in the future. The way rewards are perceived by their recipients will largely determine how they affect satisfaction and performance. Because feelings of inequity are based on individual perceptions, it is not the reward's absolute value or what a manager thinks that counts. It is what the recipients think that determines motivational outcomes. Rewards perceived as equitable should have a positive result; those perceived as inequitable may create dissatisfaction and reduced performance.

From the above-mentioned methods of reducing inequity it is clear that some involve behavioural responses (like stealing) while others involve psychological responses (like thinking differently about the situation). As many people would feel uncomfortable with stealing from their organization, they might try to lessen the inequity by thinking differently about the situation. This implies some kind of psychological process of altering their perception.

Most of the research about the equity theory thus far has concentrated on pay/salary equity/inequity. Strong support was found for equity theory. However, recent research suggested that people respond to inequities created not only by the money they receive, but by other rewards as well (Baron and Greenberg, 1990). Work and organizational psychologists should understand the basis on which people receive rewards, whatever form these rewards may take. It should be remembered that people take a multifaceted view of their rewards; they perceive and experience a variety of rewards, some tangible and others intangible. Furthermore, people's feelings of equity and inequity are based upon their subjective perceptions of reality (Moorhead and Griffin, 1989).

Expectancy theory

Expectancy theory is about expectations that people hold, and how these expectancies influence their behaviour in organizational settings. Expectancy theory is regarded as one of the theories which perhaps gives the best explanation of the complexities of human motivation in organizations.

There are different expectancy theories. The first person to develop an expectancy theory directly aimed at work motivation was Victor Vroom (1964). According to expectancy theory, motivation is the result of three different types of beliefs that people have. Each of these beliefs also implies a certain relationship. Expectancy theory asks a central question: What determines the willingness of an individual to work hard at tasks important to the success of the work unit and the organization? To answer it, expectancy theory is based on the logic: 'People will do what they can do when they want to'. Vroom (1964) suggests that the relationships among the three expectancy factors should be understood. They are:

- **Expectancy (E):** A person's belief that working hard will result in a desired level of task performance being achieved (effort–performance expectancy). If a person believes that the harder he or she works, the more he or she will accomplish, then one can say that such a person holds a high effort–performance expectancy. On the other hand a person might be able and willing to work hard, but might not have the necessary skills or training, or has to work with faulty equipment. In this case such a person is more likely to hold a very low effort–performance expectancy.

- **Instrumentality (I):** A person's belief that successful performance will be followed by rewards and other potential outcomes (performance–outcome expectancy). Even if a person works hard and performs at a high level, his or her motivation is likely to decrease if that performance is not suitably rewarded by the organization. In this instance the person is likely to hold a low belief that high performance is instrumental in bringing about rewards. A case in point is when a person has reached the top of his or her salary scale, and no further advancement opportunities exist for him or her.

- **Valence (V):** The value a person assigns to the possible rewards and other work-related outcomes (rewards–personal goal relationship). Valence refers to the degree to which organizational rewards satisfy an individual's personal goals or needs and the attractiveness of those potential rewards for the individual. If a person would rather like to receive a promotion as a reward for his or her efforts, but knows that the reward will (only) be in the form of a bonus, such a person is likely to hold a low rewards–personal goal belief. Such a person's motivation is likely to be low.

$$\textbf{Motivation} = \textbf{E} \times \textbf{I} \times \textbf{V}$$

Note that a zero at any location at the right side of the equation will result in zero motivation. The manager must give attention to each of the components of motivation. Consider the following ways (see Focus box 3.3):

Focus 3.3

Applying expectancy theory

Maximize expectancy: Make the person feel competent and capable of achieving the desired performance level. This can be done by selecting workers with ability, training workers to use their abilities, supporting work efforts and clarifying performance goals.

Maximize instrumentality: Make the person confident in understanding which rewards and outcomes will follow performance accomplishments. Clarify psychological contracts, communicate performance outcome possibilities and explain that rewards are contingent on performance.

Maximize valence: Make the person understand the value of various possible rewards and work outcomes. Identify individual needs and adjust rewards to match these needs.

According to expectancy theory, motivation is not equal to job performance. Motivation is only one of several factors which influence job performance. Skills and abilities, and role perceptions also play an important role in job performance. In one of the examples we have already mentioned something about the role of skills and abilities. Role perceptions have to do with what people think is expected of them. If a person thinks that he or she is expected to carry out certain tasks, but his or her supervisor expects him or her to do other tasks, then such a person might be seen as not performing his or her work adequately (Baron and Greenberg, 1990).

Next, an 'extended' version of expectancy theory, namely that of Porter and Lawler, (1968) will be discussed.

Initially an individual's effort to a great degree depends upon the attractiveness (valence) of the potential reward he or she can expect if he or she exerts him or herself, and upon the perceived probability (expectancy) that the effort will lead to a certain reward. Together with the individual's abilities and traits and role perceptions, effort leads to performance, which in turn leads to receiving of rewards. The individual then judges how equitable the rewards are. If the rewards are perceived as being equitable, the individual will feel satisfied. Next time around, the degree of satisfaction with the rewards (a bonus) influences the value that the individual attaches to the rewards. Also, the performance that followed from the effort influences the way in which the individual perceives the probability that a certain effort will lead to certain rewards.

According to the 'extended' expectancy theory, performance leads to rewards, and these in turn lead to satisfaction with the rewards. It is also clear that satisfaction indirectly influences (future) performance. Also, it is clear that this version of expectancy theory incorporates some of the notions of **equity theory**. Porter and Lawler recommend that one should attempt to measure the values of possible rewards, the perceptions of effort–reward probabilities, and role perceptions. Organizations should also take a critical look at the way in which employees are rewarded. They also stress that one should look closely at the relationship between levels of satisfaction and levels of performance.

Regarding the relationship between motivation and performance, barriers to performance should be overcome by ensuring that: a) people possess the necessary abilities, skills and knowledge to do their jobs; b) it is physically and practically possible for people to carry out their jobs; c) the interdependence of jobs with other people or activities is taken into account; and d) ambiguity surrounding the job requirements is kept to a minimum. Regarding the relationship between performance and satisfaction the following guidelines have been suggested: a) determine what rewards each employee values; b) define what the desired standard of performance is; c) make it possible for employees to attain the desired standard of performance; and d) link the valued rewards to the attained levels of performance.

Goal-setting theory

Task goals in clear and desirable performance targets form the basis of the goal-setting theory of Locke and Latham (1984). According to this theory, task goals can be highly motivating if they are specific and not too difficult. Goals affect performance through four mechanisms (Locke and Latham, 2002), namely:

- they direct attention and effort to goal-relevant activities and away from goal-irrelevant activities;

- they have an energizing function;

- they affect persistence; and

- they affect action indirectly by leading to arousal, discovery and/or use of task-relevant knowledge and strategies.

Moderators of the goal–performance relationship include the following (Locke and Latham, 2002):

- **Goal commitment.** The goal–performance relationship is the strongest when people are committed to goals. Workers tend to be committed to goals when they regard them as important and when their levels of self-efficacy are high.

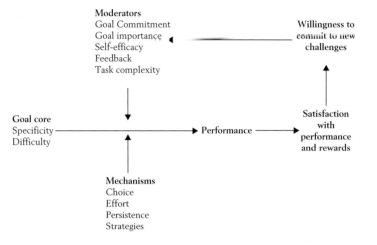

Figure 3.2 Elements of goal-setting theory and high performance.
Source: Locke, E. A., & Latham, G. P. (2002). Building a practically useful theory of goal setting and task motivation: A 35-year Odyssey. *American Psychologist, 57,* 705–717.

■ Feedback. For goals to be effective, people need summary feedback that reveals progress in relation to their goals.

■ Task complexity. Goal effects are dependent upon the ability to discover appropriate task strategies.

The essential elements of goal-setting theory and high performance are illustrated in Figure 3.2.

A manager must work with subordinates to set the right goals in the right ways. The following guidelines can be used:

■ Set specific goals. They lead to higher performance than more generally stated ones such as 'do your best'.

■ Set challenging goals. As long as they are viewed as realistic and attainable, more difficult goals lead to higher performance than easy goals.

■ Build **goal acceptance** and commitment. People work harder towards goals that they accept and believe in; they tend to resist goals that seemed forced on them.

■ Clarify goal priorities. Make sure that expectations are clear as to which goals should be accomplished first, and why.

■ Reward goal accomplishment. Do not let positive accomplishments pass unnoticed; reward people for doing what they set out to do.

Implications of motivational theories

Next, the implications of motivational theories and research findings will be discussed, based on the theories as discussed in this chapter as well as recent reviews of the topic (Latham and Pinder, 2005).

Personal motives and values

A motivating environment can be created by ensuring that the motives and values of the worker match those of the organization and the job. This can be done by giving a realistic preview of the job or training the worker to accept these motives and values. Jobs might be simple, repetitive and require little brain power to do. If someone for this type of work is found, the candidate should be told exactly what the job entails and then a candidate who will be satisfied doing that kind of work should be selected.

Goal setting

Work and organizational psychologists can assess the motivational climate of their working environment by asking, 'Do workers understand and accept performance expectations?'. The foundation of an effective motivation programme is proper goal setting. Effective goal setting has three critical components: goal setting process, goal characteristics and feedback.

- **Goal setting process**. Goals must be understood and accepted if they are to be effective. Workers are more likely to accept goals if they feel they were part of the generation process. This is especially important if the work environment is unfavourable for goal accomplishment (for example when the goal is inconsistent with accepted practice or when it requires new skills).

- **Goal characteristics**. Research has shown that goal characteristics significantly affect the likelihood that the goal will be accomplished. Effective goals are specific, consistent and appropriately challenging. Specific goals are measurable, unambiguous and behavioural.

- **Feedback**. Feedback provides opportunities for clarifying expectations, adjusting goal difficulty and gaining recognition. Therefore, it is important to provide benchmark opportunities for individuals to determine how they are doing. These progress reports are particularly critical when the time required to complete an assignment or reach a goal is very long.

Facilitating subordinates' performance

One key ingredient of an effective goal programme is a supportive work environment. After goals have been set, the work and organizational psychologist's focus should shift to helping accomplishment. Help may come in many forms, including making sure that the worker has the required abilities for the job, providing the necessary training, securing needed resources and encouraging cooperation and support from other work units. In other words, work and organizational psychologists should assist in making the paths leading towards the targeted goals easier for workers to travel.

Appropriate use of rewards and discipline

An important step in developing an effective motivational programme is to encourage goal accomplishment by linking performance to outcomes (rewards and **discipline**). Two principles are important, namely: a) rewards should be linked to performance, rather than seniority, or membership; and b) discipline could be used to decrease counterproductive behaviour and rewards could be used to reinforce constructive behaviour.

If an organization is rewarding all people the same or on some basis other than performance, then high performers are likely to feel that they are receiving less than they deserve. The most important individuals in any organization are its high performers. Therefore, motivational schemes should be geared to keeping high performers satisfied. This principle raises a voice of caution regarding the practice of eliminating distinctions between workers. Although there are obvious motivational benefits to employees who feel they are receiving the same rewards despite seniority level or level of authority, this philosophy, when carried to an extreme, ends up demotivating high performers.

Managers and supervisors must recognize that their daily interactions with subordinates are important motivators (Clawson, 2006). The following types of responses to employee behaviour must be considered:

■ **Extinction**. Extinction is behaviour followed by no response at all, but can be a difficult strategy to carry out. Often a non-response is interpreted as either a positive or negative response. If behaviour persists, it is reinforced. Thus, if an employee is chronically late or continually submits sloppy work, the manager must ask where the reinforcement for this behaviour is coming from.

■ **Disciplining**. Discipline involves responding negatively to an employee's behaviour with the intention of discouraging future occurrences. Discipline should be used to extinguish unacceptable behaviour. However, once an individual's behaviour has reached an acceptable level, negative responses will not push the behaviour up to the exceptional level. Failure to reprimand and redirect inappropriate behaviour may lead to undesirable outcomes. It poses a serious threat to the work unit's morale, and it does not improve the poor performer's behaviour.

■ **Rewarding**. The rewarding approach consists of linking desired behaviour with employee-valued outcomes. For example, when a worker completes a report in time, the manager praises their promptness. It is only through positive reinforcement that workers have control over achieving what they want.

Providing attractive rewards

It is a mistake to assume that all workers value the same outcomes. Workers could be allowed to select from a benefits menu. A flexible reward system helps managers not to project their own preferences onto subordinates.

External motivators are controlled by someone other than the worker. The manager or supervisor can show appreciation for a job well done, offer job security, show personal loyalty to workers and provide good working conditions. Although managers control the components of a job, they have no direct control over whether a specific worker finds a job interesting. The outcomes associated with an interesting job come from internal motivators – factors inherent in the job itself, not from any particular actions of the manager or supervisor.

No matter how many externally controlled rewards managers or supervisors use, if workers find their jobs to be uninteresting, and unfulfilling, performance will suffer. Attention to internal motivators is particularly critical in situations where managers or supervisors have relatively little control over the organizational incentive system. Job design is the process of matching job characteristics and workers' skills and interests. According to the model of Hackman and Oldham (1976), internal satisfying tasks are high on skill variety, task identity, task significance, autonomy and feedback. These core job characteristics result in three critical psychological states, namely experienced meaningfulness, experienced responsibility and knowledge of results. These critical psychological states promote job satisfaction, internal work motivation and work performance. Autonomy and feedback have a greater impact on the motivational potential of a job compared to the other three characteristics.

The more variety in skills a person can use in doing the work, the more the person perceives the task as meaningful. The more an individual can do a complete job from beginning to end (task identity), and the work affects the work or lives of other people (task significance), the more the employee will view the job as meaningful. The more autonomy in the work (freedom to choose when and how to do the job), the more responsibility they feel for their successes and failures. Increased responsibility results in increased commitment to one's work. Autonomy can be increased by beginning flexible work schedules, decentralizing decision making or removing selected formalized controls, such as ringing of a bell to indicate the beginning and end of a workday. The more feedback individuals receive about how well their jobs are being done, the more knowledge of results they have. Knowledge of results may be enhanced by increasing employees' direct contact with clients or by giving them feedback on how their jobs fit in and contribute to the total operation of the organization.

Other models of job design are the **job demands–control model** (Karasek, 1979) and **psychological empowerment** theory. The job demands–control model proposes that job demands might be less harmful and demotivating when they are accompanied by high levels of control. Psychological empowerment theory (Spreitzer, 1995) distinguished empowerment practices (e.g. job enrichment) from psychological empowerment (the cognitive-motivational states that arise from these practices). Psychological empowerment theory proposes that competence or self-efficacy (meaning believing that goals to be accomplished are meaningful), choice (feeling a sense of self-determination and choice over tasks) and impact (believing that actions make a difference) mediate the link between objective work conditions and psychological outcomes. This model implies that the psychological states (rather than just the objective work conditions) can be measured and promoted.

Equitable distribution of rewards

Once the appropriate rewards have been determined for each worker, the work and organizational psychologist must assist managers and supervisors in considering how to distribute the rewards. Any positive benefits of attractive rewards will be cancelled if workers feel that they are not receiving their fair share. Equity refers to the workers' perceptions of the fairness of rewards. Evaluations of fairness are based on a social comparison process in which workers individually compare what they are getting out of the work relationship (outputs) to what they are putting into the work relationship (inputs).

If workers experience feelings of inequity, they will behaviourally or cognitively adjust their own, or fellow workers', inputs and/or outputs. This may lead to a decrease in motivation and performance. For example, if workers believe that they are underpaid, they may as part of a cognitive strategy rationalize that they are not really working as hard as they thought they were, thus they reduce the perceived value of their own inputs. Or they may convince themselves that their co-workers are working harder than they thought they were. Behaviourally workers can request a pay raise, or they can decrease their inputs by leaving a few minutes early each day, decreasing their effort, deciding not to complete an optional training programme or finding excuses not to accept difficult tasks.

Subordinates' perceptions of equity should be monitored, because they may uncover faulty comparison processes. For example, people may be using inappropriate comparisons (with more senior or better-educated individuals), they may misunderstand the value placed on various inputs (e.g. experience versus expertise, quantity versus quality) or they may have unrealistic views of their own performance. The important thing to keep in mind about equity and fairness is that we are dealing with perceptions. Whether these perceptions are accurate or distorted, until proven otherwise they are accurate in the mind of the perceiver.

Providing timely awards and accurate feedback

It is the timing of the reinforcement that lets the worker know which behaviour is being encouraged. Giving a reward at the wrong time can increase undesirable behaviour. For example, giving a long-overdue, fully warranted raise to a worker during an interview in which he or she is complaining about the unfairness of the reward system, may reinforce complaining rather than good work performance. Moreover, failure to give a reward when desired behaviour occurs will make it even more difficult to increase that behaviour in the future.

Formal administrative procedure in organizations often delays for months the feedback on the consequences of worker performance. This delay between performance and feedback decreases the effectiveness of rewards or discipline. Immediate and spontaneous rewards are important.

Social and group factors

The interpersonal and group process must support the worker's efforts to achieve objectives. The use of self-managed work groups and giving responsibility for a whole task can motivate workers. The motivational climate in the group can be improved by giving attention to the composition of the group. The homogeneous composition of groups, team building and the selection and development of leaders can affect motivation.

Job satisfaction

In this section we shall be looking primarily at the relationship between satisfaction and motivation.

Definition of job satisfaction

Locke (1976) defines job satisfaction as a pleasurable or positive emotional state resulting from the appraisal of one's job or job experience. Job satisfaction is the result of employees' perception of how well their job provides those things that are viewed as important. Job satisfaction has the following three dimensions (Luthans, 1992):

- Job satisfaction is an emotional response to a job situation. Therefore, it cannot be seen. Inferences have to be made from workers' behaviour to determine whether they are satisfied or dissatisfied. Questionnaires can also be used to assess job satisfaction.

- Job satisfaction is often determined by how well outcomes meet or exceed expectations. Thus, if some workers feel that they are working much harder than some of their co-workers but that they are receiving fewer rewards than the less hardworking co-workers, they will most probably be quite dissatisfied with their work, their supervisor and/or their co-workers.

- Job satisfaction represents several related attitudes about job characteristics, namely the nature of the work, pay, promotion opportunities, supervision and co-workers.

Factors which influence job satisfaction

The work itself seems to be a major source of job satisfaction, especially characteristics such as feedback, interesting and challenging work, and work which provides status to the employee. Pay seems to be a major factor in job satisfaction, because the money a person receives not only gives him or her the opportunity to satisfy their basic needs, but also to satisfy higher-level needs. Promotional opportunities seem to have a varying effect on job satisfaction. Supervision is a moderately important source of job satisfaction. It seems as if there are two dimensions of supervision that influence job satisfaction, namely worker-centredness and participation (Luthans, 1992). It seems as if co-workers are a modest source of job satisfaction. Relationships with co-workers are not essential to job satisfaction. However, if the work group is difficult to get along with, it will have a negative effect on job satisfaction. Working conditions seem to have a modest effect on job satisfaction. If working conditions are fine, there will be no job satisfaction problems: if they are poor, there will be. It actually seems as if employees generally do not give much thought to working conditions, unless they are extremely bad. A person's needs and aspirations can affect satisfaction. If a person wants to be in a high-status position, gaining such a position will probably enhance that person's level of job satisfaction. The instrumental benefits of the job, or the extent to which it (the job) enables the employee to achieve other ends also play an important role in satisfaction (Moorhead and Griffin, 1989).

The consequences of job satisfaction and job dissatisfaction

It seems as if there is a moderate inverse relationship between satisfaction and *turnover*. High job satisfaction does seem to help to keep turnover low, but will not, in and of itself, keep it low (Luthans, 1992). If, on the other hand, there is high job dissatisfaction, turnover is likely to be high. The reason for this moderate relationship between satisfaction and turnover is the fact that other factors (e.g. the state of the economy) play a role in an employee's decision to keep or quit his or her job.

There is an inverse relationship between satisfaction and *absenteeism*. That is, when employees are highly satisfied, they tend to be less absent from work; when they are highly dissatisfied, they tend to be more absent from work. Again, there are other factors which influence this relationship. One such factor might be the degree to which an employee feels that his or her work is important. If a person feels that his or her work is important, he or she will be less likely to be absent from work (Luthans, 1992).

There is recent large-scale research (Faragher et al, 2005) which indicates a strong relationship between job satisfaction and employee health.

A more 'problematic' relationship is that of satisfaction and *performance*. Research results showed that in some cases there is a negative relationship between satisfaction and performance, in some cases there is a positive relationship between satisfaction and performance, and in some cases there are very few signs of such a relationship. During the mid 1950s Brayfield and Crockett (1955) found that the median correlation between satisfaction and performance was about 0.12, which is rather low. In the most recent examination by Judge et al (2001) a correlation of 0.30 between satisfaction and performance was found (which is a small but meaningful association). It is probably better to assess the relationship between satisfaction and motivation, rather than satisfaction and performance. The link between motivation and performance is not a simple one, because there are many other important factors which influence employee performance, besides motivational levels. These factors include job design, the functioning of machines and equipment, group norms and group coordination.

Application 3.1

The perils of money and other extrinsic motivators

Katherine Lawrence argued during the Conference on Promoting Markets in Creativity: Copyright in the Internet Age (2003) in Washington, DC, that although money is a symbolic way of showing employees that they are valued it might also be a dangerous motivator. She pointed out that there are three ways in which money can have serious repercussions for the creative process:

1. **Financial rewards can distract employees from the organization's underlying goals**. It is often difficult for employees within large organizations to see direct connections between their efforts and the final results. To make these connections clearer, some bonus reward systems tie individual compensation to overall firm performance. For example, stock options are thought to encourage employees to work harder as 'owners' of the firm. However, a recent study by Julia A. Welch (*Good Intentions Gone Awry: A Field Study of Stock Options in the High-Tech Industry*, unpublished dissertation, University of Michigan, 2003) shows that stock options can become a carrot that lures employees completely off track, causing them to be so obsessed with the hour-to-hour fluctuations in stock value that their effort and motivation fluctuate accordingly. Instead of working, employees in one firm spent hours of work time each day preoccupied with their personal stock portfolios. Rather than focusing employee effort and responsibility, stock options can be a damaging extrinsic motivator. Businesses need to consider meaningful, non-financial ways of sustaining motivation throughout the creative process.

2. **Employees may not put forward their best work if they are 'bought out' for limited rewards**. Often, people produce creative work in exchange for a salary or a fixed contract, resulting in the employer owning their 'copyrights'. If creativity has the potential to produce ongoing income to the firm, individual contributions should be rewarded in kind. For example, some organizations allow individuals within the organization to hold copyrights or patents and perhaps earn royalties from them. Financial rewards aside, this simple recognition may offer a sufficient incentive. In addition, the opportunity to reap the benefits for the years that their creativity continues to be profitable may bolster existing intrinsic motivations.

3. **Extrinsic rewards such as money can actually damage intrinsic motivation** because employees begin to focus on the reward rather than on the work, and lose interest in going the extra distance. Knowledge workers – those responsible for many of the creative products protected by copyright – typically have intrinsically motivating work, and it is important to preserve that intrinsic value as an incentive. Intrinsic motivation is encouraged through exciting opportunities, supportive work environments and recognition. As Eric Raymond, an evangelist for the open-source software movement, has said, 'You cannot motivate the best people with money ... The best people in any field are motivated by passion ... When are programmers happy? They're happy when they're not underutilized – when they're not bored ... This is a general preference in creative work. People are

happiest when they're the most productive'. The open-source software movement is proof that money is not the sole motivator. Given that fact, it is important to identify what else might motivate a particular individual – whether that might be more varied projects, a chance for learning and challenge, or greater autonomy – and reward accordingly.

Extract from Lawrence, 2004.

Summary

- In different definitions of motivation, the following words are often used: desires, wants, wishes, aims, goals, needs, drives, motives and incentives. Motivation in organizations is the willingness to exert high levels of effort towards organizational goals, conditioned by the effort's ability to satisfy some individual need.

- There are different theories that try to explain motivation. These theories can be divided into two main groups, namely the content theories and the process theories. The content theories try to explain what motivates people, while the process theories try to explain the processes that play a role in motivated behaviour.

- A motivating environment can be created by a) ensuring that the motives and values of the worker match those of the organization and the job; b) proper goal setting; c) facilitating subordinates' performance by creating a supportive work environment; d) appropriate use of rewards and discipline; e) providing attractive rewards; f) providing timely awards and accurate feedback; g) attending to social and group factors.

- Job satisfaction is defined as a pleasurable or positive emotional state resulting from the appraisal of one's job or job experience. The main factors influencing job satisfaction are organizational factors (pay, promotions, the work itself and working conditions), group factors (the role of the supervisor and of co-workers) and personal factors (needs and aspirations and how these are met, and how an individual views the instrumental benefits of the job). The relationship between satisfaction, motivation and performance/productivity is rather complex, and some kind of model is needed to explain it.

Definition of terms

A **group** is defined as a collection of two or more people who are involved in face-to-face interaction, are interdependent, perceive themselves and others as part of the group, have a stable pattern of relationships between them and strive towards a common goal (Johnson and Johnson, 1994).

A group is composed of two or more people in social interaction. In other words, the members of the group should have some influence on each other. The interaction between the people may be verbal (such as giving ideas to solve a problem) or non-verbal (such as exchanging smiles in the hallway). In addition to having social interaction, a group must possess a stable structure. Although a group can and does change, there must be some stable relationship between members which keeps a group together and functioning as a unit. A gathering of people which constantly changes (such as the gathering of people inside an office waiting room) cannot be thought of as a group.

The members of groups share common goals. Groups are often formed because of some common goals or interests that individuals could not realize on their own. For example, a soccer team is a group that may be sustained by the mutual interests of its members in winning a championship. Individual members must perceive themselves as a group. Groups are composed of members who recognize each other as a member of their group and can distinguish these members from non-members. Shoppers in a checkout line are probably not recognized as members of a group. Although they stand physically close to each other and may interact, they have little in common.

It seems that there are differences between a work group and a work team (Robbins, 1996). A work group is a group which interacts primarily to share information and to make decisions to help each member perform within his or her area of responsibility. Work groups have no opportunity or need to engage in collective work which requires joint effort. A work team generates positive synergy through coordinated effort. Their individual efforts result in a level of performance which is greater than the sum of individuals' inputs.

Figure 4.1 A team generates positive energy through coordinated effort.
Source: James Nesterwitz/Alamy.

Types of groups

There are various types of groups such as work groups in organizations (e.g. production groups or marketing groups), committees and informal groups. In the next few paragraphs we will distinguish between various ways to classify groups.

Groups can be classified on the basis of their formality. Groups can either be formal or informal. Formal groups are defined by the organization structure, with designated assignments establishing tasks. The members making up an airline flight crew are a formal group. So are the members of a production team in an organization or a department at a university. Informal groups are alliances which are neither formally structured nor organizationally determined. These groups appear naturally in response to the need for social contact. Three employees from different departments who regularly eat lunch together are an example of an informal group.

Sundstrom et al (1990) classify organizational groups as follows:

- **Advice and involvement groups** include **decision-making** committees, quality circles and employee involvement groups which are being used as vehicles for employee participation.

- **Production and development groups** use technology to generate products or services, as in assembly lines, maintenance, construction, mining, commercial airlines and sales.

- **Project and development groups** of white-collar professionals such as researchers, engineers, designers and programmers often collaborate on assigned or original projects.

- **Action and negotiation groups** include sport teams, surgery teams, musical groups and other highly skilled specialist teams cooperating in brief performance events which require improvisation in unpredictable circumstances.

Explaining work group behaviour

Why would some groups be more successful than others? The answer to this question is complex. A study of the variables which explain group behaviour in Figure 4.2 will, however, shed more light on this issue.

Next we will focus on each of the factors that explain work group behaviour.

Group member resources

Various **group member resources** (e.g. age, gender, physical characteristics and personality characteristics) may affect work group behaviour. Research showed that an increase in age is accompanied by an increase in the frequency of social contact, higher selectivity in interpersonal contact, a tendency to want to serve as leader and a decrease in conforming behaviour (Szilagyi and Wallace, 1983). Regarding the influence of gender on group behaviour, it can be

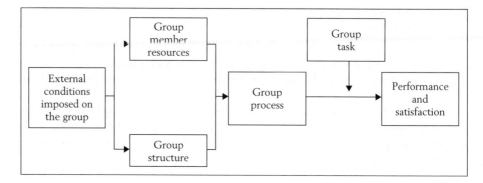

Figure 4.2 Variables which explain work group behaviour.

concluded that females (compared with males) are more inclined to conform to **group norms,** and are more communicative in bargaining situations (Reynolds, 1984). These characteristics are, however, a function of cultural norms regarding the role of females in the society (that may change). Sexual attraction between males and females may change the group dynamics, complicate leadership and cause resistance towards leadership (Bormann and Bormann, 1988).

The abilities and skills of an individual may affect his or her functioning in a group. More intelligent individuals (compared with the less intelligent) tend to be more active in groups, conform less, are more self-confident and resist efforts of others to influence them (Jewell and Reitz, 1981). Intelligent group members are more effective in leadership positions, but leadership effectiveness decreases if the leader is substantially more intelligent than group members.

External conditions imposed on the group

External conditions imposed on the group which may affect group member behaviour include organizational culture, task design and technology.

Organizational culture

Groups are influenced by the culture of the organization. **Organizational culture** is defined as the internal consistent pattern of affirmations, confirmations and limitations which lead people to act, judge and justify themselves according to sanctioned ways (Weick, 1985). The organization culture could have an inhibiting or facilitating effect on the behaviour in a group. Group effectiveness can be promoted if the current organization culture is supportive of innovation and shared expectations of success. It is important to enquire about social rules which may inhibit group work, and to identify existing norms for group gatherings and problem solving within the specific organization culture and the society.

Task design and technology

The effect of the nature of the task can be determined by considering the complexity of technical demands (knowledge and skills) and social demands (interaction between group members). To perform well, the group must divide

Research methods 4.1

Personality traits and group behaviour

Personality traits such as sociability and independence are related to productivity, morale and cohesion of the group. Characteristics such as dominance and unconventionality are negatively related to productivity, morale and cohesion (Robbins, 1996). Research by Barry and Stewart (1997) suggests that individual group member personality is related to the way in which groups function. Groups are most effective when group member personality characteristics are congruent with the roles they fulfil. The role of personality may be particularly important in self-managed work teams. Extraversion is the key personality-based correlate with individual impact on group performance as perceived by other group members. Groups having 20–40 per cent high extraversion members outperform groups with either fewer or more members. Barry and Stewart (1997) found no direct role for conscientiousness in group situations. It seems that conscientiousness may become less important in team-based tasks because groups are able to recognize and compensate for the lack of conscientious individuals. It may also be that conscientiousness plays a smaller role in conceptual tasks (e.g. creative tasks and decision-making) and a more important role in behavioural tasks (planning, performance or competition). Group effectiveness is improved when members are socially sensitive, assertive and not too anxious.

the skills, inputs and strategies available in such a way that it would fit the technical and social demands of the task. The quality of group performance decreases when the task becomes too complex or too simple.

Task design and social organization depends on the technology of the organization. The mechanization of work in a coal mine may for instance cause those individuals have to work in teams rather than on their own. Some technologies may implicate that one group member has to master all the tasks, while others are so complex that a member could only master one (e.g. a symphonic orchestra).

Optimal fit between the task, technology and social organization requires that technical processes be divided in sub-units of reasonable size. Ideally spoken, each group has to be responsible for the total manufactured product, to help them to see the end results of their work. The task should be significant, challenging and require a variety of skills. The group should be responsible for the results, be interdependent and must be able to learn and get feedback. Frequent and reliable performance feedback must be built into the task.

Organization strategy

An organization's overall strategy, put into place by top management, outlines the organization's goals and the means for attaining these goals. It might direct the organization towards reducing costs, improving quality, expanding market share or shrinking the size of the total operation. The organization's strategy may influence the power of various work groups, which will determine the resources which the organization's top management is willing to allocate to it for performing the tasks. The communication of the mission of the organization is especially important for work teams the work of which is closely related to those of other work units. Group members will be more motivated to strive for group goals if they accept them. Resistance and self-oriented behaviour arises if group members do not accept the goals.

Performance feedback

The effectiveness of a group (work team) depends on accurate and timely **performance feedback.** This requires reliable measurement systems, especially when the group produces quantifiable outputs and has a short work cycle (e.g. mining teams and the assembly line). It is, however, difficult to give feedback when the work cycle is long and when outputs are produced infrequently.

Reward and recognition

The nature of the reward may affect the productivity and functioning of the group. Rewards which encourage cooperation between group members have a positive effect on the motivation and interpersonal relations of group members, especially if they are interdependent. A well-structured reward system may reinforce the motivating nature of a well-designed task. Difficult, but realistic performance objectives must be set, and the group should receive feedback about their efforts to reach these objectives. Objectives must support (rather than replace) task-based motivation. Rewards and objectives which focus on group behaviour (rather than individual behaviour) may increase the effort of group members. Conflict arises when specific individuals in the group are targeted for rewards. This problem is often experienced in organizations which rewarded individual performance in the past.

Physical environment

The seating arrangements, illumination, ventilation and physical environment where work takes place may affect the processes and results of the group. Group interaction is promoted when group members are placed near to each other. The seat taken by the group member indicates at what distance he or she feels comfortable with others. Interaction is facilitated by face-to-face seating arrangements. Although positive causal relationships have been found between productivity and group functioning on the one hand, and light intensity, size of rooms, the use of music, and noise on the other hand, these effects are mediated by the attitudes (and expectations) of group members. Orienting group members positively towards environmental variables can control their effect.

Authority structures

Organizations have authority structures, which define who reports to whom, who makes decisions, and what decisions individuals or groups are empowered to make. This structure determines where a given work group is placed in the organization's hierarchy, the formal leader of the group, and formal relationships between groups. While a work group might be led by someone who emerges informally from within the group, the formally designated leader – appointed by management – has authority which others in the group do not have.

The informal relationships in an organization may undermine the formal structure. For example, the personal relationship between the director of an organization and the manager of one department (of a specific division) may undermine the formal authority of the head of the division.

Inter-group relationships

The degree of interdependence between various groups in the organization varies. Organizations represent a complex structure of groups imbedded in other groups. Members try to satisfy their personal needs, as well as those of other groups to which they are affiliated to in the group (Putnam, 1988). Each group is, to an extent, dependent on other groups in an organization, because everyone contributes to the final output. Performance of one group may also be dependent on outputs of other sections or groups. Poor performance of one group may block the performance of others, which may cause frustration.

The principle of competition between groups is often used to increase the productivity of groups and individuals. Excessive competition between groups (departments and sections) may lead to a subtle application of sanctions and sabotage of other groups in the organization. Tension, frustration and conflict arising from this spread to every individual in the group and delay the group interaction process.

Group structure

Work groups are not unorganized mobs. They have a structure which shapes the behaviour of members and makes it possible to explain and predict individual behaviour in the group.

Composition of the group

It is advisable to consider selecting people who are able and willing to function in a group. Two specific aspects should be mentioned in this regard, namely the heterogeneity of the group members and the compatibility of interpersonal needs of group members.

- **Heterogeneous versus homogeneous group composition**. When a group is heterogeneous in terms of gender, personalities, opinions, abilities, skills and perspectives, there is an increased probability that the group will possess the characteristics needed to complete its tasks effectively. The diversity in the group, however, increases the possibility of conflict in the group.

- **Compatibility of interpersonal needs**. According to Schutz (1978), human beings have three interpersonal needs, namely inclusion, control and affection. Interaction between people could be explained by wanted and expressed behaviour in the areas of inclusion, control and affection. Heterogeneity of group members regarding inclusion, control and affection may cause conflict between group members. However, more learning and change occurs in these groups. Two individuals are compatible if each individual shows the behaviour that the other wants. Compatibility regarding affection leads to improved cooperation and productivity between group members in interpersonal learning contexts.

Application 4.1

Group cohesiveness

'High cohesiveness in groups leads to higher group productivity.' Do you agree or disagree? Explain.

Group size

The productivity of the group can increase if the group size is increased. If, however, the group size is too large, productivity may be reduced. Larger groups are more effective if it is necessary to gather facts. Smaller groups (of approximately seven members each) are, however, more able to use inputs productively (Robbins, 1996). The optimal group size varies between four and ten members. As group size increases, communication becomes more difficult, discussions are dominated by some group members, some members feel threatened, subgroups are formed, and it becomes difficult to reach consensus. Groups with an uneven number of members are preferable to those with an even number. Groups with five or seven members utilize the advantages of both smaller and bigger groups (Bormann and Bormann, 1988).

An important finding regarding group size is **social loafing**. Social loafing is the tendency for individuals to expend less effort when working collectively than when working individually. It challenges the logic that the productivity of the group as a whole should at least equal the sum of the productivity of each individual in that group. Social loafing develops because of the belief of some group members that others do not pull their weight. Social loafing is also caused by the belief of group members that it is impossible to measure their contributions. The implication is that where managers utilize collective work situations to enhance morale and team work, they must also provide means by which individual efforts can be identified.

Roles of group members

A **role** refers to a set of expected behaviour patterns attributed to someone occupying a given position in a social unit. In any group there would initially be a period of self-oriented behaviour caused by unresolved emotional issues interfering with the task (Napier and Gershenfeld, 1987). If these issues stay unresolved, the group's behaviour will be directed at **self-oriented behaviour**, including: a) aggressive coping, which manifests in behaviour such as arguments, interrupting other group members, ignoring others and hostile humour; b) seeking for support, which manifests in group members trying to find members who agree with them, to form a subgroup; and c) withdrawal or denial, which manifests in suppression of tension and feelings, as well as passiveness and indifference (Dimock, 1987).

Task-orientated roles aim specifically at accomplishing a group goal. When groups gather to solve problems, make decisions, plan activities or determine policy, they are frequently hampered by group members' random behaviour. Sometimes one person monopolizes the conversation while others remain silent. Leaders in the group make use of the following behaviours to help the group reach its goals:

- Initiating, to get the group to begin and giving direction to the discussion.

- Coordinating, to help group members see the results of their efforts and reduce their uncertainty about the group, its problem and its solutions.

- Summarizing, to help move the group towards its goals.

- Elaborating, to explore the problem more fully and to help the group reach its goal.

Process-oriented roles help maintain a satisfactory interpersonal climate within a group, and include the following roles:

- Tension release, to reduce the tension in the group.

- Gatekeeping, to keep the communication channels in the group open.

- Encouraging, to increase the esteem of group members and raise their hopes, confidence and aspirations.

- Mediating, to resolve conflict between group members and release the tension associated with conflict.

Regarding work teams, Margerison and McCann (1990) distinguished nine **team roles** which people prefer to play (see Focus box 4.1).

Work and organizational psychologists need to understand the individual strengths which each person can bring to the team, select members with this in mind, and allocate work assignments which fit members' preferred styles. The researchers who developed this framework argue that unsuccessful teams have an unbalanced portfolio of individual talents, with too much energy expended in one area and not enough in other areas.

Group norms

The term 'norm' comes from the word 'normal'. Behaviour is normal if it seems to fall within the guidelines which a particular group accepts as appropriate for itself. Norms evolve only if they receive collective support. A norm can be defined as a collection of expectations held by the members of a group that specify the type of behaviour which is regarded as right or

> ### Focus 4.1
>
> **Team roles**
>
> - Creator-Innovators are usually imaginative and good at initiating ideas or concepts.
> - Explorer-Promoters like to take new ideas and champion their cause.
> - Assessor-Developers have strong analytical skills. They are at their best when given several different options to analyse and evaluate before a decision is made.
> - Thruster-Organizers like to set up operating procedures to turn ideas into reality and get things done.
> - Concluder-Producers are also concerned with results. Only their role focuses on insisting that deadlines are kept and ensuring that all commitments are followed through.
> - Controller-Inspectors are people with a high concern for establishing and enforcing rules and regulations.
> - Upholders-Maintainers hold strong convictions about the way in which things should be done.
> - Reporter-Advisors perform an important role in encouraging the team to seek additional information before making decisions and discouraging the team from making hasty decisions.
> - Linkers can play the roles played by any of the previous eight. Linkers are coordinators and integrators.

wrong, good or bad, relevant or irrelevant, permissible or impermissible in the group (Feldman, 1984). Group norms emerge from the values of a group and are standards of behaviour which are imposed upon members. The group norms are the do's and don'ts that result from the interactions of group members over time. A **norm,** then, is a standard model, or pattern of behaviour.

Norms are set regarding task and process issues, but are not always stated explicitly. There is usually an unspoken expectation that group members know the responsibilities and limitations of individual behaviour in the group. Although these implicit norms regulate group behaviour, few individuals are aware of them until they are broken.

Norms develop through communication with others. Norms develop by subtle, subliminal, beyond-awareness processes of inference from raised eyebrows, or hearing supportive 'uh-hums' or watching how others gain approval. They may evolve through an interpersonal process of negotiation as we attempt to follow the rule of fitting in. Within each group there is a history of what is accepted behaviour, which has developed over time in that situation, and which members learn and understand.

According to Feldman (1984), norm enforcement which groups are likely to bring under normative control are only those behaviours that a) ensure group survival; b) increase the predictability of group members' behaviour; c) prevent embarrassing interpersonal situations; or d) express the group's central values. These group norms, though, directly affect decision-making in the group (Chen et al, 2002).

Once norms are developed and agreed upon, they are difficult to change. Changing group norms not only increases the forces in the direction of the desired change, but also involves holding the resistant forces constant or reducing them. Problems may arise when the values, objectives and beliefs are in conflict with group norms.

Application 4.2

How Sherif and Sherif conquered the 'Wild-West' towards group dynamic research

Stages of group dynamics: The contributions of Sherif and Sherif

Much of the work on groups and teams was originally done in the 1940s and 1950s by two researchers called Sherif and Sherif. In their most important work they took two street gangs off the streets of New York City and gave them a summer vacation at a resort in upstate New York. One group was favoured while the other one was subtly discriminated against so it appeared as if the group was always second best. As an example, one gang was given accommodation close to the meal hall while the other group slept over half a mile away. The meals were on a first-come, first-served basis which meant that the groups further away were already operating at a disadvantage. In addition, both groups were given small housekeeping tasks which had to be done before they could go to meals. The people inspecting the two gangs were given instructions to speed on the first group while slowing the second. The first gang always beat the second to the meal hall and had first choice of the meals. As you probably suspected, there was not enough tasty food to go around and the meals the second gang received were repetitive and not very appetizing.

When the two gangs competed in games with each other, the first gang was always judged the winner. Over the course of the first week Sherif and Sherif noticed the morale, cohesion and performance of the first gang increased while that of the second gang went down dramatically. Tensions rose between the two gangs as a result of various incidents. One night, the first gang pelted the house the second gang lived in with unripe apples until all the windows were broken. Fights broke out between the gangs, and even within the second gang. Matters reached a head when one gang member from the second gang pulled a switchblade knife on a member of the first gang. The initial stage of the experiment ended at this point.

For the follow-up to the first part of the experiment, Sherif and Sherif decided to attempt to get the two gangs to operate together not only peacefully, but as one group. They changed the nature of the games from group competitions to tasks which required more members than were in either of the two gangs. Preferential treatment of the first gang was eliminated and the boys from both gangs were treated equally. The speed at which former antagonisms were forgotten and the two gangs merged resources surprised Sherif and Sherif.

- Sherif and Sherif summations:
- The availability of resources and rewards has an impact on the morale, group unity and productivity.
- Recognition and effort impact group development.
- Increased productivity maintains group effectiveness.

Source: www.peak.ca/articles/

Group processes

Group development stages

The model of Lacoursiere (1980) is one of the most comprehensive models on **group development stages** and incorporates both the recurring phase theories and sequential stage theories. It represents most of the stages found in the literature of group development and consists of the following five stages:

- **Orientation stage ('Forming')**. At the start of a group's life cycle the participants generally have positive expectations that something good will come from participation in their group. At the same time there is a certain amount of anxiety and concerns as individuals try to discover why they are there, what they will get out of it, and what the stated purpose of the group means. Group members are quite dependent on the situation and on whoever is in authority.

- **Dissatisfaction stage ('Storming')**. After some time, the participants learn that what they hope for or want from the experience and what they feel is actually happening do not coincide. The earlier dependence on the authority is found unsatisfying. This leads to unpleasant feelings of frustration, sometimes anger against the task, and usually also against the authority figure. These negative feelings usually become stronger and more prominent than the earlier feelings of eagerness and hope of gaining from the experience.

- **Resolution stage ('Norming')**. What happens at this stage is some compromise between expectations and the realities (task, leader, abilities and other members) and also some increase in skills to complete the task, either as originally construed or as redefined. Sufficient mastery of the situation and new skills allow positive feelings of increased self-esteem and pleasure in accomplishment and exceed the earlier negative feelings of frustration and anger.

- **Production stage ('Performing')**. The production stage is characterized by the positive feelings of eagerness to be part of the experience and hope for a good outcome exceeding the negative feelings of discouragement, frustration and anger of the earlier dissatisfaction stage. This all leads to more efficient use of time, with less time spent in struggling against the leader, the other group members or the task itself. Roles become flexible and functional, and group energy is channelled into the task.

- **Termination stage ('Adjourning')**. As the end of the experience approaches, the participants begin to concern themselves with what they have accomplished and with the impending dissolution of the group. Sometimes the feelings of loss or anticipated loss are largely denied or covered up in some way, such as joking (sometimes about death) or missing the final meeting. The work on the task during the termination stage generally decreases.

Considering the variety of relationships between work teams and organizational contexts, it seems unlikely that a single sequence can describe the development of all kinds of teams. Each team has to deal with certain developmental issues, but the order of precedence depends on the circumstances. The sequential stage model is supported by research results with training and laboratory groups, which cannot necessarily be generalized to work teams (Sundstrom et al, 1990).

Studies of more than a dozen field and laboratory task force groups confirmed that groups do not develop in a universal sequence of stages (Gersick, 1988). The timing of when groups form and change the way they work is highly consistent. It has been found that:

1. The first meeting sets the group's direction.
2. The first phase of group activity is one of passivity.
3. A transition takes place at the end of the first phase, which occurs exactly when the group has used up half of its allotted time.
4. The transition initiates major changes.
5. A second phase of passivity follows the transition.
6. The group's last meeting is characterized by markedly accelerated activity.

The **punctuated equilibrium** model characterizes groups as exhibiting long periods of inertia interspersed with brief revolutionary changes triggered primarily by their members' awareness of time and deadlines. The group begins by combining the forming and norming stages, then goes through a period of low performing, followed by storming, then a period of high performing and, finally, adjourning.

Group cohesion

Group cohesion is defined as the sum of the attraction of the group for members, and the ability of the group to stay together (Bormann and Bormann, 1988). It is a result of individuals' satisfaction with the group. A cohesive group is not necessarily a more productive group. Cohesion develops even if the group has a norm of low productivity. Cohesion involves the total forces acting on members to remain in the group compared to those directing people away from the group. Group cohesion can be defined, then, in terms of both the positive rewards which you derive from being in the group and the expectancy that your outcomes would be lower if you did not belong to the group.

Highly cohesive groups are more productive, have higher morale and communicate better than low cohesive groups. Cohesive groups do more work because members take the initiative and help one another. They distribute the workload among themselves and volunteer to help one another. They pay attention to the group's problems, and spend time and effort in favour of the group. The more cohesive the group, the more effective the communication within the group. Cohesiveness encourages feedback, disagreements and questions. Members of high cohesive groups indicate when they do not understand, and disagree among themselves (Bormann and Bormann, 1988).

Members of groups with low cohesiveness are quiet, bored, apathetic, tensed and uncomfortable. They seldom disagree, and there are few give-and-take discussions. Important decisions are made quickly. Members of low cohesive groups lack initiative and tend to stand around and wait for assignments. They do only what they are told to do and no more (Bormann and Bormann, 1988).

Group cohesion can be encouraged by the following factors:

1. When group members collaborate to reach a common objective and when there is a real or imagined threat in the group's environment.
2. The more satisfied group members are, the higher the group cohesion will be.
3. Cohesion is higher in a small group than in a large group.
4. More interaction between group members promotes the group cohesion.
5. The more similar the members are in terms of background and attitude, the more likely it is that group cohesion will be enhanced.
6. Group cohesion is also influenced by leadership style. A participative style will enhance cohesiveness.

Communication

Group communication can be defined as face-to-face communication among a small group of people who share a common purpose or goal, who feel a sense of belonging to the group and who exert influence upon one another. Regardless of a group's size its members must be able to talk and respond to one another. They must be sensitive to the needs and feelings of other group members. Schein (1969) states that the communication process is one of the most important processes which take place in the group and is observable. He makes the following distinction of communication processes that take place within the group: a) who communicates, how often, for how long; b) who communicates to whom; c) who talks after whom, who interrupts whom; d) communication style; non-verbal communication; e) levels of communication; and f) filters.

Group decision-making

Individual and group **decision-making** both have strengths. Neither is ideal for all situations. Groups have the following advantages:

- More complete information and knowledge. By aggregating the resources of several individuals, there is more input into the decision process.

- Increased diversity of views. Groups can bring heterogeneity to the decision process. More approaches and alternatives could be considered.

- Increased acceptance of a solution. Decisions often fail because people do not accept them. If people are able to participate in a decision which affects them, they will be more likely to accept it and encourage others to accept and support it.

- Increased legitimacy. Group decision-making is consistent with democratic ideals and may be perceived as being more legitimate than decisions made by a single person.

Groups have the following disadvantages:

- Time consuming. Groups take more time to reach a decision than would be the case when an individual makes a decision. This may limit quick and decisive action.

- Pressures to conform. The desire by group members to be accepted and considered an asset to the group can result in conformity.

- Domination by a few members. One or a few members can dominate group discussions. If these members have low ability, the group's overall effectiveness would suffer.

- Ambiguous responsibility. It is often difficult to determine who is accountable when group decision-making is used.

- Groupthink. **Groupthink** describes situations in which group pressures for conformity deter the group from critically appraising unusual, minority or unpopular views.

- Polarization. In discussing a given set of alternatives and arriving at a solution, group members tend to exaggerate the initial positions they hold. In some situations, caution dominates, and there is a conservative shift. Often, however, groups tend towards a risky shift.

There are five major characteristics of an effective group decision, namely that the resources of group members are fully utilized, the time is well used, the decision is correct, or of high quality, and the problem-solving ability of the group is enhanced, or at least not inhibited. A decision is effective to the extent that these five criteria are met; if all five are not met, the decision has not been made effectively. According to Johnson and Johnson (1994), consensus decision-making is the most effective method of group decision-making, but it also takes the most time. Napier and Gershenfeld (1987) state that reaching a decision through consensus represents the ideal in terms of group participation, but it is by no means the most efficient or least tension producing approach to decision-making. It simply indicates that each member is willing to go along with the decision.

Summary

- Groups are defined as a collection of two or more interacting individuals with a stable pattern of relationships between them who share common goals and who perceive themselves as being a group. Various types of group, including formal and informal groups, are distinguished.

- Predictions about a work group's performance must begin by recognizing that work groups are part of a larger organization. Factors such as the organization culture, strategy, authority structures and rewards may influence the group's behaviour and results. For example, if an organization is characterized by distrust between management and workers, it is likely that the work group will restrict their efforts. Characteristics of group members may also influence the results of the group.

- Roles represent the typical pattern of behaviour in a specific social context. Roles are often differentiated into task roles and maintenance roles. In the early stages of group development, the group may be dominated by self-oriented behaviour, which is caused by unresolved emotional issues. Norms, a set of generally agreed upon informal rules, have profound effects on organizational behaviour. Cohesiveness refers to pressures faced by group members to remain in the group and is influenced by various factors. Cohesiveness aids performance if the group's goals are consistent with management's interests. Groups develop through stages. Although different models of group development can be distinguished, one popular model classifies the stages as forming, storming, norming, performing and adjourning.

Key concepts and terms

Communication	Norm
Decision-making	Organizational culture
Group	Performance feedback
Group cohesiveness	Process
Group composition	Punctuated equilibrium
Group development stages	Role
Group member resources	Self-oriented behaviour
Group norms	Social loafing
Group size	Task design
Group structure	Task-orientated role
Groupthink	Team
Inter-group relationships	Team role
Interpersonal needs	

Sample essay titles

- Which processes occur in work groups?
- How could group effectiveness in organizations be improved?

Further reading

Books

Kozlowski, S.W. and Bell, B.S. (2003). 'Work groups and teams in organizations.' In: W. Borman, D. Ilgen and R. Klimoski (Eds), *Handbook of Psychology*. New York: Wiley, 333–375.

Levi, D. (2001). *Group Dynamics for Teams*. Thousand Oaks, CA: Sage.

Journal articles

Kauffeld, S. (2006). Self-directed work groups and team competence. *Journal of Occupational and Organizational Psychology*, 79, 1–21.

Van Knippenberg, D. and Schippers, M.C. (2007). Work group diversity. *Annual Review of Psychology*, 58, 515–541.

5 Communication

This chapter introduces the reader to a number of basic issues concerned with the definition, importance, methods, nature and skills of communication. The first section gives the definition of communication and describes the importance of communication. We then look at various methods of communication, namely written, oral, downward, upward, horizontal and **formal communication.** The chapter then proceeds to a discussion of communication and relationship-building skills. To communicate effectively, active listening, skilful responding, good oral and **written communication,** assertiveness and non-verbal communication skills are required. Skilful responding can take place by using questions, minimal encouragement, paraphrasing, clarification, reflection of feelings, **summarizing** and **confrontation**. Relationship-building requires **self-disclosure** and **feedback, cooperation, trust,** intercultural sensitivity, a **service orientation,** self-presentation, **social influence** and conflict resolution. Finally, we look at how **power** and **conflict** could impact on organizations.

Learning outcomes

When you have completed this chapter you should be able to:

1. Define communication and explain the importance of communication in organizations.
2. Distinguish between methods of communication in organizations.
3. Explain the interpersonal skills which are needed to communicate effectively and to build relationships in the work situation.
4. Identify factors which inhibit or facilitate communication in organizations.

Definition of communication

Communication is defined as the process by which a person, group or organization (the sender) transmits some type of information (the message) to another person, group or organization (the **receiver**) (Baron and Greenberg, 1990). Two or more parties exchange information and share meaning, so that a common understanding is established between them. It is only through transmitting meaning from one person to another that information and ideas can be conveyed. It is, however, important that this meaning also needs to be understood as it was intended to be understood (Robbins, 1996).

The importance of communication in organizations

Communication seems to play an important role in the attainment of organizational goals. According to Luthans (1992), managers devote about one-third of their activities to routine communication – exchanging routine information and processing paperwork. Communication plays an important role in managerial and organizational effectiveness. It is also one of the biggest problems that modern managers face. However, for some people communication has become an easy scapegoat on which just about every problem can be blamed – even problems of a personal, national and international nature. Communication can obviously play an important role in this regard, but it is definitely not a so-called 'cure-all' for all problems which humankind experiences.

Communication does serve certain major functions within an organization, namely those of control, motivation, emotional expression and providing information (Robbins, 1996). The function of control is fulfilled in both a formal and an informal way. Organizations have formal guidelines which employees need to follow, for instance in the case of a grievance procedure. Communication helps to motivate employees by clarifying what they need to do and how it should be done. When they receive feedback on their efforts, it serves as a motivating mechanism. Sometimes communication is aimed at emotional expression by venting feelings of frustration or satisfaction. Communication facilitates decision-making because it provides the necessary information which is needed by the decision-maker. By providing information, communication serves the purpose of achieving coordinated action between different parts of an organization.

The nature of the communication process

The **source of** the communication may be a person or an object. As an object, it may take on many forms, such as a book, a piece of paper, a radio or a television set. The message can take on many forms as well, such as an instruction, a question or even a facial expression. The characteristics of the receiver influence the way in which the message is received and interpreted (Gray and Starke, 1980).

A model depicting the communication process is depicted in Figure 5.1 (Robbins, 1996).

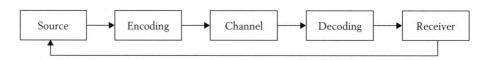

Figure 5.1 The communication process.

According to Figure 5.1, there are specific processes which play a role in the feedback that the sender receives from the receiver. This feedback takes place in order to verify the message. Encoding means that the message is translated from an idea or a thought into symbols which can be transmitted. When busy with encoding, the sender should keep the receiver and his or her characteristics in mind. The sender and the receiver need to understand the symbols in the same way. The message is the physical product which the sender wishes to communicate to the receiver. It can take on different forms: speech, writing, pictures, arm movements and facial expressions. The message is effected by the code or group of symbols that is used to transfer the meaning, the content of the message itself and the decisions regarding the selection and arrangement of codes and content. Transmission is the process through which the encoded message travels via a medium or channel or path to the receiver. These channels can be seen as pathways along which the encoded information travels. The source of the message and the way in which it is encoded play an important role in the 'type' of channel or medium which is selected. When the encoded message is delivered in a face-to-face conversation, the channel used in the transmission process is sound waves (Klikauer, 2007).

The channels (also called media) through which messages move can be of great variety. It might be an interpersonal channel, as in the case of talking and touching, to something like a fax machine, right through to something like a newspaper, a radio broadcast or a television broadcast. If one really wants to go into the technical detail, one should perhaps mention that in the case of the newspaper the way in which the message is encoded plays a particular role in the way it is perceived by the receiver. In the case of radio broadcast and television broadcast technical and electrical equipment are involved again, such as transmitters and receivers.

Decoding is the process by which the receiver of the message attaches meaning to it. In technical terms this means that the receiver must translate the symbols encoded in it into a form which he or she (the receiver) can understand, and then also in the way the sender intended it to be understood. If the receiver attaches different meanings to the message, the communication process can break down. Just as the sender has limited capacities to encode the message, so the receiver has limited capacities to decode the message.

It is important for the sender to keep the qualities of the receiver in mind when **encoding** a message and choosing the channel by which it should be transmitted. The sender should keep in mind that the receiver might be an individual, a group or an individual acting on behalf of a group. During the decoding process the receiver plays an important role in trying to understand the message as it was intended to be understood. In order to ensure that the message has been correctly understood by the receiver, it is important that the receiver gives feedback to the sender in this regard (Bundel, 2004).

Noise makes the communication process more complex. Noise refers to anything that interferes with the communication process, or which distorts the message. The message itself can also cause distortion, because of the poor choice of symbols and confusion in the content of the message. If a poor channel or medium is selected or the noise level is high, the message can become distorted. The receiver can also be a potential source of distortion. Prejudice, knowledge, perceptual skills, attention span and care in decoding are all factors which can result in distortion of the message.

Methods of communication in organizations

Written communication

Different types of written material are used in the communication process. Formal letters are usually used to communicate with someone outside the organization. Inside organizations, the so-called 'office memorandum', or 'memo' is quite prevalent. Such a memo is usually addressed to a specific person or a group of persons, and deals with a specific subject (Moorhead and Griffin, 1989).

Other types of written communication found in organizations are reports, manuals and forms. Reports are usually used to summarize the progress or results of projects, and are thus of value in decision-making. There are different kinds of manuals in organizations. These include instruction manuals which tell employees how to operate machines, policy and procedure manuals which inform employees of organizational rules and regulations, and operations manuals which tell employees how to perform tasks and to respond to work-related problems. Information is reported on standardized documents, which are called forms. Forms are used in an attempt to make communication more efficient and information more accessible, and thus to increase the efficiency of decision-making.

Oral communication

Oral communication occurs when the spoken language is used during face-to-face talks, telephone conversations, telephone messages and tape recordings. Oral communication is particularly powerful because it includes not only speakers' words but also their changes in tone, pitch, speed and volume. When people listen to messages, they use all of the aforementioned cues to understand oral messages. Moreover, receivers interpret oral messages in the context of previous communications and, perhaps, the reactions of other receivers.

Downward communication

Katz and Kahn (1978) have identified five general purposes of superior–subordinate communication in an organization. They are as follows:

- To give specific task directives about job instructions.

- To give information about organizational procedures and practices.

- To provide information about the rationale of the job.

- To tell subordinates about their performance.

- To provide ideological information to facilitate the indoctrination of goals.

To a large degree, organizations in the past concentrated only on the first two of these purposes. This leads to an authoritative atmosphere, which inhibits the effectiveness of upward and horizontal communication in organizations. The media which are used in **downward communication** include organizational handbooks, manuals, magazines, newspapers, letters, bulletin-board items, posters, standard reports, descriptions of procedures, verbal orders and instructions from superiors, speeches, meetings, closed-circuit television sets, public address systems, telephones and electronic mail systems. The key to optimizing downward communication seems to lie in understanding the important role that the receiver of information plays in the communication process. One should take into consideration that the downward flow of information could affect receivers in the following ways (Luthans, 1992):

- People's interpretations of communications follow the path of least resistance.

- People are more open to messages which are consonant with their existing image, their beliefs and their values.

- Messages which are incongruent with values tend to engender more resistance than messages which are incongruent with rational logic.

- To the extent that people positively value need fulfilment, messages which facilitate need fulfilment – are more easily accepted than messages which do not.

- As people see the environment changing, they are more open to incoming messages.

- The total situation affects communication; a message interpreted as congruent in one situation may be interpreted as incongruent in another.

- The senders of information at higher organizational levels should take note of the above-mentioned facts to make communication more effective. It is important for subordinates to receive the necessary information, because without it they cannot perform as they should.

Upward communication

Upward communication can perhaps also be called subordinate–superior or subordinate-initiated communication. This type of communication flows from a lower level to a higher level in organizations. This type of communication provides feedback to those at higher levels, informs them of the progress which has been made toward attaining goals and is used to inform those at higher levels of the problems which are experienced at lower levels. Through this type of communication those at higher levels can also get ideas on how things can be improved in the organization. Upward communication can take on different forms. These include progress reports, suggestions placed in so-called 'suggestion boxes', information gained from employee attitude surveys, information gained from grievance procedures, discussions between superiors and subordinates, and informal 'gripe' sessions where employees have the opportunity to identify and discuss problems with their superiors or with people at higher managerial levels (Robbins, 1996).

Downward communication occurs much more frequently than upward communication. It also seems as if the duration of conversations between subordinates and their superiors tends to be much shorter than conversations between subordinates and people at the same level. Furthermore, upward communication seems to be much more inaccurate. This occurs because subordinates feel the need to highlight their accomplishments, and to downplay their mistakes, so that their superiors can view their behaviour as favourable. Sometimes, subordinates are afraid to speak to their superiors for fear of being rebuked and for fear of lessening their own chances for promotion (Baron and Greenberg, 1990).

Horizontal/lateral communication

This type of communication takes place among members of the same work group, among members of work groups at the same level, or among horizontally equivalent personnel. Usually, horizontal/lateral communication tends to be easier and more friendly than downward or upward communication, because the problem of status differences is not present. Horizontal communication can also become problematic, even if it is of a formal kind. People in different departments may begin to feel that they are competing for scarce resources. Informal **horizontal communication** can cause dysfunctional conflicts if the formal vertical channels are breached, when subordinates go above or around their superiors to get things done, or when superiors find out that actions have been taken or decisions made without their knowledge.

Formal and informal communication

Formal communication is regulated by the formal channels laid down in the structure of an organization. Baron and Greenberg (1990) define informal communication as information shared without any formally imposed obligations or restrictions. Informal communication flows via informal communication networks. Informal communication networks are, of course, also found outside organizations. In this way, people are connected to each other in an informal way. Naturally, most of this communication is not necessarily work-related, but it lends itself to the very rapid flow of information. These informal channels are known as the organizational grapevine.

Information tends to flow very rapidly along the grapevine. There are mainly two reasons for this. Informal communication crosses formal organizational boundaries. Also, informal communication is mainly transmitted orally, which tends to be more rapid than written communication. Because of the oral way of communication, information tends to become distorted as it is passed along the grapevine. This does not mean that the grapevine is necessarily a bad thing. Although there are people who wish that it could be eliminated, it can sometimes be quite accurate. As long as there are people working in an organization, one will find the grapevine in operation. On the other hand, when inaccuracies enter the grapevine, it can become quite damaging. This is especially true in the case of rumours. Rumours are based on speculation, overactive imagination and wishful thinking, rather than facts (Baron and Greenberg, 1990). It is very difficult to refute a rumour. Instead, it seems to be a better strategy to concentrate on other aspects of a person or a situation, rather than directly refuting a rumour about the specific person or situation. If you directly refute a rumour, some people who did not hear it in the first place are likely to get to know about it, while others' views about it might be strengthened, perhaps only because of the rumour being denied.

For people who share in the information brought by the grapevine, it can often be beneficial. Through their access to informal information, which they would not have been able to get via formal channels and structures, people can become quite powerful in organizations. It also helps them to build informal connections with other people.

Interpersonal skills

A person is not born with interpersonal skills. These skills will also not appear automatically when they are needed. Interpersonal skills must be learned in the same way as other skills (e.g. to play the piano, to play tennis). In line with the structure suggested by Klein, DeRouin and Salas (2006), interpersonal skills are divided into communication skills and relationship-building skills.

Communication skills

Six communication skills are distinguished, namely **active listening,** responding skills, oral communication, written communication, **assertive communication** and non-verbal communication (Theobald and Cooper, 2004).

Active listening

Active listening is the conscious attempt to attend to verbal and non-verbal nuances in another person's message (Johnson, 1997). Listening is an intellectual and emotional process which integrates physical, emotional and intellectual inputs to understand the meaning of the message. It also revolves around the meaning behind the words. However, it is difficult to listen actively. It is estimated that people generally comprehend about 25 per cent of a typical verbal message (Barker et al, 1995). To listen effectively, the listener postpones his or her judgement and values, eliminates interruptions and disturbances, focuses on the contents of the message, rephrases what the speaker says in his or her own words, and looks for the important themes in what he or she says. Recurring themes must be noted. The listener tries to understand the person's message and determines what it means to him or her personally.

Responding skills

Responding skills are used to explore issues and problems in interpersonal situations. Responding skills include questioning, minimal encouragement, paraphrasing, summarizing, reflecting and confrontation (Ivey, 1988).

- **Questioning.** Open and closed questions can be used in a communication session. Open questions can be used to start a conversation, to encourage the individual to elaborate, to get specific examples of ideas, behaviour and feelings and to motivate him or her to communicate. Closed questions can be used to define the subject of discussion, to get specific information, to determine borders of a problem and to focus the session by interrupting the person who talks a lot.

- **Minimal encouragement**. Minimal encouragement refers to a direct quotation of what the individual has said, or short comments like 'uh huh' or 'Tell me more ...'. Silences can also be used.

- **Paraphrasing**. By paraphrasing, the content of the person's messages is reflected. It is a summarized repetition of what the other person says. An appropriate format for the response is: 'You say ...', 'In other words ...', 'It seems that ...', 'It appears as if ...'.

- **Clarification**. Clarification brings vague and ambiguous information into focus, encourages the person to elaborate and can be used to find meta-messages. Clarification is often put in the form of a question, such as 'Are you saying that ...?' or 'Do you mean that ...?'.

- **Reflecting feeling**. By reflecting feeling the listener demonstrates his or her understanding of the feeling of the person, whether it was expressed directly or indirectly. The feelings of the speaker can be identified by listening for feeling words and by observing the person's non-verbal behaviour. The format of a reflection of feeling is: 'You feel ...' but it must fit the person's feeling words. Add the context or situation to which the feelings are connected (e.g. 'You feel tense when you write exams').

- **Summarizing**. Summarizing refers to the shortened reflection of the speaker's behaviour. The key ideas, themes and emotions in the discussion should be summarized without adding new ideas. Summarizing can be seen as a more detailed paraphrasing and is aimed at changing the direction of the discussion, reducing the tempo, or to end the conversation and revise progress. Summarizing is used when themes are repeated and progress is not apparent.

- **Confrontation**. A **confrontation** is a verbal response used to describe contradictions, conflicts and meta-messages that are apparent in the speaker's feelings, ideas and actions. The objective of confrontation is to help the speaker see other ways of observing a situation, and to help him or her to become more aware of the incongruence in thoughts, feelings and actions.

Oral communication

It is possible that the listener will understand if the speaker's message is clear, concrete, direct and authentic. The sending of clear, concrete messages demands a conscious effort. The person who communicates effectively has a clear picture in his or her head of what he or she wants to say. He or she can clarify the message and elaborate on it. He or she is receptive to feedback, and uses it to direct his or her thoughts. Complete and specific messages, which fit the frame of reference of the person to whom the message is sent, must therefore be conveyed. A person must also accept ownership and responsibility for his/her ideas, opinions, feelings and needs by making personal statements. This is made by using personal pronouns when communicating ('I', 'My', 'Mine') rather than talking for nobody ('Some people', 'One') or to speak for somebody else ('You', 'We', 'Our').

Written communication

It is important to phrase written messages effectively. Written communication skills include the clarity of writing as well as the appropriateness of the content, tone and format (Klein et al, 2006). It is important to attend to these aspects in electronic communication. Misunderstandings occur often in mail messages because they lack the non-verbal cues which are given in oral communication.

Assertive communication

Assertive communication entails that a person describes his or her feelings, thought, opinions and preferences in an appropriate way. To be assertive, one must be aware of the difference between three concepts, namely, assertiveness, aggression and passiveness. An aggressive person believes that his or her rights are more important than those of others. The passive style is characterized by timid and self-denying behaviour and rests on a person's assumption that his or her rights are less important than those of others. The style of an assertive person is expressive and self-enhancing and rests on the assumption that his or her rights as well as the other person's rights are equally important.

Studies have shown that assertiveness is more effective than aggressiveness in both work-related and consumer contexts (Infante and Gorden, 1985; Raudsepp, 1992). Individuals should learn to be less aggressive and passive and to be more assertive. Assertive behaviour is characterized by good eye contact, a strong, steady and audible voice and selective interruptions. Assertive people should avoid glaring or little eye contact, threatening gestures and a weak voice. Appropriate verbal behaviours include direct and unambiguous language and the use of 'I' messages (Johnson, 1997).

Non-verbal communication

Non-verbal communication refers to messages sent independent of the written or spoken word. Non-verbal behaviour has been studied extensively and it was found that socially inadequate people make less use of non-verbal indicators or use them in the wrong way (Trower, 1990). It has been estimated that non-verbal communication is responsible for up to 60 per cent of the message being communicated (Arthur, 1995). Non-verbal communication has a significant impact on behaviour in organizations, including perceptions of others, hiring decisions, work attitudes and turnover (Liden et al, 1993; Wright and Multon, 1995). A person communicates by means of his or her eyes, facial movement and expressions, tone of voice, posture and body movements (Hall, 1985). Non-verbal communication is subjective, easily misinterpreted, and dependent on cross-cultural differences (Axtell, 1993). The belief that there is only one 'correct' interpretation of a non-verbal message does not promote interpersonal communication.

Relationship-building skills

Self-disclosure and feedback

Self-disclosure involves the individual sharing his or her self, thoughts, feelings and experiences with another individual and is necessary for effective communication and interpersonal relationships. A healthy relationship is built on self-disclosure. If a person hides his or her feelings from others, the tension in the relationship rises and his or her awareness of the inner experience fades. Self-disclosure leads to higher self-awareness (Johnson, 1997).

Feedback can be defined as a verbal and non-verbal process where one individual reveals to another how he or she sees the other's behaviour and how he or she feels about it. It is difficult to give feedback in such a way that the person receiving it accepts it. It is, however, a skill that is learned and for which certain guidelines exist. It is possible to reduce a person's defence against receiving of feedback and to maximize his or her ability to use it for personal growth by giving feedback in an objective way, without disturbance (Johnson, 1997).

The effects of self-disclosure and feedback in interpersonal situations can be illustrated by the Johari window model (see Figure 5.2):

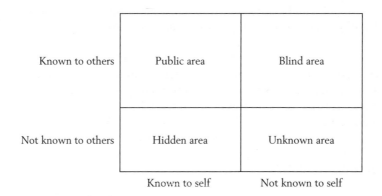

Figure 5.2 The Johari window.

Source: Luft, J. (1984, page 72). Group process: An introduction to group dynamics. Palo Alto, CA: Mayfield Publishing Co.

According to the Johari window there are certain things a person knows about him or herself, certain things about him or herself that he or she does not know, certain things others know about him or her and certain things others do not know about him or her. The more information known to a person and to other persons, the clearer communication could be. The public area can be enlarged and the blind area can be decreased through feedback from others. The hidden area can be decreased by means of self-disclosure (Luft, 1984).

Cooperation

Cooperation is defined as the offering of assistance to team members who need it, pacing activities to fit the needs of the team, and behaving in ways that are not misinterpreted by team members (Klein et al, 2006). Cooperation means that individuals engage in joint action to accomplish a goal that both want. Studies support the notion that cooperation contributes to teamwork in organizations

Trust

Trust is defined as 'the willingness of a party to be vulnerable to the actions of another party based on the expectation that the other party will perform a particular action important to the trustor, irrespective of the ability to monitor or control that other party' (Mayer et al, 1995). Trust is constantly changing as individuals interact, and it is something that is hard to build and easy to destroy. The key to building trust is being trustworthy, by self-disclosing and by being accepting and supportive of others (Johnson, 1997). Individuals who lack trust will tend to overprotect themselves and their work environment, withhold information and avoid risk-taking.

Intercultural sensitivity

Intercultural sensitivity is defined as the ability to recognize multiple perspectives on an event or behaviour, to recognize one's own cultural values and those of others, and to pick up on verbal and non-verbal signals. Intercultural sensitivity is necessary in order to understand that one's own preferred way of doing things is but one of several possible approaches, and that other cultures may have different perspectives and preferences. The ability to recognize the needs of listeners through verbal and non-verbal signals in communication, helps to empathize with culturally different others and to adjust to different ways of communicating.

Intercultural sensitivity requires that an individual demonstrates comfort with other cultures, positive evaluation of other cultures, understanding of cultural differences, empathy for individuals from other cultures, open-mindedness, sharing of cultural differences with others, seeking feedback on how he or she is received in other cultures, and adaptability (Dunbar, 1993).

Service orientation

Employees should have the necessary customer service skills to interact effectively with clients. Four factors underlie service orientation, namely active customer relations, polite customer relations, helpful customer relations and personalized customer relations (Fogli and Whitney, 1991).

Self-presentation

Self-presentation is the process by which a person tries to shape what others think of him or her (Johnson, 1997). An individual must establish and maintain impressions that are congruent with the perceptions he or she wants to convey to others (Goffman, 1959; Baumeister, 1982). The goal is for one to present himself or herself the way in which he or she would like to be thought of by the individual or group he or she is interacting with.

Social influence

Persuasion and politicking can be used to change others' attitudes and behaviours. Persuasion is a process that is used to guide people towards the adoption of an idea, attitude or action by rational and symbolic means. It is a problem-solving strategy, and relies on 'appeals' rather than force. Three strategies of persuasion are distinguished, namely persuasion through credibility, persuasion through logical reasoning and persuasion through emotional appeal.

Power is the capacity to change the behaviour or attitudes of another in a desired manner (Baron and Greenberg, 1990). One can have power but not impose it. It is therefore a capacity or potential. Power is a function of dependency. The greater B's dependence on A, the greater is A's power in the relationship. Dependence is based on alternatives that B perceives and the importance which B places on the alternatives which A controls. A person has power over you when he or she controls something you desire. French and Raven (1959) identified five bases of power derived from the characteristics which individuals possess and the nature of the relationship between individuals with and without power (see Focus box 5.1).

Focus 5.1

Power bases

- **Reward power**. Individuals with the capacity to control the rewards workers will receive are said to have reward power over them.
- **Coercive power**. A person has coercive power when he or she controls the punishment of others.
- **Legitimate power**. Legitimate power refers to the recognized right of individuals to exercise authority over others because of their position in an organizational hierarchy.
- **Referent power**. Individuals who are liked and respected by others can get them to alter their actions in accordance with their directives – a type of influence known as referent power.
- **Expert power**. To the extent that a person recognizes another person's advanced knowledge and skills and follows orders because that person knows best, that person is said to have expert power.

The extent to which organizational participants have a sense of personal power and control over their work has become recognized as critical to their performance and well-being. This is known as empowerment. The following strategies could empower employees: a) expressing confidence in employees' abilities and holding high expectations concerning their abilities; b) allowing employees to participate in the decision-making process; c) allowing employees freedom and autonomy in how they perform their jobs; d) setting inspirational goals for employees; e) using legitimate power in a sensible and positive way and limiting the use of coercive power (Luthans, 1992).

Organizational politics refer to actions not officially sanctioned (approved) by an organization taken to influence others in order to meet one's personal goals

(Baron and Greenberg, 1990). Organizational politics involves placing one's self-interests above the interests of the organization. This element of using power to foster one's own interests distinguishes organizational politics from uses of power which are approved and accepted by organizations. Political activity is likely to occur in the face of ambiguity. When there are clear-cut rules about what to do, it is unlikely that people will abuse their power by taking political action. Organizational politics will be more active at higher levels in the organization (Baron and Greenberg, 1990). The following political tactics are used most often in organizations (Baron and Greenberg, 1990):

- Blaming and attacking others. Blaming and attacking others is one of the popular political tactics in organizations. This manifests in looking for a scapegoat (someone who could take the blame for some failure).

- Controlling access to information. Controlling who knows and does not know certain things is one of the most important ways of exercising power in organizations.

- Cultivating a favourable impression. Another way to enhance organizational control is to ensure that the impression you make will be favourable.

- Developing a base of support. To be successful in influencing others, individuals sometimes gain the support of others in the organization. This includes lobbying for ideas before they are officially presented and ensuring that others are committed to them in advance.

- Aligning oneself with other persons who are powerful. One way of dealing with power is by connecting oneself with other persons who are powerful.

The following techniques may be helpful for dealing with organizational politics:

1. Clarify job expectations. Assignments should be well defined and the way work will be evaluated should be clarified.
2. Open the communication process. Decisions which are likely to be monitored by all are unlikely to allow any one individual to gain excessive control over desired resources.
3. Be a good role model. Managers must set an example of honest and reasonable treatment.
4. Do not ignore game players.

Activity 5.1

Coping with organization politics

In which places and conditions is political behaviour likely to occur in organizations? How can a manager cope with organization politics?

Conflict resolution

Conflict is defined as a process which begins when one party perceives that another party has negatively affected, or is about to negatively affect, something the first party cares about. Conflict is common in most modern organizations. Its effects are too costly to ignore. Managers report that they spend almost 20 per cent of their time dealing with conflict and its consequences. Destructive conflict may cause resentment and broken relationships. Conflict is therefore a very important topic for work and organizational psychologists.

Opposing (incompatible) interests lie at the bottom of organizational conflict. Yet conflict involves more than this. Disputes sometimes erupt in situations where the interests of the two sides are not clearly opposed, while in other cases conflict fails to develop despite the existence of deep divisions between opposing parties. The parties to it must perceive conflict; whether or not conflict exists is a perception issue. There must also be some form of interaction for conflict to exist.

Functional conflict is a constructive form of conflict which supports the goals of the group and improves its performance. Dysfunctional conflict is a destructive form of conflict which hinders group performance. The criterion which differentiates functional conflict from dysfunctional conflict is group or organizational performance. Conflict would be functional if it furthered the objectives of the group. According to Robbins (1996) the conflict process has five stages, namely potential opposition, cognition and personalization, intentions, behaviour and outcomes.

- **Stage 1: Potential opposition or incompatibility**. The first step in the conflict process is the presence of conditions which create opportunities for conflict to arise. These conditions include communication, structure and personal variables. Semantic differences and misunderstandings may create opportunities for conflict. Structure includes variables such as size, degree of specialization of group members, member–goal compatibility, leadership style, reward systems and the degree of dependence between groups. Differences between individual value systems and personality characteristics may be sources of conflict. Individuals who are highly authoritarian and dogmatic, and who demonstrate low self-esteem lead to potential conflict.

- **Stage 2: Cognition and personalization**. If the conditions in Stage 1 negatively affect something that one party cares about, then the potential for opposition becomes actualized in the second stage. The conditions can only lead to conflict when one or more of the parties are affected by, and aware of the conflict. A conflict which is perceived is not necessarily personalized. A may be aware that B and A are in serious conflict, but it may not make A tense. It is at the felt level, when individuals become emotionally involved, that parties experience anxiety, tension, frustration and hostility.

- **Stage 3: Intentions**. Intentions intervene between people's perceptions and emotions and their overt behaviour. These intentions are decisions to act in a given way. This stage is important because individuals have to infer the other's intent in order to know how to respond to their behaviour. Conflicts are often escalated because one party attributes the wrong intentions to the other.

- **Stage 4: Behaviour**. Conflict becomes visible during this stage. This stage includes the statements, actions and reactions made by the conflicting parties. These conflict behaviours are usually overt attempts to implement each party's intentions. The following techniques can be used to manage the conflict during this stage: a) problem-solving meetings between conflicting parties; b) goal-setting where the cooperation of everyone is needed; c) expanding the resources which create the conflict; d) withdrawing or avoiding the conflict; e) playing down the differences while emphasizing common interests; f) compromising; g) using formal authority to solve the conflict; h) training people to alter their attitudes and behaviour; i) altering the structural variables.

- **Stage 5: Outcomes**. Outcomes of conflict may be functional, in that the conflict results in an improvement in performance. It may also be dysfunctional, in that it hinders performance. Functional conflict improves the quality of decisions, stimulates creativity and innovation, encourages interest among group members and provides the medium through which problems can be aired and tension released. Better and more innovative decisions will result from situations where there is some conflict. Conflict may also have dysfunctional and destructive outcomes. Uncontrolled opposition breeds discontent, which acts to dissolve common ties and eventually leads to the destruction of the group. Conflict may retard communication, reduce group cohesiveness and cause subordination of group goals to the primacy of infighting between members.

Factors which facilitate or inhibit communication in organizations

Various factors – previous life experience, individual differences and situational factors – might impact on the effectiveness of communication and interpersonal relationships of workers (Klein et al, 2006).

Previous experience

The experiences of workers during childhood and adulthood might affect their communication with others. These experiences include family relationships, peer relationships and social relationships at work (Klein et al, 2006).

Individual differences

Individual differences could impact on the effectiveness of communication and interpersonal relationships. Three individual difference variables, namely

emotional intelligence, personality traits and collective orientation can influence the nature of interpersonal relations at work (Klein et al, 2006).

Emotional intelligence

Salovey and Mayer (1990), who coined the term 'emotional intelligence', defined it as 'a form of intelligence that involves the ability to monitor one's own and others' feelings and emotions, to discriminate among them and to use this information to guide one's thinking and actions'. Salovey and Mayer initiated a research programme to develop measures of emotional significance and to assess its significance. Widespread interest in the topic of emotional intelligence arose following the publication of Goleman's (1995) book, *Emotional Intelligence*.

Emotional intelligence seems to be a controversial subject. One of the reasons for this is because differences exist over whether emotional intelligence is an ability (Mayer et al, 2000) or a personality trait (Goleman, 1995; Bar-On, 1997). Goleman (1995) and Bar-On (1997) conceived emotional intelligence as a personality trait, which implies that it involves attitudes, preferences and values. According to Goleman (1995), emotional intelligence entails a) knowing what you are feeling and being able to handle those feelings without having them swamp you; b) being able to motivate yourself to get jobs done, be creative and perform at your peak; and c) sensing what others are feeling, and handling relationships effectively. Bar-On's (1997) definition states that it is an array of non-cognitive capabilities, competencies and skills. Critics of the trait approach (Landy, 2005; Locke 2005) pointed out that the definition of emotional intelligence is constantly changing, that it has no clear measurement, that it is little more than a loose conglomeration of extant personality traits, and that research on emotional intelligence did not demonstrate incremental validity over traditional personality models. The trait approach has led to assessment devices that are based upon self-report, yielding self- and other-perceptions of these traits rather than an estimate of a person's actual emotional ability.

The ability-based conceptualization (e.g. Mayer et al, 1999) is not subjected to the same criticism as the trait approach. The ability approach suggests that a skill-based or behavioural measurement (preferably not based on self-report), which focuses narrowly and specifically on emotional skills and abilities only, has demonstrated construct distinctiveness and has demonstrated good psychometric properties be used. Emotional intelligence (according to the ability approach) includes four dimensions, namely a) Emotional Perception, which involves such abilities as identifying emotions in faces, music and stories; b) Emotional Facilitation of Thought, which involves such abilities as relating emotions to other mental sensations such as taste and colour, and using emotion in reasoning and problem solving; c) Emotional Understanding, which involves solving emotional problems such as knowing which emotions are similar, or opposites, and what relations they convey; and d) Emotional Management, which involves understanding the implications of social acts on emotions and the regulation of emotion in self and others.

Personality traits

Certain personality traits are regarded as predictors of interpersonal incompetence and communication difficulties. Examples of such traits are arrogance, selfishness, aloofness, emotional instability and compulsiveness (Klein et al, 2006). They showed that personality dimensions (extraversion, emotional stability, openness, agreeableness and conscientiousness) accounted for 20 per cent of the variance in interpersonal skills. Agreeableness is regarded as an important dimension which predicts interpersonal skills, while extraversion is an important predictor when a task requires social interaction.

Collective orientation

Individuals with a collective orientation will tend to display better interpersonal skills, and will be more willing to work with others than individuals who do not have a collective orientation (Klein et al, 2006).

Application 5.1

Too much of a good thing ...?

The **Anonymous Employee website** (www.anonymousemployee.com) was created to fill the communication gap that exists in most workplaces. It provides employees and employers with an opportunity to discuss issues that affect productivity and morale. Read the ensuing case study posted by an anonymous employee under the **poor communication** section of the website and consider solutions to their problem:

I feel weird writing a question in the 'poor communication' section of this website, but that's really what my situation is about. My company is all about communication. We offer phone and Internet services. We all have blackberries and desktop computers for use at work. The management takes communication extremely seriously, and whenever there is an issue, a memo is sent out to keep everybody on top of things. The problem is that I feel overwhelmed by the amount of communication. We each easily receive over a dozen email memos every day. When I arrive at work in the morning, I'm faced with at least five or six new memos. As much as it's well intended, I simply cannot remember everything that is sent to me in all of these memos. Policies are always changing, new services are being added, new staff members are entering, old ones are leaving, and lots of other 'issues' are always being brought to everybody's attention. There's no way to keep up. I'm a very organized person, but I don't know how to stay on top of things.

- Consider the communication process and identify the underlying cause of this employee's problem.
- Which strategies would you implement to enhance the effectiveness of the communication process in this organization?

Summary

- Communication is defined as the process by which a person, group or organization (the sender) transmits some type of information (the message) to another person, group or organization (the receiver).

- Communication seems to play an important role in the attainment of organizational goals. Communication does serve certain major functions within an organization, namely those of control, motivation, emotional expression and providing information.

- The source of the communication may be a person or an object. The characteristics of the receiver influence the way in which the message is received and interpreted.

- Various communication methods exist in organizations, namely written communication, oral communication, downward communication, upward communication, horizontal/lateral communication and formal/informal communication.

- Interpersonal skills include communication skills (i.e. active listening, responding, oral communication, written communication, assertive communication and non-verbal communication) and relationship-building skills (i.e. self-disclosure and feedback, cooperation, trust, intercultural sensitivity, service orientation, self-presentation, social influence and conflict resolution).

- Various factors might impact on the effectiveness of communication and interpersonal relationships of workers. These include previous life experience, individual differences (e.g. emotional intelligence, personality traits and collective orientation) and situational factors.

Key concepts and terms

Active listening	Oral communication
Assertive communication	Organizational politics
Clarification	Paraphrasing
Conflict	Power
Confrontation	Questioning
Cooperation	Receiver
Decoding	Responding skills
Downward communication	Self-disclosure
Emotional intelligence	Self-presentation
Encoding	Service orientation
Feedback	Social influence
Formal communication	Source
Horizontal communication	Summarizing
Intercultural sensitivity	Trust
Minimal encouragement	Written communication
Non-verbal communication	

Sample essay titles

- How can effective communication in organizations be ensured?
- What is the role of emotional intelligence in effective communication in organizations?

Further reading

Books

Carr, A. (2004). *Positive Psychology: The Science of Happiness and Human Strengths*. Hove: Brunner-Routledge.

Van der Molen, H., and Gramsbergen-Hoogland, Y.H. (2005). *Communication in Organization: Basic Skills and Conversation Models*. New York: Psychology Press.

Journal articles

Russell, J.A., Bachorowski, J., and Fernandez-Dols, J. (2003). Facial and vocal expressions of emotion. *Annual Review of Psychology*, 54, 329–349.

Sizoo, S. (2006). A comparison of the effect of intercultural sensitivity on employee performance in cross-cultural service encounters: London vs. Florida. *Journal of Euromarketing*, 15, 77–100.

6 Leadership

This chapter introduces the reader to the nature and theories of **leadership.** The first section focuses on the definition of leadership. We then look at reasons why leadership is important for organizations. The chapter then proceeds to a discussion of theories of leadership. We look at various approaches to leadership, including the trait approach, the behavioural approach, the contingency approach and a few recent approaches. A major breakthrough in our understanding of leadership came when researchers recognized the need to include situational factors. In addition, the study of leadership has expanded to include visionary approaches to leadership. As we learn more about the personal characteristics which followers attribute to charismatic and transformational leaders, and about the conditions that facilitate their emergence, we should be better able to predict when followers will exhibit extraordinary commitment and loyalty to their leaders and their goals.

Learning outcomes

When you have completed this chapter you should be able to:

1. Define leadership.
2. Discuss the importance of leadership.
3. Evaluate the different leadership theories (including **trait theories,** behavioural theories, contingency theories and recent developments).

Definition of leadership

In terms of the number of printed pages devoted to the subject, leadership appears to be one of the most important issues in organizational and work psychology. It is not easy to define leadership. There are almost as many different definitions of leadership as there are persons who attempted to define the concept (Bass, 1981). Bass (1997: 17) states that '... leadership has been conceived as the focus of group processes, as a matter of personality, as a matter of inducing compliance, as the exercise of influence, as particular behaviours, as a form of persuasion, as a power relation, as an instrument to achieve goals, as an effect of interaction, as a differentiated role, as an initiation of **structure,** and as many combinations of these definitions'.

Robbins (1996) defines leadership as the ability to influence a group towards the achievement of goals. The source of this influence may be formal, such as that provided by the possession of managerial rank in an organization. A person may assume a leadership role because of the position he or she holds in the organization. However, not all managers are leaders and not all leaders are managers. In general, leadership refers to non-coercive influence techniques. This implies that leadership rests in part on positive feelings between leaders and their subordinates.

Four common themes have been emphasized in the definition of leadership, namely that it is a process, that involves influencing others, that it occurs within a group context, and that it involves goal attainment (Northouse, 2001). Leadership involves an influence process and only occurs when individuals willingly adopt the goals of the group as their own. Thus, leadership concerns building cohesive and goal-oriented teams. Leadership is persuasion, not domination.

Many people struggle with the differences between management and leadership (Cooper, 2005). Most experts agree that leadership and management are different. However, the terms leader and manager are often used interchangeably. A manager is a person who takes on a management role, which comprises activities such as planning, processing information, organizing, controlling and communicating with customers or suppliers. Managers will be leaders when they exert influence over their subordinates in order to attain organizational goals. Many persons who are leaders are not managers. They operate in contexts outside the world of business and do not perform activities associated with managerial roles (e.g. organizing, controlling and planning).

Importance of leadership

There are various reasons why leadership is important. Hogan and Kaiser (2005) give the following reasons why leadership really matters:

- Leadership solves the problem of organizing collective effort. Good leadership leads to organizational success, as well as financial and social well-being of people.

- Bad leaders cause misery for people who are subject to their domain.

- Several patterns of leadership behaviour are associated with subordinates' performance and satisfaction. Reactions to inept leadership include turnover, insubordination, industrial sabotage and malingering. Studies from the mid 1950s show that 60–75 per cent of the employees in any organization report that the worst or most stressful aspect of their job is their immediate supervisor. Good leaders may put pressure on their people, but abusive and incompetent leaders cost management millions in lost productivity. The most common complaints from direct reports concern: a) managers' unwillingness to exercise authority; b) managers tyrannizing their subordinates.

- Top managers account for 14 per cent of the variance in organizational performance.

Leadership theories

Various theories have been developed to explain leadership. These theories can roughly be studied in terms of four approaches, namely trait theories, behavioural theories, **contingency theories** and recent theories (including the attribution perspective, **charismatic leadership,** and transactional and transformational leadership).

Trait theories

Trait theories focus on discovering the leadership personality and examining what it is about the character, underlying motivations and behavioural styles that make an individual a leader. The tendency to describe people in terms of traits has a long history. Throughout history many people believed that leaders are born, not made, and that great leaders are discovered, not developed. In the early twentieth century there were many strong advocates of the trait theories of leadership. Wiggam (1931), for example, concluded that the survival of the fittest and marriage among them produces an aristocratic class that differs biologically from the lower classes.

Research methods

Researching trait theories of leadership

Hundreds of studies have been conducted to identify the personal attributes of leaders. The typical research studies on trait theories have compared the characteristics of a leader (defined as an individual holding a position of authority) with the characteristics of a follower (defined as an individual not holding a position of authority). The findings of these studies are somewhat contradictory and inconclusive. Mann (1959) reviewed 125 studies of leadership and personality characteristics representing over 700 findings. He concluded that intelligence and personal adjustment seem to be correlated with leadership (Wright, 1996).

Leaders were found to score higher on tests of a wide variety of characteristics, including intelligence, personality, task motivation and performance, and social competence. These tests have, however, not proved to be reliably useful in the selection of leaders. The safest conclusions which can be drawn from trait studies of leadership is that individuals who have the energy, drive, self-confidence and determination to succeed will become leaders, because they work hard to get leadership positions (Bass, 1981). The best predictor of leadership success is prior success in leadership roles, but a previously successful leader may fail when placed in a situation which imposes demands incompatible with his or her personality. Research has shown that leaders differ from non-leaders regarding ambition and energy, honesty and integrity, self-confidence and job relevant knowledge. None of these traits will, however, guarantee success as a leader.

The implication of trait theories is that it is possible to select the right person to assume formal positions in groups and organizations. Traits of leaders may act as a moderating variable in determining leadership behaviour (Zaleznik, 1993). In certain combinations, personality traits may account for about 35 per cent of the variance in leadership behaviour (Bass, 1998). However, the trait approach is not very successful in explaining leadership because it: a) overlooks the needs of followers; b) fails to clarify the relative importance of various traits; c) does not separate cause from effect, (for example are leaders self-confident or does success as a leader build self-confidence?); d) ignores situational factors.

Behavioural theories

The **behavioural theories** focus on specific behaviour which effective leaders exhibit that might differentiate them from ineffective leaders (Burke and Cooper, 2004). The difference between trait and behavioural theories lies in the underlying assumptions. If trait theories were valid, then leadership would be inborn. On the other hand, if there were specific behaviours which identified leaders, then it would be possible to train and develop individuals to become leaders. The implication of behavioural theories is that the behaviour of individuals should be studied in order to identify leaders, and that it is possible to train leaders. Although the behavioural theories are criticized for the fact that they do not consider the situation in which leadership occurs, they added valuable insights to the field. The following behavioural theories can be distinguished: a) **Harvard studies;** b) University of **Michigan studies;** c) Ohio State studies; d) the **Managerial Grid.**

Harvard studies

Bales (1953) at Harvard University conducted research on behaviour in small groups. The research showed two types of leader behaviour in small groups, namely task leadership and socio-emotional leadership. The task leader will keep reminding the group of its aims and bringing the group back to them whenever they stray from their problem-solving purpose, coming up with new ideas when they get stuck. The social-emotional leader is particularly sensitive to other people's needs, uses praise and other forms of feedback and is more inclined to ask for suggestions than to give them. According to Bales (1953), a group member could only be a task leader or a socio-emotional leader.

Michigan studies

Studies which were done at the University of Michigan's Survey Research Center by Tannenbaum and Schmidt (1958) also tried to locate the behavioural characteristics of leaders. The researchers at this university focused on two dimensions of leadership behaviour, namely **employee orientation** and **production orientation** (see Focus box 6.1).

The classification of leader behaviour according to the Michigan researchers is represented in Figure 6.1.

The results of the Michigan researchers strongly favoured employee-oriented leaders. Employee-oriented behaviour causes high productivity and high job

Focus 6.1

Dimensions of leadership behaviour (Michigan studies)

- **Employee-oriented leaders** emphasize interpersonal relations, take interest in the needs of their subordinates and accept individual differences among members.

- **Production-oriented leaders** emphasize the task aspects of the job. Their main concern is the accomplishment of the group's tasks, and group members are seen as a means to an end.

Figure 6.1 Leader behaviour according to the Michigan researchers.

satisfaction, while production-oriented behaviour causes low productivity and low job satisfaction.

Ohio State studies

The most comprehensive of the behavioural theories resulted from the research which began at the Ohio State University in the late 1940s (Halpin and Winer, 1957). The researchers found that two independent dimensions, namely initiating structure and **consideration,** accounted for most of the leadership behaviour described by subordinates (see Focus box 6.2).

Focus 6.2

Dimensions of leadership behaviour (Ohio studies)

- **Initiating structure** refers to the extent to which a leader is likely to define and structure his or her role and those of subordinates in the search for goal attainment.

- **Consideration** refers to the extent to which a person is likely to have job relationships which are characterized by mutual trust, respect for subordinates and regard for their feelings.

The classification of leader behaviour according to the Ohio researchers is represented in Figure 6.2.

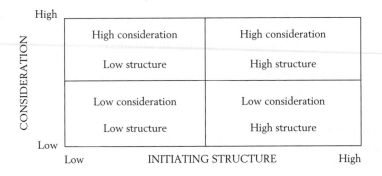

Figure 6.2 Leader behaviour according to the Ohio researchers.

Source: Hersey, P. & Blanchard, K.H. (1982, page 89). Management of organizational behaviour: Utilizing human resources. Englewood Cliffs, NJ: Prentice-Hall, Inc.

Leaders high in initiating structure and consideration achieve high subordinate performance and satisfaction more frequently than those who rate low on consideration, initiating structure or both. High scores on both these dimensions do not, however, always result in positive consequences.

The Managerial Grid

According to Blake and Mouton (1964), leadership styles are influenced by two variables, namely concern for production and concern for people. These two variables can be represented on a scale of different intensities from one to nine. Although a wide variety of leadership styles are possible, Blake and Mouton concentrate mainly on five leadership styles, i.e. 9,1; 1,9; 1,1; 5,5 and 9,9 (see Figure 6.3).

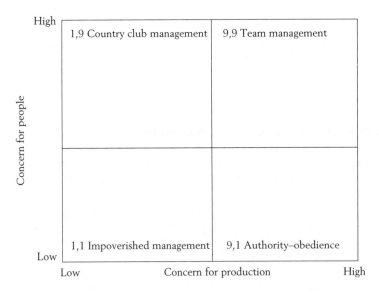

Figure 6.3 The managerial grid.

Source: Hersey, P. & Blanchard, K.H. (1982, page 89). Management of organizational behaviour: Utilizing human resources. Englewood Cliffs, NJ: Prentice-Hall, Inc.

- The **9,1 style** emphasizes concern for production to a large degree (9), while there is little concern for the human factor (1). The basic assumption is that there is an unavoidable contradiction between the needs of the organization and those of its members. The leader regards people as instruments who must be bent to perform work. Strict control is exercised, while little opportunity is given for responsibility and own initiative.

- The **1,9 style** emphasizes concern for people (9), while production must adapt to man and his or her social needs (1). Leaders give considerable attention to the attitudes and feelings of persons. People are not driven, but merely encouraged.

- The **1,1 style** emphasizes low concern for people (1) and for production (1). The leader leaves followers to work as they prefer. The leader has a messenger function and does not accept responsibility for followers.

- The **5,5 style** is a compromise style where both production and people factors receive equal attention. The assumption of this style is that people will be willing to work and obey orders if the reasons are explained to them.

- The **9,9 style** emphasizes high concern for production (9) and high concern for people. The objective of the 9,9 style is to promote the conditions which integrate creativity and high morale through concerned action.

Leaders were found to perform best under a 9,9 style, as contrasted with the other styles. According to Robbins (1996) there is little substantial evidence to support the conclusion that a 9,9 style is most effective in all situations.

Activity 6.1

Comparison of the Managerial Grid, Ohio State and Michigan studies

Contrast the Managerial Grid with the approaches of the Ohio State and Michigan studies. What are the similarities and differences?

Contingency theories

The predicting of leadership success is more complex than isolating a few traits or preferable behaviour. In organizations, contingency theory emphasizes the fit between organizational processes and the characteristics of the situation. Leadership effectiveness is also dependent on the situation. Therefore there is no best way to lead people. The best way to lead people depends on the situation. Situational variables include the degree of structure in the task performed, the quality of leader–member relations and the maturity of followers (Robbins, 1996).

The contingency theory of Fiedler

Fiedler (1967) developed the first comprehensive contingency theory of leadership. Fiedler's contingency theory suggests that leadership performance can only be understood in relation to the context in which it occurs and that success is achieved when there is a good leader–situation match. The model of

Fiedler proposes that effective group performance depends on the match between the **leader's style** of interacting with subordinates and the degree to which the **situation** allows control.

According to Fiedler, an individual's basic leadership style is a key factor in leadership success. Therefore, he begins by trying to find out what the basic style is. Fiedler developed a personality measure, the least preferred co-worker (LPC) scale, which measures whether a person is task or relationship oriented. The LPC scale contains 16 contrasting adjectives (such as efficient–inefficient, supportive–hostile). The respondent is asked to think of all the co-workers he or she has ever had and to describe the one person he or she least enjoyed working with by rating him or her on a scale of 1 to 8 on each of the adjectives. An individual's basic leadership style is determined by analysing their responses on the scale. If the least preferred co-worker is described in relatively positive terms (a high LPC score), then the person is primarily interested in good personal relations with this co-worker. High LPC leaders seem mainly concerned with establishing good relationships with subordinates. In contrast, leaders who perceive the least preferred co-worker in negative terms (a low LPC score) seem primarily concerned with attaining successful task performance and would be labelled task oriented. About 16 per cent of respondents score in the middle range. Such persons cannot be classified as either relationship or task-oriented and thus fall outside the theory's predictions. Fiedler believes that an individual's leadership style is fixed. This means that if a situation requires a task-oriented leader and the person in that leadership position is relationship-oriented, either the situation has to be modified or the leader removed and replaced if optimum effectiveness is to be achieved.

After an individual's basic leadership style has been assessed through the LPC, it is necessary to match the leader with the situation. The effectiveness of low or high LPC leaders depends on situational factors, such as the degree to which the situation is favourable for leaders (provides them with control over subordinates). Fiedler identifies three situational criteria which can be manipulated to create the proper match with the behavioural orientation of the leader, namely a) the degree to which the leader enjoys the loyalty of group members; b) the extent to which task goals and subordinates' roles are clearly defined; and c) the leader's ability to enforce compliance by subordinates. The next step is to evaluate the situation in terms of these three contingency variables. The better the leader–member relations, the more highly structured the job, and the stronger the position power, the more control or influence the leader has.

With knowledge of an individual's LPC and an assessment of the three contingency variables, Fiedler's theory proposes matching them up to achieve maximum leadership effectiveness. The leader's situational control can range from very high (positive relations with group members, a highly structured task, high position power) to very low (negative relations, an unstructured task, low position power). Low LPC leaders (who are task oriented) are superior to high LPC leaders (who are people oriented) when situational control is either very low or high. High LPC leaders have an edge when situational control falls within the moderate range. Under conditions of low situational control, groups need guidance and direction to accomplish their tasks. Since low LPC leaders are more likely to provide such structure than high LPC leaders, they will be superior in such cases. Low LPC leaders also have an edge under conditions which offer the leaders a high degree of situational control. Here, low LPC leaders realize that conditions are good and that successful task performance is almost assured. As a result, they turn their attention to improving relations with subordinates, and often adopt a 'hands-off' style. High LPC leaders, feeling that they already enjoy good relations with their subordinates, may shift their attention to task performance. Their attempts to provide guidance in this respect may be regarded as interference by subordinates, with the result that performance is impaired.

If the situation offers the leader moderate control, conditions are mixed and attention to good interpersonal relations is often needed. High LPC leaders, with their interest in people, have an advantage in such situations. Low LPC leaders may in such situations continue to focus on task performance and become even more autocratic and directive. The negative reactions of subordinates to such behaviour may have detrimental effects upon performance.

Fiedler's theory implies that leaders and situations should be matched. Individuals' LPC scores indicate the type of situation for which they are best suited. According to the theory there are two ways to improve leader effectiveness: a) change the leader to fit the situation; b) change the situation to fit the leader. This could be done by restructuring tasks or increasing or decreasing the power of the leader to control factors such as salary increases, promotions or disciplinary actions. Fiedler's model goes significantly beyond trait and behavioural approaches by attempting to isolate situations, relating his personality measure to his situational classification, and then predicting leadership effectiveness as a function of the two (Robbins, 1996).

Hersey and Blanchard's situational theory

The situational leadership theory of Hersey and Blanchard (1982) is a contingency theory which focuses on the maturity levels of followers to determine the most appropriate leadership style. Successful leadership is achieved by selecting the correct leadership style, which is contingent on followers' readiness or maturity. Regardless of what the leader does, effectiveness depends on the actions of their followers. This is an important dimension which has been overlooked in most leadership theories. The term maturity refers to the extent to which people have the ability and willingness to accomplish a certain task.

Hersey and Blanchard's theory uses the same two leadership dimensions identified by the Ohio researchers, namely task and relationship behaviour. Based on combinations of task and relationship behaviour, four leadership styles, namely telling, selling, participating and delegating are distinguished:

- **Telling (high task–low relationship)**. The leader defines roles and tells people what, how, when and where to do various tasks.

- **Selling (high task–high relationship)**. The leader provides both directive behaviour and supportive behaviour.

- **Participating (low task–high relationship)**. The leader and follower share in decision-making with the main role of the leader being facilitating and communicating.

- **Delegating (low task–low relationship)**. The leader provides little direction or support.

Hersey and Blanchard (1982) identify the following four stages of **follower maturity:**

■ **M1**: Individuals are both unable and unwilling to take responsibility to do something. They are neither competent nor confident.

■ **M2**: Individuals are unable but willing to do tasks. They are motivated but lacking skills.

■ **M3**: Individuals are able but unwilling to do what the leader wants.

■ **M4**: Individuals are able and willing to do what is expected from them.

The situational leadership theory of Hersey and Blanchard is illustrated in Figure 6.4.

As followers reach high levels of maturity (see Figure 6.4) the leader responds by decreasing control over activities and by decreasing relationship behaviour. At stage M1, followers need clear and specific directions. At stage M2, both high-task and high-relationship behaviour is needed. The high-task behaviour compensates for the followers' lack of ability, while the high-relationship

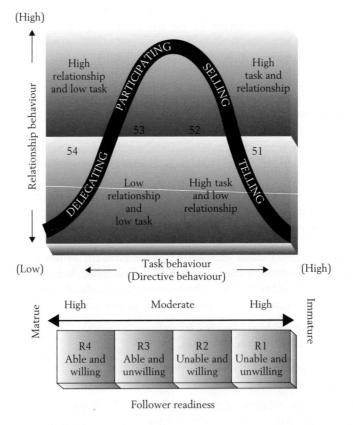

Figure 6.4 The situational leadership theory of Hersey and Blanchard.
Source: Hersey, P., & Blanchard, K. H. (1982). Management *of organizational behavior: utilizing human resources.* (4th ed.). Englewood Cliffs, NJ: Prentice Hall.

behaviour tries to get the followers to buy into the leader's desires. M3 creates motivational problems which are best solved by a supportive, non-directive leadership style. At stage M4, the leader does not have to do much because followers are both willing and able to take responsibility.

Leader–member exchange theory

Leader–member exchange (LMX) theory (Dienesch and Liden, 1986) advocates recognition of individual differences and an emphasis on dyadic relationships between a leader and each of his or her subordinates. Research focused on the quality of leader–subordinate interaction. A high quality relationship is characterized by the member having high levels of responsibility, decision influence and access to resources. Members who enjoy a high quality LMX relationship are said to be in the in-group. A low quality LMX relationship is characterized by the leader offering low levels of support to the member, and the member having low levels of responsibility and decision influence. Members who have a low quality LMX relationship are said to be in the out-group (Graen and Uhl-Bien, 1995). Leader–member relationships emerge as the result of a series of exchanges or interactions during which leader and member roles develop. This role formation process involves three phases, namely:

- **Role taking**. The member enters the organization and the leader assesses his or her abilities and talents. Based on this assessment, the leader provides opportunities for the member to 'take' a specific role. Mutual respect is essential in this stage. Leaders and members must each understand how the other views and desires respect. This might be difficult in mixed-gender relationships because men and women may interpret or define respect differently. The leader–member relationship will not develop and progress to the next stage if there is a lack of respect.

- **Role making**. The leader and the member engage in unstructured and informal negotiation. During this phase the member begins to 'make' a role. In this stage trust must be developed in order for leaders and members to further develop the relationship and influence each other's attitudes and behaviours. If trust is violated even a single time in diverse dyadic relationships, the relationship may be destroyed.

- **Role routinization**. An ongoing social exchange pattern emerges or becomes 'routinized'. Mutual obligation is formed in this phase. **Role making** has been established at this point and leaders and members have shared meanings.

The role formation process develops through a mechanism referred to as **'negotiating latitude'**. This negotiation is hypothesized to occur through the series of exchanges or interactions between the leader and the member. Work-related variables, and the leader's and the member's affective responses to their initial interaction, may be important components in the development of the LMX relationship. The affective responses are influenced by the perceived similarity between the leader and the member. The more the leader and the member perceive that they are similar, the more they will like each other and the more likely they are to develop a high quality LMX relationship. Additionally, attraction might be affected by the amount of interaction that occurs between the leader and the member. Leaders and members who share a high quality LMX relationship tend to interact more about personal topics than about work-related topics, which may result in higher levels of trust. Leaders tend to trust in-group subordinates and therefore empower them with decision-making authority.

Recent approaches to leadership

Robbins (1996) distinguishes between three recent approaches to leadership, namely an attribution theory of leadership, charismatic leadership and transactional versus transformational leadership. In these approaches, leaders are seen as managers of meaning, rather than merely in terms of their influence on subordinates.

Attribution theory of leadership

Attribution theory deals with people trying to make sense from cause–effect relationships. When something happens, they want to attribute it to something. According to attribution theory, leadership is merely an attribution which people make about other individuals. Using the attribution framework, researchers have found that people characterize leaders as having traits such as intelligence, outgoing personality, strong verbal skills, aggressiveness and understanding. The high-consideration, high-structure leader was found to be consistent with attributions of what makes a good leader (Robbins, 1996).

Charismatic leadership

The model of Conger and Kanungo (1987) proposes that charismatic leadership is an attributional phenomenon founded on subordinate perceptions of the leader's behaviour. Subordinates observe and interpret leader behaviour and traits as expressions of charisma. Charismatic behaviours and traits need not always be present to an identical degree in every charismatic leader and their relative importance will vary with the situation. Followers make attributions of heroic or extraordinary leadership abilities when they observe certain behaviour. Some examples of individuals cited to be charismatic leaders include Nelson Mandela and Martin Luther King (see Applications box 6.1).

Personal characteristics of a charismatic leader are high confidence, dominance and strong convictions in their beliefs. Conger and Kanungo (1998) identified the following behavioural characteristics of a charismatic leader:

1. Self-confidence. They have complete confidence in their judgement and abilities.
2. A **vision.** They have an idealized goal, which proposes a future better than the status quo.
3. Ability to articulate the vision. They are able to clarify and state the vision in terms which are understandable to others.
4. Strong convictions about the vision. They are perceived as being strongly committed and willing to take on high personal risk and engage in self-sacrifice to achieve their vision.
5. Behaviour which is out of the ordinary. They engage in behaviour which is being perceived as novel, unconventional and counter to the norms.

Application 6.1

Profile of Nelson Rolihlahla Mandela

Figure 6.5 Nelson Mandela.
Source: Alexander Joe/AFP/Getty Images.

Richard Sengel (*Time*, 9 May 1994) interviewed Nelson Mandela and noted the following story, which indicates his perspective on leadership.

> *'When you want to get a herd to move in a certain direction,' he said, 'you stand at the back ... A few of the more energetic cattle move to the front and the rest of the cattle follow. You are really guiding them from behind.' With a smile he added: 'This is how a leader should do his work.' (Source: Sengel, R. (1994, May 9). The making of a leader.) www.time.com/time/ time100/leaders/profile/mandela_related.html*

Nelson Rolihlahla Mandela is the most inspirational leader of the second half of the twentieth century. He was born in a village near Umtata in the Transkei on 18 July 1918. His father was the principal councillor to the Acting Paramount Chief of Thembuland. After his father's death, the young Rolihlahla became the Paramount Chief's ward, to be groomed to assume high office. After receiving a primary education at a local mission school, Nelson Mandela was sent to Healdtown, a Wesleyan secondary school of some repute where he matriculated. He completed his BA by correspondence, took articles of clerkship and commenced study for his LLB. He entered politics in earnest by joining the African National Congress in 1942. During the 1950s, Mandela was the victim of various forms of repression. After the Sharpeville Massacre in 1960, the ANC was outlawed, and Mandela, still on trial, was detained. In 1962 he left the country unlawfully and travelled abroad for several months. Not long after his return to South Africa Mandela was arrested and charged with illegal exit from the country and incitement to strike. Mandela was convicted and sentenced to five years imprisonment. While serving his sentence he was charged, in the Rivonia Trial, with sabotage. Mandela was sentenced to life imprisonment and started his prison years in the notorious Robben Island Prison. In 1988 he was moved to the Victor Verster Prison near Paarl from where he was eventually released. In the early 1990s, with great magnanimity and force of character, Mandela was able to help negotiate an end to the system of apartheid, leading to his election as president of a free and democratic society in 1994. Although retired from public life, Nelson Mandela retains a great popular appeal across the globe.

6. Perceived as being a change agent. Charismatic leaders are perceived as agents of radical change rather than as caretakers of the status quo.
7. Environmental sensitivity. They are able to make realistic assessments of the environmental constraints and resources needed to bring about change.

Conger and Kanungo (1998) proposed a charismatic leadership process including environmental assessment and vision formulation, communicating a vision, building trust and demonstrating how to achieve the vision. The process begins by the leader articulating an appealing vision. The leader then communicates the vision and high performance expectations and expresses confidence that the followers can attain them. Next, the leader conveys a new set of values, and by his or her behaviour sets an example for followers to imitate. Finally, the leader demonstrates how to achieve the mission using empowerment, modelling and unconventional tactics.

Experts believe that people can be trained to exhibit charismatic behaviour (Robbins, 1996). Charismatic leadership may not always be needed to achieve high levels of employee performance. It may be most appropriate when the follower's task has an ideological component. That is probably the reason why charismatic leaders are likely to surface in politics, wartime, religion and when a business firm is transforming.

Transactional versus transformational leadership

Bass (1985, 1990) defined transformational leadership in terms of how the leader affects followers, who are intended to trust, admire and respect the transformational leader. He identified three ways in which leaders transform followers, namely a) increasing their awareness of task importance and value; b) getting them to focus first on team or organizational goals, rather than their own interests; and c) activating their higher-order needs. Charisma is seen as necessary, but not sufficient, for leadership. Two key charismatic effects that transformational leaders achieve are to evoke strong emotions and to cause identification of the followers with the leader. This may be through stirring appeals. It may also occur through quieter methods such as coaching and mentoring.

Transformational leadership is grounded in moral foundations that are based on four components, namely idealized influence, inspirational motivation, intellectual stimulation and individualized consideration (Bass, 1998). Transformational leadership is not seen as being sufficient for effective organizations. It must be accompanied by effective management (transactional leadership). Transactional leaders guide or motivate their followers in the direction of the established goal by clarifying role and task requirements. The Ohio State studies and Fiedler's model have concerned transactional leaders. Transformational leaders inspire followers to transcend their own self-interests for the good of the organization, and are capable of having a profound and extraordinary effect on their followers. They pay attention to the concerns and development needs of individual followers, they change followers' awareness of issues by helping them look at old problems in new ways, and they are able to excite, arouse and inspire followers to put out extra effort to achieve group goals.

Research indicates that transformational leadership is more strongly correlated than **transactional leadership** with lower turnover rates, higher productivity rates and higher employee satisfaction (Bass, 1998). The criticism against **transformational leadership** is that it has poorly defined parameters, and that it treats leadership as a personal predisposition rather than as a behaviour that can be learned.

Application 6.2

A good leader does the right things right!

UNSKILLED
Can't communicate or sell a vision
Not a good presenter
Can't turn a good phrase or create compelling one liners
Uncomfortable speculating on the unknown future
Isn't charismatic or passionate enough to excite and energise others
Can't simplify enough to help people understand complex strategy
May not understand how change happens
Doesn't act like he/she really believes in the vision
More comfortable in the here and now
SKILLED
Communicates a compelling and inspired vision or sense of core purpose
Talks about possibilities
Is optimistic
Creates mileposts and symbols to rally support behind the vision
Makes the vision sharable by everyone (inclusive approach)
Can inspire and motivate entire unit or organisations
OVERUSED SKILL
May leave people behind
May lack patience with those who don't understand or share his/her vision and sense of purpose
May lack appropriate detail-orientation and concern for administrative routine
May lack follow-through on the day-to-day tasks

Figure 6.6 Skills.

Managing a vision and purpose is one of the big challenges facing leaders. Leaders need certain skills to achieve this successfully and to create trust in their ability to lead. Nelson Mandela is regarded as a symbol of visionary and charismatic leadership because he is so innately skilled to present and manage vision and purpose! Lombardo and Eichinger (2000) profiled the skills necessary to manage vision and purpose (see below). Assess your own ability (or skills gaps), and that of a leader in your environment, to manage vision and purpose according to the skills profile in Figure 6.6.

Lombardo and Eichinger (2000) provide remedies for skills gaps and it might be beneficial to consult their book if you lack certain skills.

Source: Lombardo, M.M. and Eichinger, R.W. (2000). For Your Development: A Development and Coaching Guide, (3rd Ed.) p. 389.

Summary

- Leadership is the process whereby one individual influences other group members towards the attainment of defined group or organizational goals. Leaders generally use non-coercive forms of influence and are influenced, in turn, by their followers. Not all managers function as leaders. Conversely, not all leaders are managers. The two terms should therefore not be treated as synonyms.

- Leadership plays an important role in understanding individual, group and organizational behaviour, for it is the leader who usually provides the direction towards goal attainment. In this study unit, different approaches to the study of leadership were described, distinguishing between the trait approach, the behavioural approach, the contingency approach and a few recent approaches.

- Various theories have been developed to explain leadership. These can roughly be studied in terms of four approaches, namely trait theories, behavioural theories, contingency theories and recent theories (including the attribution perspective, charismatic leadership, and transactional and transformational leadership).

- A major breakthrough in our understanding of leadership came when researchers recognized the need to include situational factors. In addition, the study of leadership has expanded to include visionary approaches to leadership. As we learn more about the personal characteristics which followers attribute to charismatic and transformational leaders, and about the conditions that facilitate their emergence, we should be better able to predict when followers will exhibit extraordinary commitment and loyalty to their leaders and their goals.

Key concepts and terms

Attribution theory	Michigan studies
Behavioural theories	Negotiating latitude
Charismatic leadership	Production orientation
Consideration	Role making
Contingency theories	Role routinization
Employee orientation	Role taking
Follower maturity	Structure
Harvard studies	Trait theories
Leadership	Transactional leadership
Leader–member exchange	Transformational leadership
Managerial grid	Vision

Sample essay titles

- Do you think there is one best leadership theory? Evaluate the different leadership theories.
- What are the differences between transactional and transformational leadership?

Further reading

Books

Burke, R., and Cooper, C. (2006). *Inspiring Leaders*. London: Routledge.

Spears, J.C., and Lawrence, M. (2004). *Practicing Servant Leadership: Succeeding through Trust, Bravery, and Forgiveness*. San Francisco: Jossey-Bass.

Yukl, G.A. (2006). *Leadership in Organizations*, (6th Ed.). Upper Saddle River, NJ: Prentice-Hall.

Journal articles

Walumbwa, F.O., Lawler, J.J., and Avolio, B.J. (2007). Leadership, individual differences, and work-related attitudes. *Applied Psychology: An International Review*, 56, 212–230.

2 | Work psychology

7 Human resource planning and job analysis

This chapter introduces the reader to human resource planning and **job analysis**. The first section focuses on human resource planning. We look at the definition of human resource planning. The chapter then proceeds to the reasons for human resource planning, and the human resource planning process. Regarding the human resource planning process, various phases are discussed, including analysing the situation, determining the characteristics of the present workforce, analysing the **demand** for and the supply of human resources, determining the human resource goals, designing and implementing human resource plans, and gathering/analysing information that can be used as feedback to update the human resource planning process. The second section focuses on job analysis. We look at the definition of job analysis, the steps in job analysis, the uses of job analysis information and methods of job analysis. Lastly, we discuss **job descriptions** and job specifications.

Learning outcomes

When you have completed this chapter you should be able to:

1. Define human resource planning and discuss the rationale for and process of human resource planning.
2. Describe the steps that have to be carried out when doing human resource planning.
3. Describe job analysis, and distinguish between job analysis, job description and job specifications.

Human resource planning

Definition of human resource planning

Human resource planning is a planned analysis of the present and future (quantitative and qualitative) human resource needs of an organization and the implementation of action plans in order to ensure the adequate supply of human resources. It is an ongoing process that it is linked to many other activities that take place inside an organization, especially human resource management activities, such as recruitment, performance appraisal and training (Coyle-Shapiro et al, 2004).

Reasons for human resource planning

The reasons for human resource planning can be summarized as follows:

- Through human resource planning it is possible to put human resources to strategic use. This means that the strategic planning of an organization can be done on a much surer base than before.

- Through sound human resource planning unnecessary risks can be avoided when strategic organizational planning is done. In this way, human resource planning is necessary in order for an organization to adapt to (expected) changes in the environment. These changes can be of a great variety, such as changes in legislation, in markets, in products or services, in the opening up of new markets, in technology and in competition from other organizations.

- Because organizations usually make use of a visual model of their human resource system when doing human resource planning, it is easy to see when problems will be encountered. In this way the necessary adjustments in plans can be made as soon as these problems are visualized. These problems might be in the form of an over- or an under-supply of particular workers at a given stage in the future.

- Through human resource planning more effective use over the short term and over the longer term can be made of an organization's available human resources. When the human resource is utilized effectively, it also means that other resources, such as time, machines and money, can also be utilized more effectively.

- Human resource planning gives organizations the opportunity to develop high-level personnel to take up the positions of those that leave senior level and management jobs. Organizations that make use of a large number of technical or professional workers or highly-skilled managers need to know when these types of workers are to be replaced in future, because these workers are frequently in short supply.

- Human resource planning allows an organization to continually upgrade the skills and abilities of its entire workforce by concentrating on activities such as recruitment, selection, placement, training and development and career management.

- Human resource planning activities ensure that the top management team of an organization is able to gain a scientific view of, and also the necessary insight into the interaction between the organization's strategic planning and its complex and expensive human resource.

- Human resource planning places the management of an organization in a position to manage the human resource in a way that complies with all the legal requirements and to effectively counter any actions instituted by workers or labour unions.

- Human resource planning has a direct influence on the quality of work life that workers experience. It gives the workers a sense of security and builds a sense of trust in an organization as an employer. This usually leads to workers being less absent from work, being involved in fewer accidents, doing better quality work and being less prone to leave the organization (Schabracq, 2005).

The human resource planning process

Next, an overview will be given of the main steps that should be followed in doing human resource planning.

Situational analysis/scanning the environment

The first phase in human resource planning is linking the human resource function in an organization with its strategic plan. The strategic plan should be in line with the current environmental conditions, as well as with the long-term changes in these conditions. The human resources of an organization are one of the mechanisms that can be used to adjust the organization to changing environmental conditions. That is why the human resource manager should preferably be a member of the team that does the strategic planning for an organization.

An organization should gather as much relevant information about its environment as possible. It should set (or adjust) its goals in terms of marketing, production and finances on the basis of this environmental scanning. The goal of human resource planning is to make a contribution towards the efficiency of an organization. For that reason it should be integrated with the organization's short- and long-range business goals and plans.

The length of the planning period should also be considered. Organizations tend to do short-range human resource planning, perhaps because there is less danger of being wrong about one's prediction if one sticks to a planning period of not more than one year, or at least not more than two years. A planning period of up to two years is usually called a short-range period. A planning period of two to five years is usually called a medium- or intermediate-range period. When one goes beyond the five-year period, one is thinking about long-range planning. The longer the time frame being used, the more difficult it becomes to anticipate the different factors that will influence the planning process.

It is of the utmost importance that human resource managers and line managers work together to develop business plans and to determine the need for human resources. They should also determine what the characteristics of the workforce should be if it is to fit in with the (future) business strategies. It will most probably also be necessary to develop programmes in order to ensure that the strategies can be carried out.

An analysis of the current human resource situation

Usually the next step in the human resource planning process is to determine the characteristics of the workers employed by the organization at the present time. This means that an inventory of present personnel must be developed. Sometimes such an inventory is also called a skills inventory or a human resource information system. To be useful, the human resource information system should be computerized. Sometimes organizations might ask a computer programmer to develop a **human resource information system** or a personnel inventory that suits the purposes of the specific organization.

The type of information that is found in a human resource information system depends on the needs of the specific organization. At the least, it should contain basic information about each employee. When one thinks of it as a skills inventory, it should contain personal information (e.g. names and ages of workers), employment history, present job or position and job grade, present salary and salary scale, skills, education, job experience, and training, special qualifications or achievements, results of performance appraisals or other indicators of potential, and personal career goals. From the information found in a skills inventory, the skill levels of the present employees and the extent to which they can be developed can be assessed.

An analysis of the demand for and the supply of human resources

The second step in human resource planning is to analyse the future demand for and the supply of human resources. Demand in the case of human resource planning refers to the number of workers needed at a specific time and place and the characteristics that they need to possess. Characteristics refers to the abilities, skills and experience that the workers need to fill the particular positions. Supply in the case of human resource planning refers to the number of workers and their characteristics that are available to fill the particular positions. The following questions should be answered to determine the demand and supply of human resources:

■ What are the positions that will need to be filled during the period for which human resource planning is being done? The human resource planner has to forecast how many workers will probably resign, how many positions will be made redundant and how many new positions will be created. Past tendencies concerning resignations, redundancies and the forming of new positions can be analysed. Previous attitude surveys can be linked to labour turnover to get an idea of the number of vacancies that might occur. Business plans can be used to get an idea of the number of positions that will be made redundant or be created.

■ How and where will we find the human resources needed to fill the positions that we have identified? Here it is important to determine what the characteristics of those human resources should be. After this, the characteristics of the present workforce, and also of those that might be recruited from outside the organization can be considered. The organization should have up-to-date records of retirements, advancements and appointments that have taken place in the past. When looking at the characteristics of the present workforce, it is important to develop a **skills inventory**. When determining the demand for and the supply of human resources, different quantitative methods can be used, but the forecasting methods that are usually used depend a great deal on human judgement. Various techniques that can be used during this forecasting process are the following: An expert can do the forecasting. Sometimes a panel of experts is used for this purpose. Tendencies noticed in the past can be used to make projections into the future. Sophisticated modelling techniques and multiple forecasting techniques can be used, where different factors (such as sales volumes or the gross national product) can be correlated with employment figures. These more sophisticated techniques include mathematical models, simulations and the statistical technique of regression analysis.

Human resource planning takes place on two levels, namely on the quantitative level and the qualitative level. The quantitative level has to do with ensuring that the right number of people having the right qualifications are available at the right time. The factors that influence an organization's future human resources needs include the staff turnover rate, the absence rate, retirements, changes in statutory working hours and women employees that get married or who become pregnant. This means that the factors that influence personnel turnover and absences should be studied very closely when one does human resource planning. The qualitative level has to do with having the right kind of people available, that is, the people who are able to communicate on an individual and group level, who are suitably motivated, are reasonably satisfied and loyal employees.

The motivation of workers should also be considered. This can be accomplished by ensuring that the work is performed in such a way and the work environment is of such a nature that people are able to utilize their skills and abilities. People should be trained to communicate effectively. Organizations should determine whether the employees are reasonably satisfied with their work. When selecting employees, organizations should determine whether candidates possess the qualities needed to do the work and fit into the 'culture' of the organization (Hough and Furnham, 2003).

Determining human resource goals

Once the supply of, and the demand for, human resources for a specified period of time has been determined, it is possible to compare the demand with the supply. If there is a difference between the forecasts of the demand and the supply, an organization needs to decide on the action steps needed to eliminate this difference or discrepancy. If an organization engages in short-term planning, it may be possible to quantify the goals. The following are examples of short-term human resource goals: a) increasing the number of the possible job applicants by means of a recruitment campaign; b) attracting candidates that have the necessary qualifications; c) upgrading the qualifications of people that are selected and appointed; and d) making sure that those who are appointed remain in the employ of the organization as long as possible.

The design and implementation of human resource plans

It is during this phase that the plans that can lead to the organization reaching its human resource goals must be designed and implemented. In the case of the forecasted demand being greater than the forecasted supply of human resources, these plans could include recruitment, selection, performance appraisal, training, paying attention to remuneration (salaries and wages), advancement and career development activities and instituting a system of overtime work. It is here that it is very important that all the activities of the human resources function/department should take place in a coordinated and in an integrated fashion. In the case of the forecasted demand being smaller than the forecasted supply of human resources, the following are possible strategies that can be implemented: early retirements, retrenchments, making use of a process called work-sharing (for instance where two employees each perform half of a job), working shorter work weeks and not filling positions that are vacated by people that retire or who resign.

Gathering and analysing information that can be used as feedback

Human resource planning does not stop with the implementation of strategies to reach the human resource goals. Previously it was stated that human resource planning is an ongoing process. This means that human resource planning must not be seen as something that is perhaps done once a year and is then filed away and forgotten. Throughout the period for which human resource planning was done, the human resource planning function will have to seek feedback on the progress towards the goals that were set. On the basis of the feedback received, adjustments need to be made to the human resource plan. Because short-term human resource goals are usually set in a quantitative manner (for example, the number of artisans needed to be recruited by the end of a certain period), it is usually quite easy to determine the degree to which these goals have been reached.

Factors in the environment may change during the period planning was done for. The skills inventory should also be updated. It may be that the training programmes did not bring about the necessary changes in the skill levels that were forecasted. It may also happen that because of tough economic times fewer workers opted for earlier retirement. From what has just been said, it is clear why human resource planning should be carried out on a continual basis.

Job analysis

Definition of job analysis

Job analysis is defined as the process of gathering job information by breaking the job down into its component elements, in order to identify what tasks and responsibilities a job consists of, what skills, knowledge and abilities are required to do the job, and what environmental conditions surround the job. A job description is a written summary of the key performance areas (tasks, duties and/or responsibilities) of a specific job. The job description includes a clear presentation of what is done, how it is done and why it is done. A job specification is a written explanation of the minimum requirements needed for effective performance on a given job. It includes knowledge, skills, abilities, traits and other characteristics needed for effective job performance.

Steps in job analysis

The job analysis process involves a number of steps:

- Step 1: Decide who should conduct the job analysis. If an organization only has an occasional need for job analysis information, it may hire a temporary job analyst from outside. Other organizations will have job analysis experts employed on a full-time basis. Still other organizations will use supervisors, job incumbents or some combination of these to collect job analysis information. Regardless of who collects the information, the individual should thoroughly understand people, jobs and the total organization system.

- Step 2: Examine the total organization and the fit of each job. This step provides a broad view of how each job fits into the total structure of the organization. Organization charts and process charts are used to complete this step.

- Step 3: Determine how the job analysis information will be used. Different uses of job analysis information call for different approaches. For example, if management's purpose is to ensure that a selection test is valid by proving that the content of the test reflects the content of the job, then job analysis will focus on the job's work activities. On the other hand, the objective of developing a performance evaluation system that will be defensible in court may require gathering of information about behaviour that results in more and less successful performance.

- Step 4: Select the jobs to be analysed. Since it is usually too costly and time consuming to analyse every job, a representative sample of jobs needs to be selected. The manager of the specific department must be contacted, and the objectives of the process discussed with him or her. It is essential to get his or her cooperation. Since job analysis plays a central role in the management of people, it should be conducted when a new job is introduced in the organization, and when the job's major tasks and thus worker performance requirements change.

- Step 5: Collect data by using acceptable job analysis techniques. Techniques like interviews, observation and questionnaires are used to collect data on the characteristics of the job, the required behaviour and the employee characteristics needed to perform the job.

- Step 6: Prepare the job description and job specification.

The knowledge and data collected in steps 1–6 are used as the foundation for other human resources activities.

Uses of job analysis

Job analysis is the foundation of human resource management. Job analysis can be used in each of the following human resource activities:

- Job analysis can be used to prepare **job descriptions**. A complete job description contains a job summary, the job duties and responsibilities, and an indication of working conditions.

- Job analysis is used to write **job specifications**. The job specification describes the individual traits and characteristics required to do the job well.

- Job analysis makes it possible to **organize** and integrate the total workforce based on duties and responsibilities.

- The **staffing** programme of an organization rests on the information supplied by the job analysis. Job analysis information can be used to help recruiters to seek and find the type of people that will fit into the organization, to supply information about the nature of the job, to set standards that applicants must reach, to determine which selection techniques can be used, and to establish criteria for the selection process.

- The analyst can use the information gathered through job analysis for **training and development** purposes (e.g. the training needs of employees, the content of training courses, and relevant training methods).

- Job analysis supplies the basic data needed to do a **job evaluation**. Job evaluation is a systematic process to determine the value of a job relative to all other jobs in an organization.

- Job analysis is used to determine the criteria and requirements for **performance appraisal** of a job holder. Without an adequate job analysis, it is possible that the success of a given employee will be judged in terms of behaviours that may appear important, but in fact have little bearing on whether the worker is successful.

- Job analysis can be used in **career development**. The movement of individuals into and out of positions, jobs and occupations is a common procedure in organizations.

- Working conditions and **safety** can be improved based on the results of a job analysis. The safety of a job depends on a proper layout, standards, equipment and other physical conditions.

Job analysis methods

There are five basic methods, which can be used separately or in combination, of collecting job analysis data. These methods are observation, interviews, questionnaires, **critical incident technique** and job incumbents' diaries.

Observation

Direct observation is used for jobs that require manual, standardized and short job cycle activities. Observation will be especially useful in jobs that demand few skills, where work is controlled mechanically, which involve physical activities and where the work cycle is short. The job of an automobile assembly-line worker, an insurance company filing clerk and an inventory stockroom employee are examples of jobs which can be analysed by using observation. In contrast, observation is not appropriate for jobs that involve significant amounts of mental activity, such as a research scientist, lawyer or mathematician. Jobs involving intangible factors such as judgement, computations and decision-making present few opportunities for supplying information to the observer.

The job analyst observes what the employee does, why he or she does it, how he or she does it, which skills are used and what physical demands are placed on the employee. In order for observations to be maximally useful, an adequate, representative sample of employees needs to be observed at various times during the work period. It is useful to be as unobtrusive as possible when observation is used. Employees must not be disturbed in the execution of their duties. The job analyst must also remember that employees might change their behaviour when they are observed. The employee must have the opportunity to study the job analysis notes, and to modify incorrect observations

The interview

The **interview** is probably the most widely used data collection technique. It permits the job analyst to talk face to face with job incumbents. The job incumbent can ask questions, and this interview serves as an opportunity for the analyst to explain how the job analysis knowledge and information will be used. Reliable, accurate and comprehensive information can be gathered by interviewing employees and supervisors. Interviews can be conducted with a single job incumbent, a group of individuals, or with a supervisor who is knowledgeable about the job. Usually a structured set of questions will be used in interviews so that answers from individuals or groups can be compared.

The interview has the following advantages:

1. It allows the job analyst to gather complete and accurate work information, provided care is taken that the job is not deliberately inflated. The job analyst should also confirm the information with other job incumbents and their immediate supervisor.
2. Interviewing the employee saves him or her from providing a written description of his or her work – something that usually causes headaches for employees.
3. The interview gives the employee the opportunity to receive first hand information regarding the reasons for job analysis from the job analyst.

Interviewing a person to analyse a job has the following disadvantages:

1. It requires much time if many jobs need to be analysed.
2. It is an expensive method, because the organization must pay the salary of the job analyst, and the working time of the interviewee is lost.
3. It is impossible to involve all the workers. If questionnaires are used it is possible to involve many employees.
4. Inaccurate information may be collected. For example, if a job incumbent believes that the job analysis interview will be used to set the job's compensation level, he or she may provide inaccurate information. It is necessary to interview more than one person, to plan the interview carefully, to use relevant questions and to establish rapport with the interviewee.

The questionnaire

The job analyst can construct a questionnaire to send to employees and supervisors. The information gathered by using the questionnaires is checked to ensure that it is accurate and complete. The job holder and his or her supervisor are usually asked to complete the questionnaire. The questionnaire includes specific questions about the job, job requirements, working conditions and equipment. The format and degree of structure that a questionnaire should have are debatable issues. There is really no best format for a questionnaire. It should be kept as short and simple as possible, its objectives should be explained, what it is being used for – people want to know why it must be completed, and it should be tested before it is used.

The questionnaire has the following advantages: a) It makes provision for maximum participation, because each employee and supervisor can complete a questionnaire. b) It prepares employees for follow-up interviews (if interviews are used), because it gives them time to think about the different aspects of their jobs. c) It saves time and money if questionnaires are completed accurately. However, questionnaires have the following disadvantages: a) It is difficult to construct a good questionnaire. b) It is difficult and time-consuming to interpret the answers to the questions. c) Employees sometimes are irritated by questionnaires. This may lead to carelessness in the completion of questionnaires.

The motivation of employees to complete questionnaires is usually a problem. Many job analysts use a combination of interviews and questionnaires to analyse jobs. The combination of the questionnaire and the interview will supply more accurate information, give the employee the opportunity to elaborate on the answers given on the questionnaire, and give the job analyst the opportunity to receive first hand information regarding the reasons for job analysis.

The critical incident technique

In this method employees and supervisors are asked to report critical incidents in their work behaviour that are effective or ineffective in reaching their job objectives. The elements, the situation in which it took place, what the employee did that was effective or ineffective, and the effects of the behaviour are indicated for each incident. The advantage of this method is that real behaviour, rather than opinions or subjective impressions, is used as the yardstick of how the job must be done. The disadvantage is that it takes much time to gather, analyse and classify incidents. Using the critical incidents method, 'average' worker behaviour is often difficult to discern and it may not be possible to compile a complete job description.

Job incumbent diary

The diary is a recording by job incumbents of job duties, frequency of the duties and when the duties were carried out. This technique requires the job incumbent to keep a diary on a daily basis. Unfortunately, many individuals are not disciplined enough to keep such a diary. If a diary is kept up to date, it can provide good information about the job. Comparisons on a daily, weekly or monthly basis can be made. The diary is especially useful when attempting to analyse jobs that are difficult to observe, such as those performed by engineers, scientists and senior executives.

Job descriptions

The job description is one of the primary outputs provided by a systematic job analysis. It is a written description of what the job entails. While there is no standard format for a job description, it will include information regarding the following aspects:

- Job title. A title of the job and other identifying information such as its wage and benefits classification.

- Summary. A brief two-sentence statement describing the purpose of the job and what outputs are expected from job incumbents.

- Key performance areas. A description of the primary job duties and responsibilities in terms of *what* is done, *how* it is done and *why* it is done.

- Equipment. A clear statement of the tools, equipment and information required for effectively performing the job.

- Environment. A description of the working conditions of the job, the location of the job and other relevant characteristics of the immediate work environment such as hazards and noise levels.

The guidelines for writing job descriptions are given in Focus box 7.1.

Focus 7.1

Guidelines for writing job descriptions

1. Write about the job, not the person.
2. Describe only what is required of the incumbent.
3. Describe the what and the how of each task.
4. Begin each sentence with a present tense active verb. Try not to use adjectives.
5. Be concise, do not give irrelevant details, subjective statements or opinions.
6. Use concrete examples to explain unfamiliar or broad responsibilities.
7. Present the tasks in a logical sequence.

Job specification

The job specification evolves from the job description. It indicates the competencies (qualifications, personal traits and experience) needed to perform the job effectively. The job specification is especially useful for offering guidance for recruitment and selection.

Job specifications can be compiled in three ways:

1. The job analyst judges which competencies are important for good performance. This approach saves time, but is subjective. Although this method indicates which competencies are essential for work success, it does not indicate the relative importance of these competencies for work success.
2. A group of specialists who know the job determine the competencies needed for the job in behavioural terms. This approach starts with a list of competencies (knowledge, aptitudes, skills and personality characteristics) that are defined and judged by specialists after they have studied the job description. In this way one will get a profile for each job. This approach is more objective, but requires more time.

Job title	Secretary.
Previous experience	Two years office experience.
Dexterity	Precise movement of hands and fingers required to operate computer. Minimum 60 wpm typing speed.
Visual demand	Concentrated vision required 50% of the time to take dictation, read incoming mail, keep records, type letters.
Physical demand	Under 5 kg lifting or carrying. Normal work position is seated.
Judgement	Judgement required to decide course of action from complex facts, determine whether to interrupt supervisor in meeting, to compose routine letters, establish filing system, deal with executives, supervisors and visitors.
Working conditions	No unpleasant or stressful environment conditions, air-conditioned office.
Hazards	No probable injury or health hazard.
Other requirements	Must have a good command of English, verbal and written, know correct grammar and spelling.

Figure 7.1 Example of a job specification.

3. Psychometric tests are used to determine job specifications. First, current employees are tested with a range of psychometric tests. Second, their work performance is assessed to determine who is more successful and less successful on the job. Next, the differences between the psychometric tests of successful and less successful groups are analysed to determine the job specifications.

Regardless of the method used to determine job specifications, two aspects should be considered, namely that a) minimum acceptable standards should be specified, and b) flexibility should be shown in the application of job specifications. It serves as a guideline and may be adapted if there is a limited supply of candidates for a vacant job. Job specifications include the following aspects: a) educational and training required; b) experience needed; c) special skills required; d) physical and mental abilities required; e) emotional characteristics required. An example of a job specification is set out in Figure 7.1.

An example of a job description and job specifications is set out in Figure 7.2.

JOB IDENTIFICATION	
Job title	HR Manager
Company	Company X
Location/Workplace	Head Office
Job title of immediate supervisor	HR Executive
Job title(s) of subordinate(s)	Organizational Development Manager, Training Manager, Personal Assistant
Job level	7

JOB SUMMARY
Primary Output: To ensure the HR needs of Company X are met

JOB DUTIES AND RESPONSIBILITIES	
Key Performance Areas	Accountabilities
1. Implement HR strategies	❑ An annual HR tactical plan in support of the strategic goals of the company. ❑ Ensure sound employee support systems that enhance the culture of the company. ❑ Ensure the implementation of proactive organizational development strategies. ❑ Ensure effective management and quality assurance of processes in the HR department, i.e. administrative processes, recruitment and selection, policies and procedures, leave management, communication and performance management.

JOB SPECIFICATIONS	
Qualifications	Masteris degree in either Human Resource Management or Work and Organizational Psychology
Experience	At least five years experience in HR development and management

JOB-SPECIFIC BEHAVIOURAL DIMENSIONS	
1.	**Quality orientation:** Accomplishing tasks by considering all areas involved, no matter how small; showing concern for all aspects of the job; accurately checking processes and tasks; being watchful over a period of time.
2.	**Work standards:** Setting high standards of performance for self and others; assuming responsibility and accountability for successfully completing assignment or tasks; self-imposing standards of excellence rather than having standards imposed.
3.	**Technical professional knowledge:** Having achieved a satisfactory level of technical and professional skill or knowledge in position-related areas; keeping up with current developments and trends in areas of expertise.

Figure 7.2 A job description and job specifications.

Summary

- Human resource planning was defined as ensuring that an organization has the right number of suitably qualified workers available at the right time. In order to achieve this, human resource planning has to be linked to the strategic planning process and to the business plan of an organization. The reasons for human resource planning were described. The human resource planning process may take on many forms, one of which was described. It consists of analysing the situation (scanning the environment), determining the characteristics of the present work force, analysing the demand for, and the supply of human resources, and determining the human resource goals. It further consists of designing and implementing human resource plans to reach these goals and gathering and analysing information that can be used as feedback to update the human resource planning process.

■ Job analysis is defined as the process of gathering job information by breaking the job down into its component elements, in order to identify what tasks and responsibilities a job consists of, what skills, knowledge and abilities are required to do the job, and what environmental conditions surround the job. There are six steps in job analysis, starting with examining the total organization and the fit of jobs, and concluding with the preparation of the job specification. The uses of job analysis include strategic planning, recruitment, selection, training, compensation and job design. It is clear from the above discussion that amateurs should not conduct job analysis. Training is essential before a person can analyse a job. Before conducting a job analysis, organization charts should be studied to acquire an overview of the organization. The techniques that can be used to analyse a job include observation, interviews, questionnaires, diaries or a combination of these.

■ A job description concentrates on the job. It explains what the job is and what the duties, responsibilities and general working conditions are. A job specification concentrates on the characteristics needed to perform the job. It describes the qualifications that the incumbent must possess to perform the job. Recruitment has been defined as the process of attracting suitable candidates to apply for vacancies that exist in an organization.

Key concepts and terms

Critical incident technique	Job specification
Demand	Observation
Human resource information system	Occupation
	Position
Human resource planning	Questionnaire
Interview	Situational analysis
Job	Strategic plan
Job analysis	Supply
Job description	Task
Job incumbent diary	

Sample essay titles

- Is there a link between human resource planning, strategic planning and the business plan? Motivate your answer.
- Do you agree with the following statement? 'Job analysis is the cornerstone of human resource management.' Motivate your answer.
- Which techniques can be used to analyse the job of a financial manager in an organization?

Further reading

Books

Armstrong, M. (2006). *A Handbook of Human Resource Management Practice*. London: Kogan Page.

Brannick, M.T., and Levine, E.L. (2002). *Job Analysis: Methods, Research, and Applications for Human Resource Management in the New Millennium*. Thousand Oaks, CA: Sage Publications.

Whetzel, D.L., and Wheaton, G.R. (2007). *Applied Measurement: Industrial Psychology in Human Resources Management*. Mahwah, NJ: Lawrence Erlbaum.

Journal articles

Conte, J.M., Dean, M.A., Ringenbach, K.L., Moran, S.K., and Landy, F.J. (2005). The relationship between work attitudes and job analysis ratings: Do rating scale type and task discretion matter. *Human Performance*, 18, 1–21.

Macfarlane, D., Fortin, P., Fox, J., Gundry, S., Oshry, J., and Warren, E. (1997). Clinical and human resource planning for the downsizing of psychiatric hospitals: The British Columbia experience. *Psychiatric Quarterly*, 68, 25–42.

8 Recruitment and selection

This chapter introduces the reader to **recruitment** and **selection**. The first section focuses on recruitment. We look at the definition of recruitment and describe **recruitment planning** and the development of a **recruitment strategy.** In developing a recruitment strategy it is necessary to determine who will do the recruiting, what kind of recruiting will be used, where it will be done, and what sources and methods of recruitment will be used. The chapter then proceeds to the actual recruitment process, **preliminary screening** and evaluation of the recruitment efforts. The second section focuses on selection of staff. We define selection and describe the factors that should be considered before making selection decisions. Then we look at the **selection procedure** (including the preliminary screening interview, completion of the applicant blank, **psychometric tests,** the selection **interview, reference** checks and physical examinations) and requirements for selection predictors. We describe the factors that should be considered when rejecting applications and auditing the selection process.

Learning outcomes

When you have completed this chapter you should be able to:

1. Define recruitment and describe recruitment planning.
2. Develop a recruitment strategy by considering the type of recruiters needed, kind of recruitment, place of recruitment, and sources and methods of recruitment.
3. Identify the factors that should be considered during the actual recruitment process.
4. Define selection and motivate why selection is important for organizations.
5. Describe the factors which affect selection decisions and explain the requirements for selection predictors.
6. Evaluate the suitability of different selection predictors for different jobs.
7. Discuss the considerations when applicants are rejected and develop a strategy to audit the selection process.

Recruitment

Definition of recruitment

Recruitment is defined as a process of seeking and attracting suitable candidates from within the organization or from outside the organization for job vacancies that exist. 'Suitable candidates' means those who possess the required characteristics that will enable them to perform satisfactorily in the specific job.

Recruitment planning

Before any recruitment can be done, an organization needs to decide what the nature and number of job vacancies are. This information comes from human resource planning and job analysis. In recruitment planning that information is used to decide on the number and characteristics of potential candidates that need to be attracted. Organizations try to recruit more candidates than the number they wish to employ. Some candidates will most probably be overqualified for the specific positions, while some might not really be interested in obtaining a position.

An organization needs to keep a balance between setting recruitment standards that are too high or too low. When an organization is operating in a so-called 'tight labour market' (where there are few candidates for the number of job openings), it might be tempted to lower standards regarding the candidates' qualifications. This might lead to other undesirable outcomes. An organization might decide to retain high standards and to spend much time and money to attract suitable candidates. It seems that when organizations retain higher standards, fewer candidates apply for jobs, but then these candidates are also better qualified (Kepes and Delery, 2006).

From past experience, organizations usually know how many potential candidates they need to reach through their recruitment efforts in order to have a sufficient number of applicants from which to choose. The number will most probably vary with the type of vacancy or job. The type of recruitment source and the recruitment method will also have to be taken into consideration when deciding on the number of candidates that have to be reached.

Developing a recruitment strategy

When developing a recruitment strategy, an organization must answer the following questions:

- Who will be doing the recruiting and how should they be prepared?

- What kind of recruiting will be used?

- Where will the recruiting be done?

- What sources and methods of recruitment will be used?

Recruiters and their preparation/characteristics

In most organizations the human resource department is responsible for the coordination of the recruitment process. Because recruiters come into direct contact with possible candidates, it is of great importance that they should be knowledgeable about the organization in general and about the specific jobs that are vacant. Often, recruiters are the main source of information that potential candidates make use of in deciding to apply for a position. The reason for this is that potential applicants know so little about the organization. They have to make use of the information supplied by recruiters when deciding to apply for a position. The ideal recruiter is someone who can make potential applicants enthusiastic about the organization. A recruiter should have very good interpersonal skills and should be able to supply realistic information to possible applicants. He or she should be a likeable person, be enthusiastic and must show personal interest in applicants (Rosenfeld et al, 2002).

Kind of recruitment

Both positive and negative aspects about the organization and job should be provided to applicants. When an organization (through its recruiting efforts) gives applicants both positive and negative information about the organization and job in a balanced and objective way, it is called **realistic job previews**. One of the main reasons for giving a realistic job preview is to reduce the 'reality shock' and disappointment when a newcomer eventually joins an organization and finds that his or her expectations are not being met and/or that circumstances are quite different from those which were envisaged. Unless the applicant has no other option than to take the job offered to him or her, a realistic job preview gives the applicant the chance to 'opt out', without losing face, because the decision to 'opt out' is based upon realistic information. It also seems that if an applicant, in the face of a realistic job preview, still decides to join an organization, such a person will most probably be a more committed employee.

Place of recruitment

Organizations tend to recruit managerial and professional employees on a country-wide or a regional basis, technical employees/artisans on a regional or a local basis and clerical and manual workers on a local basis. Generally speaking, organizations make use of past experience to decide where to concentrate their recruitment efforts, and to get the best return on the money invested in recruitment.

The basis of recruiting will also depend on the job-seeking behaviour of applicants. One aspect of job-seeking behaviour is, for instance, the distance a person will travel, looking for a job. Another aspect might be the media a potential candidate might use when searching for a job. The state of the labour market will also play a role. If, for instance, there are very few qualified clerical workers available locally, an organization will concentrate its recruitment efforts on a regional basis.

Sources and methods of recruitment

Sources refer to the segment(s) of the labour market where applicants can be found, such as schools, colleges, universities, other organizations and sources of unemployed people. Methods refer to the specific way(s) of obtaining applicants. Here one can think of something like direct applications or so-called 'write-ins' or 'walk-ins', referrals by present employees, advertising using different media, private and public employment agencies and so-called 'executive search agencies/firms'. It seems safe to say that sources do influence the methods used.

Internal recruitment

Internal recruitment has various advantages: a) Most people, at one time or another, expect to be appointed to some higher position, having a greater status and paying a higher salary. If an organization appoints from within, it can lead to an increase in the morale of employees, because their expectations are being met. b) It is possible to more accurately assess the knowledge, skill and personality characteristics of an organization's present employees than those of outside applicants who have to go through a selection process. c) The recruitment and selection process is simplified, because, with a few exceptions, candidates from outside sources are only needed for entry-level jobs. d) The career development of employees can be planned far more systematically and suitable career paths for them to follow can be more easily identified. e) The candidates already know how the organization operates. f) The investment already made in present employees is continued.

Recruiting and subsequent appointing from within also has some disadvantages: a) It leads to inbreeding that can prevent the development of new ideas and much needed creativity. b) An organization needs to have very good training programmes in place through which the knowledge and skills of employees can be upgraded in order for them to be promoted to the vacant positions. c) If an organization wants to appoint from within, it needs to ensure that when candidates are first employed, they have the potential to be promoted. Otherwise, people might be promoted to a point where they are unable to carry out the duties of the job successfully. d) It might lead to 'infighting' amongst colleagues, something that does the morale of employees no good.

There are different **internal recruitment** methods that an organization can use.

■ An informal search for a suitable candidate can be conducted. This method is not recommended, because it does not give everybody that might be interested or qualified a fair chance to apply for the specific job.

■ A system of job posting and job bidding can be used. Job posting simply means that vacancies are advertised internally in such a way that everyone that is eligible is able to take notice of the vacancy.

■ When vacancies occur, the human resource information system can also be searched. Such a system contains up-to-date information on each employee's skills, abilities and personal characteristics. When vacancies do occur, use will also have to be made of the human resource plan. If career paths are in place for employees, it will also be clear which employees could be promoted to the vacant positions.

External recruitment

An organization makes use of a number of different recruitment methods to attract suitable candidates from outside the organization. It might be cheaper to hire certain categories of employees from outside than to train present employees, the pool from which one can select is much greater, and people appointed from outside bring in new ideas. On the negative side recruiting from outside sources might be quite costly. Candidates from outside sources need more time to become orientated and adjusted to their new surroundings. Resentment can also develop in present employees when candidates from outside rather than themselves are appointed.

The following **external recruitment** methods can be used:

- **Advertisements**. Many organizations make use of advertisements in newspapers, magazines and professional journals/periodicals and over the radio and television to attract suitable candidates. When recruitment advertisements are used, the following goals should be kept in mind: first, to reach the 'right' audience (target population) and, second, to attract sufficient suitable candidates and as few (unqualified) candidates as possible. This means that one has to understand the characteristics of the target population and what motivates them to apply for a vacancy. If one receives too many applications for a specific vacancy, then it shows that there is something wrong with the communication process. An effective recruitment advertisement appear to require the following conditions: a) It should be based on a thorough job description and must provide details about the job and about the job specification. b) In order to ensure that a realistic job preview is given, it is important that the necessary unfavourable information about the job is also provided. c) One should be specific in describing tasks and the remuneration package. d) The facts should be presented in a positive way.

- **Private employment agencies**. These agencies have information of a large number of possible candidates on computer which can be matched against the job specifications of vacant jobs. If they do not have suitable candidates on file or on computer, they do the necessary advertising to attract the required candidates. A private employment agency is able to do a lot of the administrative work associated with recruitment, but they tend to charge large fees for their services.

- **'Walk-ins' or 'write-ins'**. This simply means that sometimes applicants write in to the organization to apply for jobs, even though no such jobs have been advertised. Sometimes applicants come in person to apply for jobs which have not been advertised.

- **Referrals by employees**. It often happens that the information that a vacancy exists is passed along by means of word of mouth among colleagues and their friends. The advantage of this recruitment method is that it is very time and cost effective. Unfortunately, it might lead to inbreeding and the forming of cliques.

- **Educational institutions**. Organizations can let recruiters visit different educational institutions to recruit suitable candidates. Sometimes an organization is looking for candidates who possess specific scholastic, academic or professional qualifications. In order to reach these candidates, it is important for organizations to build up relationships with these educational institutions, who will be more than willing to supply information on suitable candidates.

- **Executive search firms**. These concentrate on the recruiting of middle and top managers. In order for them to attract suitable candidates, these executive search firms take much care to ensure that the job specifications are clearly stated. Middle and top managers recruited by means of this method are often drawn away from other organizations. That is why this method of recruiting is often called 'head-hunting'. It is nothing out of the ordinary for them to ask a fee that amounts to one-third of a successful candidate's annual salary.

- **Other methods**. There are a variety of other methods an organization can use to recruit suitable candidates: a) An organization may make use of direct-mail recruiting, by obtaining mailing lists from different professional bodies or societies, and sending the specific advertisements to all the people on these mailing lists. b) Recruiters may set up stands at job fairs or career exhibitions. c) Many organizations also make use of the services of temporary-help agencies.

The actual recruitment process

Once an organization has decided on a recruitment plan and a recruitment strategy, the following two broad steps have to be carried out: the potential sources of recruitment must be activated and the 'sales' message must be communicated to qualified applicants.

Activating the sources of recruitment

No recruitment is done before a request has been received from line management that a vacancy has occurred or is about to occur. Heneman et al (1989) point out that the recruitment process at this point in time can become an administrative and logistic nightmare for an organization, because the following tasks have to be performed:

- Preliminary screening of applicants has to be done to eliminate those candidates who are clearly unsuitable.

- Candidates have to be transported to the organization and will have to be housed for the duration of the selection process.

- Line managers must be ready to interview candidates.

- Candidates who have been unsuccessful must be notified to that effect.

- Formal employment offers must be sent to successful candidates.

- The acceptance or rejection of such offers must be processed.

- A well-functioning record system which can be utilized at any moment to check what progress has been made in the recruitment process needs to be in place.

Communicating the 'sales' message to potential applicants

An organization should not 'oversell' itself to potential candidates. The organization should take note of the factors that influence a person's decision to apply for a job and to join an organization. It appears that the message and the medium through which it is communicated play a significant role in this regard.

- **The message**. A potential candidate is likely to apply for a job, and to keep on working at that job, if there is something in the remuneration package that attracts him or her. This has implications for the nature of the message that has to be communicated to the potential applicant. Although there is no clear-cut answer as to what should be included in this message, the following can be used as pointers: a) Salary and the nature of the work play a role in most candidates' decision to apply for a job. b) The geographical area in which the organization is located and the possibilities for advancement are important for people who apply for managerial or professional positions. c) Job security is an important factor for unschooled or lower-schooled workers. d) Working conditions, hours of work and the nature of supervisors and co-workers are often of no great concern when applying for a job.

- **The medium**. The effectiveness of a recruitment message also largely depends on the medium through which the message is delivered. It seems that the credibility or 'believability' of the medium plays an important role in getting the message across. Credibility of media is based on trust, perceived expertise and personal liking. Therefore, media such as personnel agencies and recruitment advertisements have the least credibility, while the smaller and more intensive media, such as friends and personal contacts, have the most credibility.

Preliminary screening

There are several ways to go about doing preliminary screening. It might consist of doing a quick check on the application blanks that were returned by applicants. One can also do a check on curricula vitae and testimonials that were sent in by applicants. It might even consist of doing some reference checking on applicants. In the case of **'walk-ins'** the screening might consist of an interview with the applicant.

Evaluation of recruitment

Several methods can be used to evaluate the recruitment effort of an organization. For instance, the outcomes of the recruitment effort could be studied. The following questions should be answered: a) Have all the vacancies been filled? b) What is the nature of the work performance and labour turnover of applicants that have been accepted? c) What is the average cost incurred for every candidate that has been appointed? Is this cost in accordance with that what has been planned for? Did everything in the recruitment process go according to plan? These are the type of questions usually asked when doing a

utility analysis of the recruitment effort. A utility analysis of the different recruitment methods or media that were used can be done to get an indication of the relative costs and benefits of the different methods or media.

Selection

Definition of selection

Selection involves the sorting out of applicants for a vacant job and the elimination of those applicants who do not fit the requirements of the job and/or the organization. The content of different jobs differs, as do the abilities and skills required. For example, the abilities and skills that are required of a telephone operator differ from those required of the manager of a retail store. Applicants also differ regarding their abilities, aptitudes, skills, experience, age and education. Therefore, the objective of selection is to assess which applicant will best fit a specific job (Cooper et al, 2003).

The importance of selection

Selection is a major expense for organizations. A lot of money is spent on recruitment, selection and training. In addition to these costs, there is the cost incurred by the new employee's inability to meet performance requirements while learning the job. Often, it takes a year before the employee actually deserves the salary for the position. The costs are even greater if the wrong person is hired.

Despite the high costs of selection, research has shown conclusively that good selection pays off. Sometimes good selection methods are expensive to develop and refine, which can discourage organizations from investing in them. Selection, however, affects the quality of personnel and their task performance. Training will also be more successful if you select the right quality people. Poor selection causes a poor fit between the job and the individual, which contributes to job dissatisfaction, poor performance and high labour turnover.

Factors that influence the selection decision

There are three factors that may influence the selection decision: the job description and job specification, the organization and social environment, and the successive hurdle or the multiple correlation approach.

Job description and job specification

If a selection programme is to be successful, the employee characteristics stated in the job specification must accurately summarize what is necessary for effective performance on the job. An accurate list of characteristics can only be generated after the organization has conducted a thorough job analysis. Job specifications which are important for selection purposes include education and training, experience, physical characteristics, and personal characteristics and competencies.

Organization and social environment

The organization and social environment refer to the values of the organization, the way things are done, social cliques, openness to new employees and the personality of the manager. The objective of selection will be to assess whether the applicant would adapt to these values and conditions. A match between the values of the employee and those of the organization contributes to his or her commitment.

The selection approach

Three approaches – the successive hurdles approach, the compensatory approach and the **combined approach** – can be used during selection.

- **The successive hurdles approach.** Using the successive hurdle approach, the candidate must fit the requirement of each step in the selection process (for example, the application form, psychometric testing or medical examination) to be considered for appointment. This approach saves time and money because it prevents unsuitable applicants going through the whole selection process.

- **The compensatory approach.** The compensatory approach allows very high performance on one selection procedure to compensate for low performance on another.

- **The combined approach.** It is possible to combine the successive hurdles approach and the compensatory approach. In this case the abilities and motivation that are critical for success are first assessed. If the applicant does not fit these requirements, his or her application is rejected. If he or she fits the critical requirements, he or she goes through the whole selection process, and then the selection decision is made.

Selection procedure

A systematic selection procedure must be followed to make selection decisions. Selection procedures refer to procedures or actions that can be used to acquire and integrate information to make a recommendation and/or final human resource decision. The assumption of a selection procedure is that the procedures used predict an important and relevant behavioural requirement or job performance.

The selection procedure is given in Figure 8.1. The procedure may be adapted depending on the job requirements. If physical requirements (for example eyesight, fitness and hearing) are important requirements then the medical examination may take place earlier. Another important consideration is that the application form and psychometric tests must be administered prior to the selection interview to verify the results obtained during the interview.

The next section focuses on the predictors that can be used as part of the selection procedure.

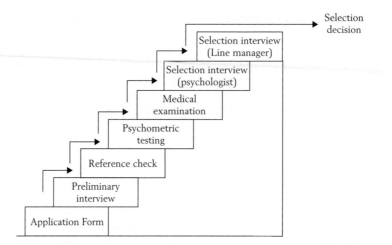

Figure 8.1 The selection procedure.

Requirements for selection predictors

Personnel selection is based on individual differences between people. The work performance of different individuals also differs. This stresses the importance of individual differences in the selection of the right person for the right job. Before a selection predictor is used, it must be valid, reliable and fair.

Validity

The term **validity** refers to how well a measure assesses the attribute it is being used to assess. An intelligence test is valid if it measures intelligence as it is defined.

The validity of a predictor is not absolute but is relative to its intended use. It is valid as long as it successfully measures the attribute that the user intends it to measure. In other words, a measure that is valid for one purpose may not be valid for another. An aptitude test that is used for the selection of university students may not be valid for the selection of managers. The term **validation** refers to the process of assessing the validity of a measure. Validation indicates whether it is justifiable to make a particular inference from a score obtained on the predictor. A validity coefficient is a correlation coefficient between a predictor measure (e.g. a psychometric test) and a criterion measure (e.g. work performance) applied to the same group of individuals. The **correlation coefficient** expresses the degree to which two sets of numbers are in agreement, or correlated, with each other.

The following types of validity are distinguished:

■ **Criterion-related validity**. Criterion-related validity measures scores on a predictor, which is usually a selection device. It also measures scores on a criterion (or a set of criteria), which is usually job behaviour such as performance, absenteeism and training success. A predictor score and criterion score are obtained for each person in a sample, and the statistical relationship between the two sets of scores is computed. Predictors in validation are usually chosen because they are similar to the actual selection techniques the organization is considering. A good predictor distinguishes applicants from each other, and does it reliably. Good criteria should be: a) affected by individuals, not determined largely by others or by technology; b) relevant to the goals of key constituents in the organization; c) measurable at reasonable cost, with adequate quality and in practical ways; d) affected by the individual differences reflected in the predictors; and e) remain stable over time. Sales performance might seem a complete criterion for the validation of a selection battery for sales personnel. However, sales may be contaminated by unrelated factors (e.g. the territory assigned to individuals). Sales performance may also be deficient by failing to reflect important factors (e.g. working as part of a team and completing paperwork). Two types of criterion-related validity – **concurrent validity** and **predictive validity** – can be computed (see Focus box 8.1).

Focus 8.1

Types of criterion-related validity

Concurrent validity. In the case of concurrent validity the predictor scores (e.g. scores on IQ tests) of current employees are correlated with their job performance (e.g. quantity and quality of work). The predictor and criterion data are gathered at the same time (which is why it is called concurrent validity). The correlation coefficient between the predictor and criterion is called the concurrent validity of the predictor (in this case the IQ test). Organizations use this method because time and cost considerations make it impossible to determine the predictive validity of a predictor. The disadvantage of the concurrent validity design is that poor performers are not included in the study, and that employees may perform better on the predictor (because of their experience).

Predictive validity. Predictive validity indicates if a predictor (e.g. an IQ test) can be used to predict future behaviour. Predictor scores are gathered from a sample of applicants (not current employees). Next, selection decisions are made regarding these applicants, without considering their scores on the predictor. (The applicants are selected by using methods used in the past, excluding the predictor that you want to validate.) Criterion scores (e.g. quality and quantity of work, ratings of supervisors) are gathered after the employees have been working for a while (e.g. six months). After that, the correlation between the predictor and criterion is calculated. Predictive validity is indicated if the employee who scored high on the predictor performs well on the job. This method eliminates the disadvantages of the concurrent validity design, but requires more time and administration. The results are also not immediately available.

- **Content validity**. A predictor has content validity if its items are representative of important aspects of a dimension or the job. (For example, are the items of an IQ test representative of what can be defined as intelligence? Does the application form include questions about the most important aspects of the applicant in relation to the job?)

- **Construct validity**. A predictor (e.g. an intelligence test) has construct validity if it correlates with a specific construct (e.g. intelligence). It takes time to assess the construct validity of a test, because the relationship between a predictor and other measuring instruments must be determined.

- **Face validity**. Face validity is a non-statistical type of validity, which indicates what the test measures on face value. It refers to the judgement of the validity of a predictor by the person on whom it is administered. An engineer who is tested may easily assess the material used in the predictor and identify irrelevant aspects. High face validity is necessary to create a positive attitude towards the predictor.

Reliability

The **reliability** of a predictor refers to the consistency of performance of the same individual on the predictor at different times. For example, if you test a person's blood pressure with a device today, and you test it again after two weeks, the device must give the same results (if there was no change in the person's blood pressure). A predictor must be reliable. Statistical procedures are used to obtain a numerical estimate of a measure's reliability. The most common numerical estimate is called a reliability coefficient. Basically the reliability coefficient measures the extent of agreement among two or more applications of the same measurement device to the same group of individuals. To be reliable, the test must have a reliability coefficient (r) higher than 0.95.

The reliability of a measurement device (predictor) is not a guarantee of its validity. Reliability only indicates the consistency of measurement, and not the extent to which it measures what it is supposed to measure. However, a predictor cannot be valid if it is unreliable. Reliability of a predictor is essential, but not adequate for its validity. The reliability of a predictor must be indicated in its manual.

Different types of reliability are defined in Focus box 8.2.

Fairness

Fairness is a perceptual variable along which people will differ. There are several variables that affect perceptions of fairness, and some potential outcomes associated with these perceptions (Arvey and Faley, 1988).

- **The processes and procedures used**. A selection procedure will be perceived as fair when: a) Subjective decision-making by the employer is minimized. b) The selection process is consistent across applicants, e.g. interview questions should be the same for males and females. c) The selection process is not subject to manipulation. Applicants should be examined against a common set of standards. d) The selection process is developed and managed

Focus 8.2

Types of reliability

Test–retest reliability indicates the relationship between scores of the same people on the same predictor on different occasions.

Parallel forms reliability indicates the correlation between predictor scores of the same people in equivalent forms of the test on different occasions.

Inter-rater reliability is assessed by calculating the correlation between the ratings of answers on a predictor by different assessors (e.g. in projective personality tests). This type of reliability gives an indication of the objectivity of scoring procedures.

Internal consistency reliability indicates the homogeneity of the items of the predictor. Although items are independent, they must focus on the same content area. High internal consistency is the result of high correlation coefficients between items and equal difficulty of items.

by professionals. Professionals often rely on sets of selection standards that help to ensure fairness. e) The organization maintains the confidentiality of data supplied by the candidate. f) The review of applicant information is made by several individuals who represent different perspectives and constituents.

- **The nature of information used**. Variables that are explicitly illegal would be perceived as unfair by most candidates. Variables based on merit (e.g. talent, abilities, experience) are considered more fair than variables that are not (e.g. family connection or political loyalty). Variables that are job-related are considered more fair than variables that are not. Variables that seem related to the job (content validity), show empirical relationships to important aspects of the job (empirical validity), or reflect central psychological constructs important to the job (construct validity) are perceived as more fair than variables that bear no direct relationship to the job. Information that invades the privacy of a candidate will be considered less fair than information that does not. The use of selection instruments that probe candidates' personal lives, explore sexual habits or invade these emotional components believed to be private may be perceived as unfair.

- **The relative outcomes achieved**. Perceptions of fairness have to do with whether the 'right' number of disadvantaged people (e.g. blacks, women) were selected compared to a majority group (usually white males). If these people are disadvantaged in the selection process the organization must show the job-relatedness of the selection device. This component of selection fairness emphasizes the outcomes of prediction and test use, instead of the selection procedures and information used.

- **Different constituents**. Different constituents may have different perceptions of fairness even when the procedures used, the information gathered and the relative outcomes achieved are kept constant. What might be perceived as fair by one constituent might not be perceived as fair by another. These perceptions will differ according to whether the applicant was hired or not.

■ **Situational factors**. Perceptions of selection fairness might depend on situational factors, for instance whether an organization has a history of hiring minorities and whether the organization has enjoyed high profits and could therefore afford to hire protected group members.

Types of selection predictors

The most important selection predictors will be discussed next.

The application form

The **application form** consists of questions designed to provide information on the general suitability of applicants for jobs they are seeking. The questions address the applicant's educational background, previous job experience, physical health and other areas that may be useful in judging a candidate's ability to perform a job. The application form serves as a means for deciding if the applicant meets the minimum requirements of a position, and assessing the candidate's strengths and weaknesses. It serves as a basis for the selection interview and supplies information for human resource information systems.

A problem with application forms is the possibility that the applicant will provide inaccurate information. When people are competing for a job, they may distort information that they give in order to 'look good'. Distortion can range from inflation of school and university grades to outright lies involving types of jobs held, companies for whom they worked or educational degrees earned. This happens especially when it is difficult, timely and costly to verify the information. If the candidate supplies false/misleading information, the organization may terminate his or her application.

Psychometric testing

A psychometric test is a systematic, standardized and objective procedure to observe a sample of an individual's behaviour and to quantify it on a scale. A score, which indicates the individual's score on a continuum, is awarded on the basis of his or her performance on the test. Each item is an observation of the individual's behaviour. The test of n items is a representative sample of the total spectrum of the concept measured. For example, a test that measures the ability to solve arithmetic problems represents a sample of a universe of arithmetic problems. It measures a representative sample of an individual's arithmetic ability. Psychometric tests are subject to mistakes because a sample of observations (which may not be representative of the universe) is used.

Psychometric tests can be classified in different ways, namely administrative considerations and test content. The following classification of psychometric tests can be made on the basis of administrative considerations:

■ **Speed tests versus power tests**. Speed tests usually have demanding time limits. The amount of work completed per time unit is manifested in the scores on these tests. Speed tests are used when individuals must solve problems in a short time span. Speed is also a factor in certain skills (e.g. typing). Power tests have no rigid time limits. The individual gets sufficient time to complete the test, and if a time limit is used, it is usually for the convenience of the tester.

- **Group tests versus individual tests**. Group tests are administered at the same time on a group of people. These tests are especially used for selection and placement purposes because they allow many candidates to be tested on one day. Individual tests are administered on an individual basis and are expensive. Individual tests are used for high-level selection and when interpersonal rapport with the candidate is important.

- **Paper and pencil tests versus performance tests**. Paper and pencil tests are used for selection purposes. The individual's scores on these tests are not related to the manipulation of physical objects or equipment. Examples of these tests include the verbal comprehension test and a mechanical insight test. These tests are increasingly being replaced by computers. Performance tests require that the individual respond by manipulating specific physical objects or equipment. The individual's scores on a performance test are related to the quantity and quality of manipulation of the objects or equipment (e.g. a practical driving test).

- **Aptitude versus proficiency tests**. An aptitude test measures an individual's future potential for a specific activity. The objective of a proficiency test is to assess the applicant's level of proficiency at the time of the testing (for example a knowledge test).

The following classification of psychometric tests can be made on the basis of test content (Hough and Oswald, 2000):

- **Ability tests**. Ability tests measure individual characteristics that could lead to learning specific skills. It indicates which tasks the individual will be able to perform if he or she receives the necessary training, and which tasks he or she is able to perform currently. Ability tests include cognitive tests, mechanical and spatial tests, perceptual accuracy tests, motor tests and physical tests (see Focus box 8.3).

- **Personality tests**. Personality tests include objective tests and projective tests. Objective tests (personality questionnaires) are paper and pencil tests with a clear stimulus (e.g. statements regarding preferences for different life styles) and clear responses that may be selected. Personality questionnaires are concerned with measures of emotional adjustment and tendencies towards extraversion or introversion. The five-factor model of personality enjoys considerable support in personnel selection (Clarke and Robertson, 2005).

- **Interest questionnaires**. Interest questionnaires can be used to determine likes and dislikes for various activities. Some people would rather work indoors than outdoors; some like to deal with people, others prefer working with machinery; some crave responsibility, others strive to avoid it. By matching interests and vocations, it is quite apparent that job satisfaction and motivation, at least, can

Focus 8.3

Types of ability tests

Cognitive tests include intelligence tests and aptitude tests. Intelligence tests measure abilities that can be used in different situations and jobs. Most items measure some combination of vocabulary, symbol manipulation, mathematics, reading comprehension and reasoning. Aptitude tests measure abilities that are more situation and job specific (e.g. verbal comprehension, word fluency, general reasoning, perceptual speed and memory).

In **perceptual accuracy tests** (which are especially important in clerical jobs) it is expected from the individual to compare a standard stimulus with a test stimulus to determine the differences.

Mechanical tests measure the individual's comprehension of mechanical principles.

Spatial tests measure the ability to manage concrete material through visualization (that is, the ability to determine the appearance of an object if it is rotated).

Motor tests measure physical abilities (e.g. finger dexterity, speed of arm movement, arm–hand stability, finger speed and reaction time).

Physical tests include fitness tests (cardiovascular power, muscle power) and physical ability (for jobs that are physical demanding).

be increased. As in other questionnaires, the respondents can fake the results if motivated to do so.

- **Work sample tests**. Work sample tests are samples of tasks that are performed in a specific job. The assumption of these tests is that performance results acquired from realistic simulations of the job are the best predictor of work performance. Most studies in which work samples were used report validity coefficients higher than 0.50.

Research methods 8.1

Validity of selection predictors

Research shows that ability tests are supported by favourable validity data. Ability tests (including intelligence and aptitude tests) are valid predictors of work performance and success in training programmes (in various jobs and occupations). Personality tests and interest questionnaires have lower validity for selection purposes. Few studies indicated significant correlation coefficients between personality tests and interest questionnaires, and job performance. However, it seems that these tests are very useful for the selection of management and sales personnel.

References

References can be used as a predictor for selection purposes because it is not as expensive and time consuming as other methods. It is based on the assumption that past behaviour is a good predictor of future behaviour. The following references can supply information about applicants:

- **Educational institutions**. Schools, colleges and universities can be visited or contacted to enquire about the candidate's marks, position in the class, extracurricular activities, motivation and emotional adaptability.

- **Previous employers**. Previous employers can supply information about the applicant's quality and quantity of work, participation, personality characteristics, initiative and interpersonal relationships. The accuracy of the information supplied by the candidate can be verified, as well as jobs held, salary and reason for quitting.

- **Testimonials**. The candidate can be asked to nominate friends as references. Friends are usually not able to assess a candidate's job behaviour. Few validation studies were done on references and testimonials, which makes it difficult to judge the validity thereof. These reports are usually favourable and do not discriminate between good and poor candidates. The problem may be overcome by informing the suppliers of the reports about the information needed, and by giving feedback to them regarding the usefulness of their information.

Physical examinations

Some organizations require that those most likely to be selected for a position complete a medical questionnaire or take a physical examination. The reasons for such a requirement include: a) In case of later workers' compensation claims, physical condition at the time of hiring should be known. b) It is important to prevent the hiring of those with serious communicable diseases. This is especially so in hospitals, but it applies to other organizations as well. c) It may be necessary to determine whether the applicant is physically capable of performing the job under question (Beach, 1985).

These purposes can be served by the completion of a medical questionnaire, a physical examination or a work physiology analysis. The last of these is neither a physical examination nor a psychomotor test. It is used for the selection of manual workers who will be doing hard labour. The purpose of work physiology analysis is to determine, by physiological indexes (heart rate and oxygen consumption), the true fatigue engendered by the work.

Physical examinations have not been shown to be very reliable as a predictor of future medical problems. This is at least partially due to the state of the art of medicine. Different physicians emphasize different factors in the exam, based on their training and specialities. There is evidence that correlating the presence of certain past medical problems (as learned from a medical questionnaire) can be as reliable as a physical examination performed by a physician and probably less costly.

Interviews

Interviewing is probably the most popular – and most criticized – method of employee selection. This popularity seems to prevail at all job levels, from unskilled to executive. Despite its popularity, the interview has been criticized as unreliable and invalid. The lack of reliability and validity raises potential legal hazards; if an interview appears to discriminate unfairly, management may face an uphill battle in court because of the generally low validity of most interviewing approaches. Besides, the interview is often a subjective process that allows the intrusion of personal biases, and this factor arouses the suspicion of courts.

A selection interview can be defined as a conversation with three objectives, namely: a) to provide information about an applicant's suitability for a job and organization to the interviewer; b) to provide information about the job and organization to the applicant; and c) to treat the applicant in such a way that a positive attitude towards the organization is maintained.

Interviews may be unreliable and invalid, partly because they are often done in a haphazard way. Therefore specialists are urging employers to use structured rather than unstructured interviews (see Focus box 8.4).

Focus 8.4

Structured versus unstructured interviews

A **structured interview** is an interviewing method in which the content, format and evaluation of the interview are specified in advance and followed by the interviewer. The structured interview is generally more reliable and valid than the unstructured interview, perhaps because more attention is paid to the purpose of the interview and more time is spent in planning it.

An **unstructured interview** is an interviewing method in which the content, format and evaluation of the interview are not specified in advance. Unstructured interviews may lead to a hasty evaluation of the candidate. The advantage of the unstructured interview over the structured interview is that it yields more detailed information about the applicant's experiences, feelings and values. This format allows interviewers to consider factors and initiate discussions that they might not have planned in advance.

The following recommendations can be made regarding selection interviews (Heneman et al, 1989):

- **Restrict the use of interviews to characteristics and behaviour that interviews can assess most effectively.** The interview is appropriate to measure personal relations characteristics (e.g. sociability and verbal fluency) and good citizenship characteristics (e.g. dependability, conscientiousness and stability).

A third characteristic, job knowledge, has also been evaluated in interviews, but other predictors may be more suitable for this purpose.

- **Incorporate more structure in the interview format**. The reason for structure is to ensure that the interviewer consistently gathers information about all relevant requirements from each applicant. Because the interviewer has information from each applicant on the same characteristics, it is easier to choose among the applicants.

- **Use job-related questions**. The most useful questions provide direct, specific information about characteristics required on the job – detailed questions about the applicant's participation in work, training or educational activities relevant to the job.

- **Make the scoring formal**. The most commonly used formal systems require the interviewer to rate the interviewee on a series of characteristics. The rating scales have a number at each point, each with an adjective (for example, not acceptable, marginal, minimal, good and superior) or a brief description.

- **Use a panel interview**. In a panel interview, several interviewers meet as a group with the applicant. Panel interviews are frequently used to hire technical or highly skilled personnel. Planning is essential to the success of the panel interview. One interviewer should be the chairperson, and each interviewer should question the applicant in turn. There should be assigned areas for each interviewer to question, and evaluations should be completed separately by each interviewer.

- **Train the interviewer**. The main skills of an interviewer include accurately receiving information, critically evaluating the information received, and regulating his or her own behaviour in asking questions.

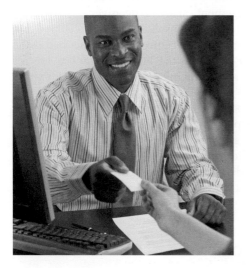

Figure 8.2 Interviewers should be well trained before they conduct selection interviews.

Source: Jupiter images/Comstock Images/Alamy.

Assessment centres

An **assessment centre** is not a building or a place. An assessment centre is defined as a multi-method, multi-trait and even multimedia technique. It is a series of individual and group exercises in which a number of candidates participate while being observed by several specially trained judges (Kraut, 1976). Assessment centres are designed to provide a view of individuals performing critical work behaviours. The candidates are asked to complete a series of evaluative tests and exercises, and to attend feedback sessions. The popularity of the assessment centre can be attributed to its capacity for increasing an organization's ability to select employees who will perform successfully in management positions. In assessment centres a wide array of methods including several interviews, work samples and simulations, and many kinds of paper-and-pencil tests of abilities and attitudes are used.

Most assessment centres are similar in a number of areas:

- Groups of approximately twelve individuals are evaluated. Individual and group activities are observed and evaluated.

- Multiple methods of assessment are used. These include interviewing, objective testing, projective testing, games, role plays and other methods.

- Assessors doing the evaluation are usually a panel of line managers from the organization. They can, however, be consultants or outsiders trained to conduct assessments.

- Assessment centres are relevant to the job and have higher appeal because of this relevance.

As a result of candidates participating as part of a group and as individuals, completing exercises, interviews and tests, the assessors have a large volume of data on each individual. Individuals are evaluated on a number of dimensions, such as organization and planning ability, judgement, analysis, decisiveness, flexibility and resistance to stress. The rater judgements are consolidated and developed into a final report. Each candidate's performance in the centre can be described if the organization wants this type of report. Portions of the individual reports are fed back to each candidate, usually by one or more members of the assessment team.

The assessment centre report can be used to determine the suitability of individuals for particular positions, the promotability of individuals, individuals' functioning in a group, and training and development needs of candidates. Research on assessment centres has indicated that they are a valid way to select managers. Assessment centres can predict future success with some accuracy. The disadvantages of assessment centres are that they are a relatively expensive managerial selection technique. In some circumstances less costly and complicated techniques may sometimes be just as effective.

Making the final selection decision

The final step in the selection process is choosing one individual for the job. If there is more than one qualified person, a value judgement based on all of the information gathered in the previous steps must be made to select the best candidate. In many organizations, the human resource department handles the completion of application forms, testing, interviewing and reference checking, and arranges physical examinations. The final selection decision is usually left to the manager of the department with the job opening.

Rejecting applicants

Interviewers, being no different from other people in this respect, frequently find it difficult to inform an applicant, directly to his or her face, that he or she does not measure up to the organization's standards.

A person may feel rejected when his or her application is rejected. If those responsible for making the employment decision are sure in their own minds that the applicant should not be hired, there is no justification to holding out vague hopes. If it is a well-qualified individual but there are no openings at present for his or her talents, but it is expected that there will be openings in the near future, it makes sense to inform him or her.

The interviewer has the threefold objectives of maintaining the person's ego and self-concept, maintaining goodwill towards the organization, and definitely letting the applicant know that he or she is rejected. There are a number of ways of communicating to the person that he or she is being rejected. If the applicant can clearly see that his or her vocational aptitudes and interests or wage level needs are totally incompatible with the situation, he or she may withdraw. If the individual possesses certain skills and abilities that might be appropriate in another job situation, he or she may be informed that while the pattern of his or her skills, interests and abilities is good, he or she does not match the particular job for which the organization is hiring.

If the person possesses all the required technical abilities but is rejected because of personality, this presents a difficult challenge to the interviewer. Since personality traits cannot be measured objectively, there is a danger of creating the feeling that the candidate is discriminated against if he or she is told that his or her personality is unsuitable. This situation demands real skill on the part of the interviewer to diplomatically convey the message that the interviewee is being rejected. At times it is best to imply that the organization is going to pick just one or a very few out of a number of good candidates. The competitive situation will mean that just the top few will be hired.

Auditing the selection effort

In order to ensure that the selection process accomplishes the results expected, a comprehensive audit should be conducted. The following issues can be examined in such an audit:

- Does the selection programme meet affirmative action standards?
- Is there a delay in filling job openings?
- What percentage of those who apply are hired?
- What percentage of those hired resign or are discharged during the probation period?

- What is the cost of the selection per person hired?

- How well do the predictions derived from each of the selection techniques correlate with job performance?

- How well do those hired perform at the job?

- Has feedback been obtained from applicants regarding treatment received throughout the selection process?

Application 8.1

In the news!

Removing bias from recruitment

Public Service Review: Home Office Issue 15 – Wednesday, 21 March, 2007.
[www.publicservice.co.uk].

Peter Thickett, Director of Human Resources at Lothian and Borders Police, reports on how the Scottish Police Forces are initiating screening for racial biases when recruiting.

Following the BBC's *The Secret Policeman* programme in 2003, which revealed very serious issues concerning attitudes to race among police trainees at a non-residential training centre in NW England, the Association of Chief Police Officers in Scotland (ACPOS) initiated a review of the recruitment and training processes for the country's eight police forces. Following the reviews, which were thought to be robust, the eight Scottish Police Forces reported that they had, over the years, rejected a small number of applicants on the grounds of concerns about attitude to race. It was noted, however, that Forces had not been keeping records of such rejections or at what stage in the process applicants were rejected. As all police recruits to Scottish Forces attend the Scottish Police College (SPC) at Tulliallan for lengthy residential training, SPC instructors are able to observe trainees in both work and social situations and to take action to tackle inappropriate language and behaviour. ACPOS then reviewed what other organizations had done to add race screening to the selection processes but discovered that little had been done, and what had been done looked unreliable.

Multi-choice questionnaires were thought to be untrustworthy and responses easily faked. Candidates could be expected to guess what the correct answer might be, or to find ways of communicating the 'right' answers to others (through the internet, for example). The Association was looking for a tool to provide additional quality assurances to the recruitment selection processes. In pursuit of improved consistency between Forces, Scottish Police Forces have in recent years introduced a national application form and recruitment standards, including up-dated medical standards. The ideal tool turned out to be a psychometric test being developed by a

Glasgow-based company, Human Factors Analysts Limited (HFAL), whose approach had been developed from leading research in the rail and nuclear industries. ACPOS has worked in close collaboration with HFAL to develop a tool that meets demanding technical requirements but also makes sense to recruiters and police managers. Additionally, ACPOS identified that Scottish Police Forces needed to assure potential BME (Black and Minority Ethnic) recruits that 'we meant it when we said' that police forces sought to exclude people with racist attitudes from engagement. And the Association wanted to signal to all recruits what Forces were aiming to achieve – to deter bad candidates and encourage good ones.

The Commission for Racial Equality (CRE) has stated that it believes that Forces are making genuine and sincere efforts to recruit from minority communities, but that perception of the police as an employer in these communities needs to be changed. The test is not a pass or fail. It provides cues for interviewers to investigate further within the selection process and adds to all the other information collected about candidates, from application form, familiarization evenings, standard entrance tests, assessment centres, criminal record and intelligence vetting and first and final interviews.

ACPOS and the Scottish Police Service make no apologies for the care with which police officers are selected and will continually seek to monitor results and improve the selection processes. No selection process can guarantee 100% success but ACPOS and the Scottish Police Service will work robustly to minimize the risks.

Summary

- Recruitment has been defined as the process of attracting suitable candidates to apply for vacancies that exist in an organization. Recruitment forms a crucial part of the overall human resource provisioning or employment process. It is thus very important to carefully plan the recruitment process. An organization needs to decide whether it will primarily use inside or outside sources when doing recruiting. It is therefore also important to develop a recruitment strategy. When developing such a strategy, one has to look into the characteristics of recruiters, the kind of recruiting to be done, where recruiting will be done and what sources and methods of recruiting will be used.

- The objective of selection is to obtain the employees who are most likely to meet the organization's standards of performance and who will be staffed and developed on the job. The following points were stressed:

- Selection is influenced by job and organization factors.

- Reasonable criteria for the choice must be set prior to prediction.

■ The selection procedure includes the preliminary screening interview, completion of the applicant blank, psychometric tests, the selection interview, reference checks and physical examinations.

■ The predictors used must be valid, reliable and fair.

■ Using a greater number of accepted methods to gather data for selection decisions increases the number of successful candidates selected.

■ Larger organizations are more likely to use sophisticated selection techniques.

■ Even if the most able applicant is chosen, there is no guarantee of successful performance on the job.

Key concepts and terms

Ability test	Personality test
Application form	Predictive validity
Assessment centre	Preliminary screening
Combined approach	Private employment agency
Compensatory approach	Psychometric test
Concurrent validity	Recruitment
Construct validity	Recruitment planning
Content validity	Recruitment strategy
Criterion-related validity	Reference
External recruitment	Reliability
Executive search firm	Selection
Face validity	Selection procedure
Fairness	Successive hurdle approach
Interest questionnaire	Test–retest reliability
Internal consistency	Utility analysis
Internal recruitment	Validity
Inter-rater reliability	Walk-ins
Interview	Work sample test
Parallel forms reliability	

Sample essay titles

- Which factors should be taken into account when trying to give realistic job previews?
- What factors influence an organization's choice of selection methods?
- How can an organization improve the validity of its interviews?
- What is an assessment centre? How will you develop an assessment centre?
- What can be done to promote fair selection in organizations?

Further reading

Books

Edenborough, R. (2007). *Assessment Methods in Recruitment Selection and Performance: A Manager's Guide to Psychometric Testing, Interviews and Assessment Centers*. London: Kogan Page.

Voskuijl, O., Evers, A., Anderson, N., and Smit-Voskuijl, O. (2005). *Blackwell Handbook of Personnel Selection*. Oxford: Blackwell Publishing.

Journal articles

Bertua, C., Anderson, N., and Salgado, J.F. (2005). The predictive validity of cognitive ability tests: A UK meta-analysis. *Journal of Occupational and Organizational Psychology*, 78, 387–409.

DeGroot, T., and Kluemper, D. (2007). Evidence of predictive and incremental validity of personality factors, vocal attractiveness, and the situational interview. *International Journal of Selection and Assessment*, 15, 30–39.

9 Induction, training and development

This chapter introduces the reader to **induction**, training and development in organizations. The first section focuses on the definition of terms. The chapter then proceeds to induction (i.e. the introduction of new employees to an organization). We look at the objectives of induction, investigate who should be responsible for induction, focus on the content of an induction programme, and describe how induction programmes can be evaluated. The third section focuses on training and development of employees. We focus on the goals of training, and the **training cycle** (i.e. needs assessment, the **development** and presentation of training programmes, and the evaluation of training programmes).

Learning outcomes

When you have completed this chapter you should be able to:

1. Define induction and training.
2. Discuss the content of an induction programme.
3. Discuss the follow-up and evaluation of an induction programme.
4. Discuss the goal and objectives of training.
5. Explain the training cycle.
6. Discuss the identification of **training needs.**
7. Explain **learning principles** and evaluate different training methods.
8. Distinguish between the four levels of evaluation of training programmes.

Induction

Definition of terms

Training is a process that involves the acquisition of **knowledge, skills and attitudes** to increase the performance of employees (Warr, 2002). **Training** is directed at the improvement of skills, including motor skills, cognitive skills and interpersonal skills. Economic, social, technological and governmental changes influence the objectives and strategies of all organizations. Changes in these areas can make the skills learned today obsolete in the future. Planned organizational changes and expansions can also make it necessary for employees to update their skills and acquire new ones.

A formal training programme is an effort by the employer to provide opportunities for the employee to acquire job-related knowledge, skills and attitudes. **Learning** is the act by which the individual acquires knowledge, skills and attitudes that result in relatively permanent changes in **behaviour**. **Knowledge** is divided into declarative and procedural knowledge (Warr, 2002). **Declarative knowledge** refers to factual information about a specific topic, while **procedural knowledge** refers to routines on how to do something. An individual should have declarative knowledge before he or she can have **procedural knowledge**. Any behaviour that has been learned is a **skill**. Attitudes are evaluative tendencies towards an object.

Training is often distinguished from **education** (Beach, 1985). **Education** has a broader scope. Education is considered to be formal education in a school, college or university, whereas training is vocationally orientated and occurs in a work organization. **Management development** is a systematic programme by which individuals gain and apply knowledge, skills, insights and attitudes to manage work organizations effectively (Beach, 1985).

Bryars and Rue (1991: 200) define **induction** as '... the introduction of new employees to the organisation, work unit and job'. One finds that some writers talk about induction, while (most) others mention orientation. Induction includes relinquishing certain attitudes, values and behaviours as the new recruit learns the organization's goals, the means of attaining those goals, basic job responsibilities, effective job behaviour and work rules. Much of this is learned on the job from co-workers and work teams. Induction is geared towards the 'fitting in' of the new employee with the way in which an organization operates. It is a learning process which starts during recruitment and continues after the new employee is placed in the job. It is correctly regarded as forming part of the training and development process.

Induction as a human resource management activity

The objectives of induction

Induction has three objectives: first, learning job procedures; second, establishing relationships with co-workers (including subordinates and superiors) and fitting into the employer's way of doing things, for which purpose realistic job expectations and a positive attitude towards the employer are developed; and, third, to give the employee a sense of belonging by showing him or her how the job fits into the overall organization (Milkovich and Boudreau, 1994).

Induction has the following objectives (Gerber et al, 1995):

■ It helps to create realistic employee expectations, especially in the case of new employees who have a long professional training period which provides much practical work experience. During their training period people such as attorneys and general practitioners learn to a large extent what to expect in the actual work situation.

- It helps to make the new employee become productive sooner. This happens when the new employee is taught how the work is to be done, how the organization functions and how he or she fits into the organization.

- It helps to reduce the fear, anxiety and insecurity experienced by the new employee. New employees are unsure whether they will succeed on the job. A well-organized induction programme will tend to put these fears at rest.

- It helps to reduce the possibility that the new employee may leave soon after joining the organization. Staff turnover tends to be rather high during the first few months after new employees join an organization. If a new employee can see that he or she can make a positive contribution towards the activities of the organization, this tendency to leave will be reduced.

- It helps to create job satisfaction and a positive attitude towards the organization. If, during the induction programme, the new employee senses that the organization takes an interest in him or her as a human being, wants to make the job climate a pleasant one and that he or she is being treated with dignity, he or she will tend to develop a positive attitude towards the organization.

- It saves the time of superiors and co-workers, because during a well-planned and well-executed induction programme the new employee is taught what is expected of him or her and how his or her tasks have to be carried out. If this happens, it means that there is very little need to correct mistakes later.

Who is responsible for induction?

The decision about who should be responsible for induction depends on the particular circumstances, for instance, the size of the organization, the size of the human resource department, the role that a labour union and its officials play in the induction process and the general policy of the organization regarding induction. In bigger organizations it appears to be a shared responsibility. In this case the responsibility is shared between the human resource department and the managers or supervisors. The responsibility of the human resource department is for the general orientation of new employees, while that of the managers or supervisors may be termed departmental and job orientation. Beach (1985) points out that in some organizations the human resource department exerts staff control over line supervisors by requiring them to fill out a checklist form to show which specific orientation tasks they have provided for each new employee. Bryars and Rue (1991: 201) also refer to the so-called '... "buddy system" in which the job orientation is conducted by one of the new employee's fellow workers'.

The content of induction programmes

The content of an induction programme depends upon the particular circumstances. Besides providing new employees with a well-structured orientation programme, it is also advisable to issue them with written material that they can always refer back to. It is desirable for each new employee to receive an orientation kit, or packet of information, to supplement the verbal orientation programme. This kit is normally prepared by the human resource department and can provide a wide variety of materials. Care should be taken in the design not only to ensure that essential information is provided but also that too much information is not given.

Some orientation materials that might be included in an orientation kit include the company organization chart, a map of the company's facilities, a copy of the policy and procedures handbook, a list of holiday and fringe benefits, copies of performance appraisal forms, dates and procedures, copies of other required forms (e.g. expense reimbursement form), emergency and accident prevention procedures, sample copy of company newsletter or magazine, telephone numbers and locations of key company personnel, and copies of insurance plans. Many organizations require new employees to sign a form indicating that they have received and read the orientation kit (Bryars and Rue, 1991). This is done to protect the organization if a grievance should arise and the employee should allege that he or she had not been aware of certain organizational policies and procedures.

Follow-up and evaluation of induction programmes

It is important to follow up any induction activities. It is of very little use if the human resources manager tells the new employee that he or she 'should drop by if any problems occur'. The human resource department should have a scheduled follow-up one month after the new employee has been placed. The supervisor/manager should also check how well the new employee is doing. The supervisor/manager should also answer any questions that the new employee has to ask about aspects that have arisen since he or she attended the orientation programme.

The human resource department should also on an annual basis evaluate the total induction programme. This should be done to determine whether the programme is meeting the needs of the organization, as well as the needs of new employees. Data gathered during such an evaluation can be used to improve the present programme.

Feedback from new employees can be used to evaluate the effectiveness of a programme (Bryars and Rue, 1991). Various methods can be used to obtain feedback, namely a) unsigned questionnaires that are completed by all employees; b) in-depth interviews with randomly selected new employees; c) group discussion sessions with new employees who have settled into their jobs. From the above-mentioned feedback that is received an organization can adapt its induction programme. An organization should make use of the suggestions that employees made during the feedback sessions. This is important, because the induction process has a definitive impact on the performance of the new employee.

Training

The goals of training

Training is only one component of the development process that includes all of the experiences that enhance and build employees' employment-related characteristics (Sonnentag et al, 2004). The problem is, however, that a training programme frequently occurs because a few people decide it is needed, or because the latest fad can be sold to top management. They find the money to get it started and measure success by how many people participate. Effectiveness is seldom measured.

The best companies integrate training within a systematic set of human resource activities, including selection, rewards and job design. Training can be used as a strategic tool for attaining the goals of the organization and the employees. The link between training and strategic goals seems obvious, but it is often lost in the day-to-day struggle to implement programmes and deal with crises. In that case training becomes an activity, rather than a strategy.

Training as activity is characterized by no client, no business need, no assessment of performance effectiveness, no effort to prepare the work environment to support training, and no measurement of **results.** Training as a strategy is characterized by a partnership with the client, link to a business need, assessment of performance effectiveness, preparation of the work environment to support training, and measurement of results.

The reasons for training can be summarized as follows (Gerber et al, 1995):

- To give employees direction in their jobs and acquaint them with their working environment so that they can become productive quickly.

- To provide the human resources that are necessary for commerce and industry to be effective.

- To increase the loyalty and increase the morale of employees.

- To improve the quality and quantity of an organization's output and to reduce costs.

The training cycle

The training cycle consists of three phases (see Figure 9.1). These phases include the following (Wexley and Latham, 1991):

- Identification of training and development needs.

- Training and development.

- Evaluating the training and development programme.

Identification of training needs

Training must be directed towards the accomplishment of some organizational objective, such as more efficient production methods, improved quality of products and services or reduced operating costs. The organization should commit its resources only to those training activities that can best help in achieving its objectives.

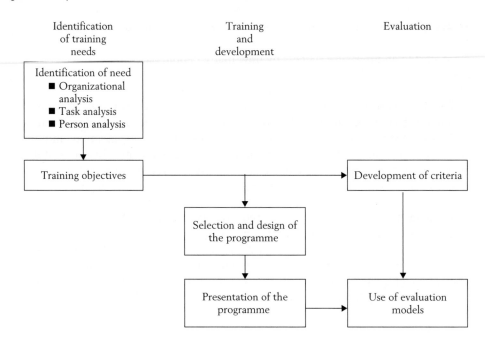

Figure 9.1 The training cycle.

Needs assessment is a systematic analysis of the specific training activities required by job holders and an organization to achieve the objectives of the job and the organization. The organizational needs assessment requires an examination of the long-term and short-term objectives of the organization. The organization's financial, social, human resource, growth and market objectives need to be matched with its human talent, structure, climate and efficiency. The knowledge, skills and abilities needed to perform the job are carefully considered. What are the tasks? What skills are needed to perform well? What does performing well mean? Data from current employees, supervisors and experts need to be collected to complete this part of the needs assessment.

The employee's needs must also be considered: ask the employee what he or she needs to competently perform the tasks. This will provide useful information. Evaluate the employee's performance against a standard or the outputs of co-workers to help identify strengths, weaknesses and needs.

Training can improve the individual's performance only when a) the employee does not have the knowledge and skills to do the job, b) the low performance is not due to a lack of practice, and c) the low performance is not due to other causes.

Wexley and Latham (1991) identified five methods that can be used to gather needs assessment information: interviews, questionnaires, observation, focus groups, and document examination (see Focus box 9.1).

By observation, asking and listening, the manager can conduct a **performance analysis.** The specific steps in performance analysis include the following:

Focus 9.1

Methods to assess training needs

- **Interviews**. Interviews with employees can be conducted by human resource specialists or by external consultants. The following questions should be investigated: a) What problems does the employee experience in the job? b) What knowledge and/or skills does the employee need to improve performance on the job? c) What training does the employee feel is needed? If interviews are to provide useful information, employees must feel that their input will be valued and not be used against them.
- **Questionnaires**. Questionnaires can be used to assess training needs. This involves developing a list of skills required to perform a particular job effectively and asking employees to check those skills in which they believe they need training. Attitude surveys and customer surveys can also be used to determine training needs.
- **Observation**. A specialist can observe the behaviour of employees in their jobs and translate these observations into training needs.
- **Focus groups**. Focus groups are composed of employees from various departments and levels in the organization. Each group investigates the following questions with the help of a facilitator: a) What knowledge/skills will employees need in order for the organization to stay competitive over the next five years? b) What problems does the organization experience that can be solved through training?
- **Document examination**. Document examination is concerned with examining organizational records on absenteeism, turnover and accident rates to determine if problems exist and to determine if problems can be solved through training. Performance appraisal information can also be studied in order to determine training needs.

a) Appraise the performance of employees in order to determine how they are doing, in comparison with how they should be doing, and determine behavioural discrepancies. b) Assess the cost and value of correcting a behavioural discrepancy. c) Determine if it is a *can't do* or *won't do* situation. It is important to determine if the employee could do the expected job if he or she wanted to. d) Set standards, because under-performance might result if an employee does not know what the standards are. e) Remove obstacles relating to time, equipment and people, which result in behaviour discrepancies. f) Allow the employee time to practise, so that he or she can perform the job better. g) Provide training if the performance analysis indicates that knowledge, skills or attitudes need to be altered. h) Redesign the job through job enrichment, job simplification or enlargement if necessary to improve performance. i) Transfer or terminate the employee's services if all else has failed. j) Create a motivational climate. Sometimes a skilled employee does not want to perform the job because of motivational problems. Rewards, punishment, discipline or some combination may be needed to create a positive climate for the optimal use of skills.

Presenting training programmes

After training needs have been determined, specific and measurable objectives must be established for meeting these needs. Effective **training objectives** should state what the organization, department or individual should achieve once training is completed, for example to improve listening and feedback skills for use in the performance appraisal programme.

Training objectives can be categorized as:

- **Instructional objectives**. What facts, principles and concepts are to be learned in the training programme? Who is to be taught? When are they to be taught?

- **Organizational and departmental objectives**. What impact will the training have on organizational and departmental outcomes, such as absenteeism, turnover, costs and productivity?

- **Individual performance and growth objectives**. What impact will the training programme have on the attitudes, behaviour and personal growth of the trainee? (What should he or she be able to do after the training?) Under what conditions should the trainee be able to perform the trained behaviour? How well should the trainee perform the trained behaviour?

Explicit objectives serve a number of purposes. They assist in developing the criteria to be used in evaluating the training outcome. Together training objectives and evaluation criteria also help in choosing relevant instructional material. During training, objectives help motivate trainees to organize their efforts in a way that will help them accomplish those objectives.

Before a training programme is presented, the presenter should ensure that sound learning principles are followed (to maximize learning). Then, the training methods that are most applicable for the specific situation must be selected (Wexley and Latham, 1991; Warr, 2002).

- **Maximization of learning**. For training to have any effect at all, trainees must learn something from it. When training is effectively designed and trainees are motivated, learning can occur. The use of sound learning principles during the development and implementation of training programmes contributes to its success.

- **Ability to learn**. Individuals enter training with different experiences, different levels of familiarity with the material, and different mental and physical abilities. The training demands should match the abilities of trainees. Training that is too difficult or too easy is likely to be less effective. Testing trainees prior to beginning training can help ensure a good match.

- **Motivation to learn**. In order to learn, a person must want to learn. Perhaps the most important motivation trainees bring to training is their desire to change their behaviour and results on the job. In the context of training, motivation influences a person's enthusiasm for training, keeps attention focused on training activities and reinforces what is learned. People strive to achieve objectives they have set for themselves. The objectives of employees include job security, financially and intellectually rewarding work, recognition, status, responsibility and achievement. The learning process is facilitated when the training programme helps employees to achieve these objectives. Supportive supervisors and the expectation that training results will be assessed later on the job contribute to higher trainee motivation.

- **Goal setting**. Individuals' conscious goals may regulate their behaviour. The trainer's job is to get the trainees to adopt or internalize the goals of the programme in the following ways: a) Convey the learning objectives at the outset and at various strategic points throughout the training programme. b) Make goals difficult enough to be a challenge. c) Supplement the overall goals with sub-goals to maintain feelings of accomplishment.

- **Reinforcement**. The idea behind reinforcement is that behaviour appearing to lead to a positive consequence tends to be repeated, while behaviour leading to a negative consequence tends not to be repeated. Learners must be rewarded for new behaviour in ways that satisfy needs, such as pay, praise, recognition and promotion. For example, a trainee who is praised for good performance is likely to continue to strive for additional praise. According to the expectancy theory, individuals are motivated to choose behaviour that has the greatest chance of producing desired consequences. Trainees must believe that acquiring the knowledge and skills from training will lead to desired outcomes and that training can provide that knowledge or skill.

- **Flow of the training programme**. Each segment of the training should be organized so that the individual can see not only its purpose, but also how it fits in with the other parts of the programme. Later segments should build on those presented earlier.

- **Modelling and self-efficacy**. The trainer can build trainees' skills by allowing them to see models of good and poor performance, and by giving trainees confidence in their abilities to apply their skills. Confidence building includes providing trainees with encouragement, guidance and feedback on how well they are doing, and providing the opportunity for practice (Bandura, 1977).

- **Practice and repetition**. Learning requires time to assimilate what has been learned, to accept it, internalize it and to build confidence in what has been learned. This requires practice and repetition of the material. After sufficient practice the skills may become automatic, requiring little conscious thought. Trainees should be given opportunities to continue practising even after they have achieved proficiency the first time. 'Overlearning' leads to a relative permanent change in behaviour and automatic responses to the learned task.

- **Spacing of sessions**. Training spread out over a period of time facilitates the learning process. The interval most conducive to learning depends on the type of training.

- **Material must be meaningful**. Appropriate material for sequential learning (for example, cases, problems, discussion outlines and reading lists) must be provided. The learning methods used should be as varied as possible. Boredom destroys learning. Any method that is overused will begin to bore learners.

- **Small training units**. The learning material should be presented in small segments or units. This format allows quick feedback to the trainee on how well he or she is doing.

- **Whole or part training**. Learning is facilitated when an overview is given to trainees, and it is then divided into portions for in-depth instruction. Whether to use whole or part learning depends also on the difficulty of the task, and the degree of relationship between sub-tasks.

- **Transfer of learning**. The trainer must do his or her best to make the training as close to the reality of the job as possible to ensure that the newly learned behaviour is transferred to the work environment.

- **Knowledge of results**. Knowledge of results (feedback) influences the learning process. Keeping employees informed of their progress as measured against some standard helps in setting goals for what remains to be learned. The process of analysing progress and establishing new objectives enhances learning. Precautions should be taken that goals are not so difficult to achieve that employees become discouraged.

- **The characteristics of the instructional environment and instructors**. The instructional environment can be designed around events such as gaining attention, informing learners of objectives, presenting the training stimulus material, providing feedback, assessing performance and enhancing retention and transfer. The instructor should have informed everyone, arranged the facilities, checked the physical requirements, secured the necessary equipment, established training objectives and studied the lesson plan to anticipate group responses and to prepare experiences.

Training methods that can be used can be classified as on-site methods and off-site methods. On-site training methods include the following (Wexley and Latham, 1991; Warr, 2002):

- **On-the-job training**. On-the-job training is probably the most widely used method of training. The employee is placed into the real work situation and shown the job and the tricks of the trade by an experienced employee or the supervisor. Although this programme is simple and relatively inexpensive, if it is not handled properly the costs can be high in damaged machinery, unsatisfied customers and poorly trained employees. To prevent these problems, trainers must be carefully selected and trained. The trainee should be placed with a trainer who is similar in background and personality. The trainer should be motivated by training and be rewarded for doing it well.

- **Apprentice training**. Apprentice training is a combination of on-site and off-site training. It requires the cooperation of the employer, trainers at the workplace and technical training institutions. The apprentice commits to a period of training and learning that involves both formal classroom learning and practical on-the-job experience.

- **Vestibule training**. In vestibule training, the trainee learns the job in an environment that simulates the real working environment as closely as possible (for example, training of pilots in a simulated cockpit of an aeroplane). A machine operator trainee might run a machine under the supervision of a trainer until he or she learns how to use it properly. Only then is the trainee sent to the shop floor. This procedure can be quite expensive if the number of trainees supervised is not large.

- **Coaching and counselling**. One of the best and most frequently used methods of training new managers is for effective managers to teach them. The coach sets a good example of what a manager does, answers questions and explains why things are done the way they are. It is the coach's obligation to see to it that the manager-trainee makes the proper contacts so that the job can be learned easily and performed in an adequate way. Although most organizations use coaching and counselling as an informal management development technique, it has problems. **Coaching** and counselling fail when inadequate time is set aside for them, when the subordinate is not allowed to make mistakes, if rivalry develops, or if the dependency needs of the trainee are not recognized and accepted by the manager.

- **Computer-based training**. Computer-based training permits self-paced learning and immediate feedback. This type of training works as follows: A trainee sits at a terminal with a monitor. The computer is programmed with the training materials. The trainee communicates by programming or using the keyboard to input commands or requests. The advantages of computer-based training include availability, self-paced features, distribution and adaptability, and work simulation.

- **Job rotation**. Trainees can be rotated through a series of jobs to broaden their managerial experience. Organizations often have developed career plans that include a mix of functional and geographic transfers.

Because of the perceived relevance of on-the-job experience, on-site training methods should be used in training programmes. Off-the-job development programmes should, however, supplement them where expertise is not readily available. Off-site training methods include:

- **Lectures**. In a lecture an instructor presents material to a group of learners. Lectures are relatively inexpensive to develop and deliver. They can impart factual knowledge quickly and efficiently. Lectures, however, lead to one-way communication, are insensitive towards learner differences and do not allow feedback to the trainer. Many of these difficulties can be overcome by a competent lecturer who makes use of discussions during the lecture.

- **Conference**. The conference is a participative method that emphasizes small group discussion in which the instructor guides rather than instructs trainees

Figure 9.2 Computer-based training permits self-paced learning.
Source: Digital Archive Japan/Alamy.

through a process of questions, answers and discussion to a desired outcome. The objectives of the conference method are to develop problem-solving and decision-making skills, present new and complex material, and modify attitudes. Topics for the discussion can be chosen by the instructor or by trainees. The leader of the session prepares for the topic in advance of the session. The training group may be given an agenda for the meeting or may develop it on their own. The conference method requires a high degree of participation from the trainees and provides immediate feedback and the opportunity to assess own learning by listening to the comments made by the instructor and other group participants. The conference method is limited in the amount of substantive material that can be covered in one session. It also requires trainees with good verbal skills and self-images so that they are not threatened by group participation.

■ **Audio, video and teleconferencing**. Recordings, films and slides can be distributed to learners and used independently or in conjunction with other training methods. It is possible to produce effective videos at low cost. The advantage of audio-visual techniques is their ability to quickly distribute a consistent training experience to a large number of individuals without being constrained by the time limits of instructors or logistical requirements. With video teleconferencing, learners are in remote classrooms equipped with televisions and microphones. The instructor provides the training from a video studio, often linked to learners via satellite. Learners can see the instructor and ask questions via audio links to the studio. Audio teleconferencing provides a similar arrangement but uses only audio connections.

- **Programmed instruction**. Programmed instruction presents the learner with a series of tasks, allows evaluation of success at intervals throughout the training, and provides feedback about correct and incorrect responses as the learner advances through the training. Programmed instruction can be incorporated into books, machines and computers. Careful attention must be given to learning sequences and objectives. Learners progress faster with programmed instruction than with lectures. Other advantages of programmed instruction are that materials can be packaged and distributed, and learners can use the material at their convenience and when they are ready. It also makes provision for self-paced learning, which allows flexibility according to different abilities.

- **Learning-by-doing**. Learning-by-doing training techniques copy the essential elements of real world situations: they allow learners to play a role or make decisions about the situation and then receive feedback about their effectiveness. Business games allow learners to make decisions about business variables, often competing against other individuals or teams. The case study presents learners with a written report of a realistic situation. The learners analyse the information and prepare solutions for discussion. Role-playing involves having trainers act out simulated roles. Interpersonal skills can be learned by using role-playing. Advantages of these training methods include the potential for a high degree of transfer to the work situation, high participant involvement, providing specific feedback and helping learners deal with incomplete information.

Evaluating training and development programmes

It is necessary to evaluate training programmes (Kraiger et al, 1993). Less effective programmes can be withdrawn to save time and effort. Weaknesses within established programmes can be identified and remedied. One way to approach the evaluation of training programmes is according to the model of Kirkpatrick (1959). According to Kirkpatrick, training programmes can be evaluated on four levels, namely **reaction**, learning, behaviour and results (see Focus box 9.2).

Focus 9.2

Kirkpatrick levels of evaluation of training programmes

Reaction. Evaluating the reaction of a training programme answers the following question: 'How well did the trainees like the programme?'. Reaction evaluation should consider topics such as programme content, programme structure and format, instructional techniques, instructor abilities and style, quality of the learning environment, extent to which training objectives were achieved and recommendations for improvement. Reaction evaluation is done directly after the training programme, or a few weeks thereafter. The shortcoming of reaction evaluation is that the enthusiasm of trainees cannot necessarily be taken as evidence of improved ability and performance (Warr, 2002).

Learning. Evaluating the learning after a training programme answers the following question: 'What facts, principles and concepts were learned in the training programme?'. Learning evaluation is concerned with how well the facts, principles and skills were understood by trainees. Paper and pencil or skill tests can be used to evaluate learning. In order to obtain an accurate picture of what was learned, trainees should be tested before and after the training programme (Wexley and Latham, 1991).

Behaviour. Evaluating the behaviour of trainees after a training programme answers the following question: 'Did the job behaviour of trainees change because of the programme?' (Warr, 2002). A systematic appraisal should be made of on-the-job performance on a before-and-after basis. The appraisal of performance should be made by the trainer, the trainees' superior, their subordinates or their peers. A statistical analysis should be made to compare performance before and after the training programme and to relate changes to the training programme. The post-training appraisal should be made several months after the training so that the trainees have an opportunity to put into practice what they have learned. An experimental group (who receive training) and a control group (who do not receive training) should be used.

Results. Evaluating the results of a training programme answers the following question: 'What were the results of the programme in terms of costs and productivity'?.

Activity 9.1

The recent training and development perspective in a 100-year-old credo!

The development and empowerment process has overtaken the training event in organizations. The focus is on learning through reframing the workplace problems, self-determined development, unfreezing barriers to learning and understanding what it means to be a learning organization (Mabey and Iles, 2001). However, if we investigate the life and philosophy of Dr Y.C. Yen it is evident that this approach is not so new ...

Dr Y.C. James Yen was born in China in 1893. He dedicated his life to mass education and rural reconstruction, first in China and then throughout the world. He committed himself to sensitizing the world's intellectual community to the tremendous losses the world suffers by ignoring the humanity of the poor, and by not acknowledging their productivity. During the First World War, he was stationed in France to supervise Chinese labourers. While there, he realized that the people's illiteracy was no fault of their own. Yen proclaimed, 'I began to realise that what these humble, common people of my country lacked was not brains, for God has given that to them, but opportunity ... They had potential powers waiting for development, waiting for release ...'.

If one considers the principles of adult learning, the training cycle and training methods, the above observation of James Yen is still applicable today! James Yen developed a Credo of Rural Reconstruction, portraying the developmental approach that should be applied; the Credo speaks as follows:

Go to the people; Live among them
Learn from them; Plan with them; Work with them
Start with what they know; Build on what they have
Teach by showing; Learn by doing
Not a showcase but a pattern
Not odds and ends but a system
Not to conform but to transform
Not relief but release.
(James Yen)

Critical thinking activity

Can you apply the approach portrayed in Yen's Credo to training and development approaches in the workplace? How?

Source: Mabey, C. and Iles, P. (2001). *Managing Learning*. London: Thompson Learning.

Summary

- Induction has been defined as the introduction of new employees to the organization, work unit and job. The idea was expressed that it should be grouped with human resource management activities/subjects of study such as training and development because orientation involves learning. The objectives of induction are seen to be learning job procedures, establishing relationships with co-workers and fitting into the employer's way of doing things, to give the employee a sense of belonging and to create favourable attitudes towards the company. Both the personnel/human resource department and line managers/supervisors are responsible for induction. The content of an induction programme can be divided into general organizational aspects and specific departmental/job aspects. Induction (programmes) should regularly be followed up and evaluated.

- Training is a form of job-specific education directed at improving the knowledge, skills and attitudes of employees. Effective organizations design their training programmes after assessing the individual's and organization's training needs and setting training objectives. Effective training programmes select trainees on the basis of their needs as well as the objectives of the organization. Various training methods can be used. Sound learning principles should, however, be applied to maximize trainees' learning.

- It is, however, important that training courses be evaluated to determine the reaction of participants, to evaluate the learning achieved, behavioural changes effected, and the impact on work results after the completion of the training course.

Key concepts and terms

Apprentice training	On-the-job training
Behaviour	Performance analysis
Coaching	Procedural knowledge
Computer-based training	Programmed instruction
Conference	Reaction
Counselling	Results
Declarative knowledge	Skill
Development	Teleconferencing
Education	Training
Induction	Training cycle
Job rotation	Training need
Knowledge	Training objective
Learning-by-doing	Vestibule training
Learning principles	
Lecture	

Sample essay titles

- What are the main objectives of an induction programme for new employees?
- Why are training programmes one of the first areas to be eliminated when an organization's budget is cut?
- If you were asked to develop a training programme for taxi drivers, how would you do it? How would you evaluate the training programme?

Further reading

Books

Elliot, C., and Turnbull, S. (2005). *Critical Thinking in Human Resource Development*. London: Routledge.

Swanson, R.A., and Holton, E.F. (2001). *Foundations of Human Resource Development*. New York: Berrett-Koehler.

Journal articles

Sue-Chan, C., and Latham, G.P. (2004). The relative effectiveness of external, peer, and self-coaches. *Applied Psychology: An International Review*, 53, 260–278.

10 Compensation Management

This chapter introduces the reader to compensation in organizations. The first section focuses on the role of compensation in human resource management. The chapter then proceeds to the requirements for an effective compensation system. We look at the influences on compensation (including external and organizational influences). The next section focuses on **job evaluation.** More specifically, job evaluation will be defined, and the objectives and advantages/disadvantages thereof will be discussed. Furthermore, job evaluation methods will be explained and the steps in implementing a job evaluation system will be described. Lastly, incentive pay systems will be discussed.

Learning outcomes

When you have completed this chapter you should be able to:

1. Discuss the role of compensation in human resource management.
2. Discuss the requirements for an effective compensation system.
3. Describe external and internal influences on compensation.
4. Explain the factors that affect the pay level decision.
5. Discuss job evaluation as a human resource management activity, and describe the steps in the implementation of a job evaluation project.
6. Evaluate different pay incentive schemes.

The role of compensation in human resource management

Employers compensate their employees to motivate them to work (Aft, 1985). Therefore a study of compensation theory starts with motivation theories. Compensation is divided into financial compensation and non-financial compensation. **Financial compensation** includes pay and benefits. Non-financial compensation includes a variety of things people value and want to receive through their work. Organizations use both financial and **non-financial compensation** to attract the quality and quantity of employees needed, retain these employees and motivate them towards organizational goal achievement. A fair and market-related financial compensation plays a key role in the organization's ability to attract, retain and motivate employee performance. A well-structured, flexible compensation package may enhance performance, especially if it is accompanied by recognition, good interpersonal relationships and other non-financial compensation (Rynes et al, 2005).

Requirements for an effective compensation system

An effective compensation system should be adequate (as set forth in minimum wage and other legislation and in line with market salaries), equitable (based on the value of a job relative to other jobs in the organization), incentive-providing (by making use of merit and raises), secure (adequate to satisfy the employee's basic needs), balanced (including pay, benefits and promotions), cost-effective for the organization and acceptable to the employee.

Influences on compensation

Compensation is influenced by external and internal factors.

External influences

The **external influences** on compensation include the government, trade unions, the economy and the labour market.

- **The government**. The government directly influences compensation through laws directed at the establishment of minimum wage rates, wage regulations and the prevention of discrimination directed at certain groups.

- **Trade unions**. Unions have tended to be pacesetters in demands for pay, benefits and improved working conditions. There is reasonable evidence to suggest that the presence of unions tends to increase pay levels, although this is more likely where an industry has been organized by strong unions. The presence of the union is more likely to increase the compensation of its members when: a) the organization is financially and competitively strong; b) the union is financially strong enough to support a strike; c) the union has the support of other unions, and d) general economic and labour market conditions are such that unemployment is low and the economy is strong.

- **The economy**. The economic conditions of the industry, especially the degree of competitiveness, affect the organization's ability to pay high wages. The more competitive the situation, the less able the organization is to pay high wages. Ability to pay is also a consequence of the relative productivity of the organization, industry or sector. If a firm is very productive, it can pay higher wages. Productivity can be increased by advanced technology, more efficient operating methods, a harder working and more talented workforce or a combination of these factors. The degree of profitability and productivity is a significant factor in determining the ability of organizations in the private sector to pay wages.

- **The labour market**. Although many people feel that human labour should not be regulated by supply and demand, it does in fact happen. In times of **full** employment, wages and salaries may have to be higher to attract and retain sufficient qualified employees; in depressions, the reverse is true. Pay may be higher if few skilled employees are available in the job market. Research evidence from the labour economics fields provides adequate support for the impact of labour market conditions on compensation.

Organizational influences on compensation

Several organizational factors, including the size and age of the organization, the **labour budget** and the goals of its controlling interests may influence pay levels. Although not much is known about the relationship between organization size and pay, it seems that larger organizations tend to have higher pay levels. Some people believe that new organizations tend to pay more than old ones.

The labour budget of an organization normally identifies the amount of money available for annual employee compensation. Every unit of the organization is influenced by the size of the budget. A firm's budget normally does not state the exact amount of money to be allocated to each employee, but it does state how much is available to an organizational unit. The discretion in allocating pay is then left to department heads and supervisors.

Another organizational influence on compensation is related to the goals of controlling interests and the specific pay strategy that managers select. The final authority in pay decisions is senior management. These are the managers that decide the overall strategic plan of the organization. Unfortunately, compensation is often an under-utilized tool in supporting overall strategic objectives. Therefore, many compensation plans have minimal impact on recruitment, motivation and retention of employees. To be part of the strategic plan, the compensation system must be directly linked to the strategic goals of the organization, provide strong incentives, not support undesired behaviour, offer valued rewards and be communicated clearly.

The views of managers and supervisors about pay differ as much as the employees' views do. Some managers and supervisors believe their employees should be compensated at high levels because they deserve it; they also accept or reject the idea that high pay leads to greater performance or employee satisfaction. These attitudes are reflected in the **pay-level strategy** chosen by the managers of the organization. Three pay-level strategies, namely high, low or comparable, can be chosen.

In the high pay-level strategy, managers choose to pay higher than average levels. In the low pay-level strategy, managers may choose to pay at the minimum level needed to hire enough employees. In the comparable pay-level strategy the pay level is set at the going wage level.

The pay-level decision

The **pay-level decision** is made by managers who compare the pay of persons working inside the organization with those outside it (Gerhart and Milkovich, 1992). The decision is affected by multiple factors in interaction with one another that affect pay levels upwards, downwards or laterally (see Figure 10.1).

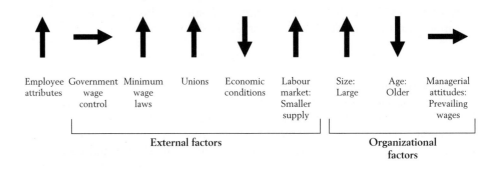

| Employee attributes | Government wage control | Minimum wage laws | Unions | Economic conditions | Labour market: Smaller supply | Size: Large | Age: Older | Managerial attitudes: Prevailing wages |

External factors   **Organizational factors**

Figure 10.1 Factors influencing the pay-level decision.

When factors such as managerial attitudes, the labour market and competition change, the pressures on pay levels shift. For example, if organizations experience little growth, it will put pressure on compensation in the downward direction. To help make the pay-level decision, managers use a tool called a pay or salary survey. Salary surveys are surveys of the compensation paid to employees by all employers in a geographic area, an industry or an occupational group. Surveys are the principal tool used in the pay-level decision. These surveys help managers to gauge the exact market rates for various positions. Obtaining valid, reliable salary surveys is critical to creating a compensation programme that supports the financial goals of the organization.

Salary surveys can be done by personal interviews. This method supplies the most accurate responses, but is also expensive. Mailed questionnaires are a frequently used method that is cheap. The jobs being surveyed by mail must be clearly defined, or the data may not be reliable. Telephone enquiries, as a follow-up to the mail questionnaires, can also be used. The organization must decide on the jobs to be covered, the employers to be contacted and the method to be used to gather data. Usually organizations compare themselves with similar competitors in their industry.

Job evaluation

The organization must not only relate pay to pay levels paid for comparable jobs in other organizations, it must also determine the pay structures for its employees having different jobs within the organization. Managers can cope with the attempt to provide equal pay for positions of equal worth by making arbitrary management decisions, engaging in collective bargaining or using job evaluation. If managers try to make these decisions without help from tools such as collective bargaining and job evaluation, unsystematic decision-making is likely to lead to perceived inequities.

Definition of job evaluation

The implementation of a job evaluation system is the first step in developing a fair compensation structure. Job evaluation is a systematic process to determine the value of a given job relative to all other jobs in a specific organization. It involves the analysis of jobs for the purpose of writing job descriptions and specifications, rating of those jobs through use of a job evaluation plan, and conversion of relative job values to definite wage rates.

Job evaluation must not be confused with performance appraisal. The objective of performance appraisal is to determine the economical value of the job holder. The objective of job evaluation is to determine the economical value of the *job*, irrespective of the job holder. Job evaluation is a systematic, rather than a scientific process. The subjective judgement of people is used to analyse, describe, assess and grade a job, which means that it is subjected to bias.

Objectives of job evaluation

The objectives of job evaluation are to:

- Establish a systematic and formal structure of jobs based on their worth to the organization.

- Justify an existing pay structure or develop one that provides for internal equity.

- Provide a basis for negotiating pay rates when an organization bargains collectively with a union.

- Provide a hierarchy of pay progression for employees.

- Develop a basis for a merit or a pay-for-performance programme.

Advantages and problems of job evaluation

The implementation of a job evaluation system has the following advantages for the organization:

- Personal bias in the determining of the value of the job is minimized.

- It forms the basis of a fair **salary structure** for all employees.

- An objective basis for collective bargaining is created.

- Job descriptions that can be used for selection, training and performance appraisal purposes are compiled.

The following problems are experienced with regard to job evaluation:

- Job evaluation can never be scientifically correct because it cannot be done according to scientific criteria.

- Pressure groups inside the organization can exercise pressure to grade certain jobs higher.

Job evaluation methods

The four most frequently used job evaluation methods include the job ranking method, the **factor comparison method**, the classification method and the point system.

- **The job ranking method**. The job ranking method is used in smaller, simpler organizations. Instead of analysing the full complexity of the job by evaluating parts of jobs, the job ranking method has the evaluator rank order in whole jobs, from the simplest to the most challenging. The problem with this method is that the difference between the highest job and the next highest job may not be exactly the same as that between the lowest and the next lowest. The method is not suitable for an organization with many jobs.

- **The job classification system**. This method groups a set of jobs together into a grade or classification. These sets of jobs are then ranked on levels of difficulty. The job evaluator decides how many categories the job has to be broken into. The next step is to write definitions of each class. Once the classes are defined, jobs to be evaluated are compared with the definitions and placed into appropriate classifications. The Paterson method (Paterson, 1972) is one of the most well-known job classification methods. This method divides jobs into levels based on decision-making.

- **The point system**. Most job evaluation systems use the point system. The point system requires evaluators to quantify the value of the elements of the job. On the basis of the job description and/or interviews with job occupants, points are assigned to the degree to which various factors are required to do the job. For example, points can be assigned based on skill required, physical and mental effort needed, degree of unpleasant working conditions involved and the amount of responsibility involved in the job. This method is reliable and assesses differentials between jobs. The disadvantage is that it is time consuming. The point system is, however, suitable in a unionized environment, because its validity can be demonstrated and union representatives can be trained in using it. The Hay system is an example of a point system.

- **The factor comparison method**. The factor comparison method permits the job evaluation process to be done on a factor-by-factor basis. It differs from the point method in that jobs are compared against a benchmark of key points. Five key factors are identified for the evaluation of jobs. Benchmark jobs are selected and the factors are then ranked in terms of their importance in each job. Monetary factors are assigned to the factors in each job. Others jobs in the organization are classified and paid in terms of their comparison to the benchmark jobs. This method can be suitable for small, homogeneous jobs, but is difficult to explain and does not allow any flexibility for prevailing market conditions.

The implementation of a job evaluation system

The steps in implementing a job evaluation system will now be discussed.

Step 1: Establish the need for a job evaluation system

It is essential to determine if a job evaluation system is really necessary before such an expensive and timely project is initiated. The following factors may indicate a need for a job evaluation system: a) An increase in the size of the organization. In a small organization it is possible to monitor salaries individually. If the organization, however, has more than 200 employees, salaries must be more structured. b) Dissatisfaction among employees because of perceived inequality of compensation, which manifests in symptoms such as poor labour relations, and high labour turnover. c) Perceived anomalies in compensation: for example, two employees on the same job level and with the same abilities earn different salaries.

Step 2: Get the support from top management

Prior to implementing a job evaluation system, top management must be convinced that the project is necessary, and that the time and cost involved is justified. Their continuous interest and support is essential to ensure the successful implementation of the project. Employees, supervisors and managers (who will be affected by the implementation of the system) want to be sure that top management supports the project, and that it is not only a fad used by someone in the human resource department.

Step 3: Select a job evaluation system

An appropriate job evaluation system must be selected. The service of external job evaluation consultants can be used if expertise regarding job evaluation is not available in the organization. The organization can contact other organizations in the industry or area to enquire about their methods and successes regarding the implementation of a job evaluation system. A system that is good for one organization will not automatically be good for another one. The reason for this is that each organization has its own 'personality', and may require different systems. If a pre-fabricated system is used, it may be necessary to modify it to suit the needs of the specific organization.

Criteria for the selection of a job evaluation system include: a) credibility, e.g. how many organizations used the system, and are still using it successfully?; b) relevancy, e.g. is the system applicable to all types of jobs and organizations?; c) simplicity, e.g. is it easy to learn and understand the language of the system?; d) objectivity, e.g. are the procedures of the system standardized?; e) comparability, e.g. is it possible to compare the results of the evaluations with other organizations?; f) flexibility, e.g. can the system be applied to all jobs that must be evaluated?

Step 4: Plan the implementation of the job evaluation system

The next step in the implementation of a job evaluation system is to finalize a time schedule. The following aspects regarding the time schedule must be considered: a) The time schedule must include all phases of the job evaluation, including communication with employees. b) The time schedule must be realistic and detailed. Interruptions affect the morale of employees and the credibility of the system. c) The job evaluation must accompany the annual salary review.

Step 5: Communicate with employees

Employees tend to resist change, especially if change may affect their status and salaries. The timing of the communication is crucial. Rumours, which can be detrimental for the project, arise if you procrastinate with the employees' introduction to the project. It is essential to communicate important aspects regarding the project at an early stage to all employees. The information that is communicated must be simple and clear. Even unskilled employees must be able to understand it. Verbal and written communication with employees must include the reasons for and advantages of implementing the job evaluation system. No person is willing to invest energy in something that would have no advantages for him or her. The employee's first concern in implementing a new method, procedure or technique is: 'Which advantage or disadvantage will it have for me?'. Advantages must be discussed with employees. The implementation of the job evaluation system must be approved by the trade union. A meeting must be held with representatives of trade unions to exchange information. Trade union representatives can also be included in job evaluation panels.

Step 6: Conduct job analyses and write job descriptions

The organization starts with the process of job analysis and job description.

Step 7: Rate and grade jobs

The rating of jobs is done by job evaluation panels. The job evaluation panel must include the following people: one or more representatives of the trade union(s), a senior representative from each department, a secretary and a neutral chairperson. The panel may include a consultant (as chairperson), a financial manager, a technical manager, the human resource manager, a organizational and work psychologist and trade union representatives.

The panel must be trained in the specific job evaluation system, and must be willing to spend time on job evaluation. The job evaluation panel must be representative of all the sectors of the organization. Each meeting of the job evaluation panel focuses on one section or department. The secretary provides copies of the job description to each member of the panel prior to the job evaluation meeting, and records decisions of the job evaluation panel. The panel discusses and rates each job and the chairperson makes the final decision if they fail to reach consensus. A total score for each job is calculated by summing the panel ratings on each dimension of the job evaluation scale. The jobs are subsequently graded.

Step 8: Develop a salary structure

After each job has been graded, a salary structure, which accommodates present salaries within the range of reasonable, market-related salaries, must be developed. The first step is to plot current salaries of employees against the new **job grades.** A salary curve which gives the best representation of the data can be drawn. This can be done by calculating the linear regression, or by drawing a curve which best represents the data. The line of best fit will be the midpoint of the new scale. Salary ranges must be developed on each side of the salary scale. This range must accommodate most salaries within the grade, but must not be too wide. The salary range would normally be in the region of 10–20 per cent.

The following factors must also be considered before the scale can be finalized: a) The scale must be in line with labour market data. National surveys could be consulted to find relevant market data and the scale should be adjusted. b) The scale must conform to wage agreements, industrial legislation or be negotiated with the trade union. It is recommended that the salary scales are introduced at the time of a general increase or wage negotiations, so that the organization can achieve the desired scales while adjusting salaries. Individual employees below the minimum should be given increases that will bring them to the minimum of the new scale. Employees above the maximum for a grade continue to receive standard increases while they are in those grades. They will be promoted or will leave the organization at some stage, and the salary curve of the organization would then be rectified.

Step 9: Communicate with employees

Employees should be notified verbally and in writing of their new grade and salary increase. They should also be informed how the grading system and salary structure operates and when increases will be given. Employees must receive a copy of their job description, and be made aware that the job description may, in time, need to be altered and re-evaluated.

Step 10: Implement the system

The following should take place during implementation: a) Salary increases should be awarded to employees. b) New grades and salaries must be entered in the human resource records. c) Procedures should be drawn up for job evaluation and updating of job descriptions. d) A job evaluation manual should be distributed to personnel who need it.

Step 11: Maintain the job evaluation system

The job evaluation system should be maintained: that is, workable and documented procedures for its maintenance must exist.

Incentive pay systems

Incentive pay plans attempt to relate pay to performance in an endeavour to reward above-average performance rapidly and directly. Although good performance can be rewarded through the salary structure – either by raising an individual's pay within the range of the job or by promoting the individual into a higher pay grade – these rewards are often subject to delays and other restrictions. Such rewards are often not viewed by the employees as being directly related to performance. Incentive pay plans attempt to strengthen the performance–reward relationship and thus motivate the affected employees (Rynes et al, 2005).

The following basic requirements are necessary for an incentive plan to be effective:

- Employees must feel that their performance is accurately and fairly evaluated. Performance is easier to measure in some situations than others. The performance of a sales representative is easy to measure, while the performance of a middle manager is difficult to evaluate. It is difficult to quantify and measure some of the results that a manager must achieve.

- Incentives must be based on performance. Employees must believe that there is a relationship between what they do and what they get. Individual incentive plans require that the employees perceive a direct relationship between their performance and subsequent rewards. Group-based plans require employees to perceive a relationship between the group's performance and the subsequent rewards of group members.

Incentive plans can be effective in the long term. If it is only effective for a short time, there may be something wrong with the way in which it was implemented. Performance must be evaluated effectively and incentives must be based on the performance of employees. Therefore, delays and other restrictions in the implementation of the incentive plans must be prevented.

Individual incentives are based on the performance of the individual as opposed to the group or the organization. The advantage of the individual incentive systems is that the employees can readily see the relationship between what they do and what they get. With group and organization based plans, this relationship is often not so clear. The disadvantage of individual incentive systems is that it may cause competition between employees, which may have negative results (Rynes et al, 2005). For example, sales personnel may not share their ideas with one another for fear that their peers might win a prize that is being offered to the top salesperson.

Because jobs are interdependent, it is sometimes difficult to isolate and evaluate individual performance. In these instances, it is wise to establish incentives based on group performance. For example, an assembly-line operator must work at the speed of the line. Thus, everyone working on the line is dependent on everyone else. With group incentives, all group members receive incentive pay based on the performance of the entire group. Many **group incentive** plans are based on factors such as profits or reductions in costs of operations.

Group incentive plans are designed to encourage employees to exert peer pressure on group members to perform. For instance, if a group member is not performing well and is lowering the production of the entire group, the group will usually pressurize the individual to improve, especially if a group incentive plan is in operation. A disadvantage of group incentives is that the members of the group may not perceive a direct relationship between their individual performance and that of the group (Rynes et al, 2005). Organization-wide incentives reward members based on the performance of the entire organization. Group incentive systems include profit sharing and gain sharing, **Scanlon-type plans,** and **employee stock ownership plans.**

Focus 10.1

Scanlon-type plans

Scanlon-type plans provide employees with a **bonus** based on tangible savings in labour costs. These plans are designed to encourage employees to suggest changes that might increase productivity. Organizations establish departmental committees composed of management and employee representatives to discuss and evaluate proposed labour-saving techniques. Usually, the bonus paid is determined by comparing actual productivity to a predetermined productivity norm. Actual productivity is measured by comparing the actual payroll to the sales value of production for the time being measured. Any difference between actual productivity and the norm is placed in a bonus fund. Any cost savings are paid to all employees, not just the employees who made the suggestions.

Summary

- Compensation is the human resource function that deals with every type of reward (financial and non-financial) that individuals receive in return for performing organizational tasks. The objective of compensation is to create a system of rewards that is equitable to the employee and the employer. Compensation should be adequate, equitable, cost effective, secure, incentive-providing and acceptable to the employee.

- Effective compensation administration is desirable in efforts to increase employee satisfaction and productivity. External influences on compensation systems include government, unions, economic conditions and the nature of the labour market. Internal influences on compensation systems include the labour budget and managerial pay strategies. Salary surveys are a valuable tool in determining the pay of employees. To ensure that salaries are internally fair, employers can compare jobs within the organization to determine their relative worth. Determining the value of a job is difficult because it involves measurement and subjective decisions. The use of systematic job evaluation procedures is recommended for determining a job's worth.

■ The most important factors that influence the salary of an employee include the job content (as measured by job evaluation), the market value of the job and individual expertise. The market value of a job refers to the average wage or salary paid in a country, area or industry. The pay level of the individual is determined by expertise, that is, the qualifications and experience of the job incumbent.

■ Incentive pay plans attempt to relate pay to performance in an endeavour to reward above-average performance rapidly and directly. Although good performance can be rewarded through the salary structure, either by raising an individual's pay within the range of the job or by promoting the individual into a higher pay grade, these rewards are often subject to delays and other restrictions. Such rewards are often not viewed by the employees as being directly related to performance. Incentive pay plans attempt to strengthen the performance–reward relationship and thus motivate the affected employees (Rynes et al., 2005).

Key concepts and terms

Bonus	Labour budget
Employee stock ownership plans	Stake
External influences	Non-cash benefits
Factor comparison method	Non-financial compensation
Financial compensation	Pay-level decision
Group incentive	Pay-level strategy
Incentive pay system	Plans based on saved time
Job classification system	Point system
Job evaluation	Salary structure
Job grade	Scanlon-type plans
Job ranking method	Stock plans

Sample essay titles

- What are the differences between the job evaluation methods?
- What can an organization do to ensure fair payment?

Further reading

Books

Armstrong, M., Cummins, A., Hastings, S., and Wood, W. (2003). *Job Evaluation: A Guide to Achieving Equal Pay*. London: Kogan Page.

Berger, L.A., and Berger, D.R. (2000). *The Compensation Handbook*, (4th Ed.). New York: McGraw-Hill.

Journal articles

Kahya, E. (2006). A revision of a job evaluation system. *Journal of Advanced Nursing*, 56, 314–324.

11 Performance appraisal

This chapter introduces the reader to **performance appraisal** in organizations. The first section focuses on the definition of performance appraisal. The chapter then proceeds to the importance of performance appraisal for employees and organizations. We look at legislation affecting performance appraisal and the conditions for the successful implementation of performance appraisal (including a supportive philosophy and strategy of management, **performance criteria** and standards, establishing the system, and performance appraisal methods). We also focus on the training of appraisers and describe the **performance appraisal interview**. Lastly, we will discuss guidelines for **performance management**.

Learning outcomes

When you have completed this chapter you should be able to:

1. Define performance appraisal and discuss the importance thereof.
2. Discuss the uses of performance appraisal.
3. Describe the conditions for the successful implementation of a performance appraisal system.
4. Explain the content and methodology of a training programme for appraisers.
5. Discuss guidelines for performance management.

Definition of performance appraisal

Performance appraisal is a human resource management activity that is used to determine the extent to which an employee is performing the job effectively. It is a process of evaluation and documentation of personnel performance in order to make a judgement that leads to decisions regarding training and development, promotion, remuneration and selection (Gerber et al, 1995).

The importance of performance appraisal

Performance management can be used to provide feedback about the strengths and weaknesses of employees, to distinguish between individuals to allocate rewards, to evaluate and maintain the human resource system of the organization (e.g. training and development, allocate rewards effectively) and to create a paper trail to document the reasons for certain actions, such as dismissing an employee.

Performance measurement and feedback are important for most individuals because they want to learn about themselves and find out whether they are making progress. Expectations can be made clear, employees can be managed more effectively, and participative management practices can be established by using performance appraisal in the correct way. Satisfaction with performance appraisal might lead to high morale, motivation and productivity (Mani, 2002). Dissatisfaction with the system, however, may lead to decreased motivation, feelings of inequity and staff turnover (Dobbins et al, 1990).

Focus 11.1

Purposes of performance appraisal

The following purposes can be served with a well-designed, formal performance appraisal system:

- **Developmental purposes**. Performance appraisal can determine which employees need more training and helps evaluate the results of training programmes. It provides feedback about the strengths and weaknesses of employees.
- **Reward purposes**. Performance appraisal helps the organization decide who should receive pay raises and promotions.
- **Motivational purposes**. Performance appraisal has a motivating effect because most employees want feedback about their performance.
- **Human resource planning purposes**. Performance appraisal data are an important input to human resource planning.
- **Communication purposes**. Performance appraisal is a basis for ongoing discussion between managers and employees about job-related matters.
- **Human resource management research purposes**. Performance appraisal can be used to validate selection techniques (e.g. psychometric testing programmes).

Employees have conflicting goals concerning performance appraisal. They want to obtain the rewards and opportunities that come with favourable appraisals, so they present their performance in the best possible light, even denying problems or inflating accomplishments. When they want help with problems, they need to honestly share their difficulties. If they paint a very positive picture, they may not get the help they need. If they overemphasize their desire to improve, they risk giving the impression that they cannot do their jobs (Barnes-Farrell, 2001).

There is a conflict between the organization's and the individual's goals with performance appraisal. This can lead to feelings of ambivalence experienced by the manager and the employee. Accurate information is needed to allocate rewards and provide feedback, but employees may share only the most positive information, for fear they will not be rewarded. Unpleasant interpersonal situations can arise because managers find it difficult to give negative feedback to poor performers.

Legislation affecting performance appraisals

The performance appraisal process can serve as a tool to manage employee performance and to safeguard against litigation. In the USA, performance appraisal played an important role in cases involving personnel actions in organizations (Martin et al, 2000). Performance appraisal practices are therefore subject to employment legislation (Werner and Bolino, 1997).

Conditions for successful implementation of performance appraisal

Philosophy and strategy of management

The management of an organization has the following responsibilities regarding performance appraisal:

- They must be committed and actively manage the performance appraisal system.

- They should link the system to the strategy and policy of the organization and set specific objectives for the system.

- They should create a performance oriented climate.

- They have to maintain a participative, motivational approach. They must first focus the system on development of employees, and later on rewards.

- They should not regard performance management as a human resource function.

Performance criteria and standards

Performance appraisal should be based on the specific tasks that the employee accomplishes or fails to accomplish (Martin and Bartol, 2000). Performance standards should be narrow and job-focused (Arvey and Murphy, 1998). Performance standards can be determined by conducting a job analysis and a job description. An important part of the job description is to state the performance dimensions and standards expected from incumbents, as well as how it can be measured. Many things could be measured to determine performance. Although not often directly observed, individual characteristics combine with tasks and organization factors to produce behaviour that can be observed. Behaviour reflects an individual's attempts to perform; individual characteristics signal the causes of the behaviour.

The dimensions of performance against which an employee is evaluated are called the criteria of evaluation. Examples include quality of work, quantity of work and cost of work. One major problem of many performance appraisal methods is that they require supervisors to make person evaluations rather than performance appraisals. The criteria should be integrated with the strategy and business plans of the organization, and based on a job analysis. Multiple criteria, that include activities (e.g. the number of calls made) and results (e.g. value of sales), must be included. Focus box 11.2 provides an overview of the different types of criteria which can be used in performance appraisal.

Focus 11.2

Criteria used in performance appraisal

- **Trait criteria**. Traits refer to observable dimensions of personality, such as initiative, friendliness and aggressiveness. Trait criteria are the most traditional performance criteria in use. Although they are convenient, they are poor criteria for performance appraisal. They confine the evaluator to making judgements strictly on ambiguous terms such as initiative, which result in unreliable appraisals among raters. Although traits may be potentially useful predictors of performance, situational and non-personality factors may also influence performance.
- **Behavioural criteria**. Behavioural criteria measure behaviour exhibited by the employee, such as asking subordinates for ideas and suggestions to solve job-related problems. These criteria permit the organization to specify the job behaviour relevant for getting the job done properly. These criteria are very useful for identifying employees' training and development needs, and communicating to them how they may improve their performance. Behavioural criteria are not useful for administrative purposes, because different behaviours may result in similar performance outcomes.
- **Output criteria**. Output criteria refer to the results of work such as sales or production volume, and number of typing mistakes in a letter. Output criteria specify the employee's contribution to the achievement of organizational goals. These criteria are objective, and there is little bias in evaluating someone's behaviour based on job results.

Output criteria are not useful for developmental purposes, because they give little factual basis for suggesting how to improve performance. It is also difficult to obtain short-term output criteria for many jobs. The closer the relationship between the employee's performance and the outcome of that performance, the easier it is to invent output measures. Another problem with output measures is that situational factors, over which employees have little control, may affect their performance. Examples of situational factors are the quality of equipment available, the availability of materials, economic changes, budgetary support and cooperation of the people whose input is needed. The use of output measures as the only criteria may have the following negative effects on performance:

- It has a short rather than a long time-frame orientation.

- It may cause a results-at-any-cost mentality.

- It may lower the commitment of employees to the achievement of goals that are beyond their control.

- It may fail to let the employee know how to behave to maintain or increase performance.

It is essential to choose the objectives, standards and key performance areas in the performance measurement system and to give attention to the following aspects:

- It must be integrated with the strategy and business plans of the organization.

- Job analysis should be done to find performance dimensions and standards.

- Both behaviour and results (outputs) are important.

- Difficult objectives and standards must be established.

- It should be possible for individual behaviour to influence measurements.

- Limit key performance areas.

- Output/behaviour expectations and standards should be clear and quantifiable.

Establish the system

Top management must be involved and should participate in the establishment, evaluation and adjustment of the system. Performance management is a key performance area of every manager. Top, middle and first level management is responsible for the management of the system. They assume ownership for the system, but ensure that it is carried over and shared. These people are important role models and should set the example. They will also be subjected to the system and process. Workers must be informed of the reasons for the system and how it works. It is important to involve them and give them a chance to participate, so that they can identify with the system.

There are two decisions to be made regarding the timing of the appraisal. One is when to do it, and the other is how often. In many organizations, performance evaluations are scheduled at arbitrary dates, such as the date the person was hired. Alternatively, each employee may be evaluated on or near a single calendar date. If the last alternative is selected, managers have to complete many performance evaluations on one day, which may lead them to quickly get it over with. It makes more sense to schedule the evaluation at the completion of a task or goal cycle. It seems better to conduct performance evaluations regularly.

Performance appraisal methods

A systematic process must be followed to ensure that accurate and reliable data are gathered. Users of appraisal systems often feel dissatisfied with these systems, not only because they are not valid, but also because they are not perceived as instruments that develop and motivate people (Latham and Mann, 2006). The requirements of a performance measurement system are given in Focus box 11.3.

Focus 11.3

Requirements of a performance measurement system

- **Valid**: measures what it intends to measure.
- **Reliable**: measures accurately.
- **Objective**: applies clear procedures.
- **Standardized**: uses the same items for each worker.
- **Practical**: simple and easy to administer.

Evaluation against common performance standards

Three performance appraisal methods are based on evaluation against common standards. These methods are graphic rating scales, checklists and behavioural rating scales.

- **Graphic rating scales**. The rating scale requires the appraiser to rate the employee's performance among selected traits, behaviour or outputs on a descriptive scale that ranges from low performance to high performance. The outcome of the rating process produces a performance assessment on each performance category, and the ratings given for each standard can be summed to get an overall evaluation of performance. The use of graphic rating scales may result in evaluation errors. These scales are often low in job relatedness, reliability and validity.

- **Checklists**. Checklists are similar to graphic rating scales. Whereas the graphic rating scale uses traits as performance criteria, the checklist uses behaviour descriptions. In contrast to graphic rating scales, which are often not based on job analysis, checklists use the critical incident method of job analysis to arrive at the items for the scale. The rater is asked to specify agreement or disagreement with behavioural statements. Checklists vary in the degree of sophistication used in their development. A simple checklist may list ten to twenty items that are believed to reflect effective and ineffective job performance. In a weighted checklist the items are weighted in terms of their importance to job performance, as judged by those familiar with the job and its tasks. These checklists permit evaluations on each performance category to be summed for an overall performance assessment and allow employees to see their strengths and weaknesses along each performance category.

- **Behavioural rating scales**. Behavioural rating scales are called behaviourally anchored rating scales (BARS) or behavioural observation scales (BOS). Although these scales are similar to graphic rating scales, they are developed on the basis of a thorough analysis of the job and constructed in a sophisticated way. The critical incident method of job analysis is used to obtain information on effective and ineffective behaviour. The scales permit evaluation of overall performance by summing the scores obtained on each performance category. They also allow the identification of strengths and weaknesses in performance.

BARS differ from BOS in the way the observed behaviour is scaled. In the BARS-scale, all behaviours are prefaced with the phrase 'could be expected to'. The intent of the phrase is to allow the appraiser to generalize what he or she has seen the employee do in the job situation to what the employee could be expected to do in a non-observed situation. BOS is a newer scale developed to overcome the complex judgements appraisers have to make in generalizing future behaviour by the BARS method. In the BOS, behaviour that measures similar concepts is grouped under a general behavioural performance category, called a performance dimension. Each behaviour is scaled from 1 through 5, and appraisers record how frequently they have observed the behaviour.

Evaluation against individualized performance standards

Appraisal systems that evaluate performance against individualized performance standards are called results-oriented, or output-oriented systems of performance management. Results-oriented systems take the organization's objectives for a given period and distribute them among the departments. The following two methods evaluate performance against individualized performance standards: the **direct index method,** and management by objectives.

- **The direct index method**. The direct index method is concerned with global outcomes of job performance. Global performance standards, that are derived from the job's required output, may be defined by the supervisor or negotiated between the supervisor and the employee. For example, a marketing job's required output may include performance goals regarding sales volume, and profit from those sales. The level of performance for each goal is objectively defined, and numerical performance ratings reflecting each performance level for the goal are specified. Overall performance is determined by summing the numerical ratings.

- **Management by objectives (MBO)**. MBO concerns itself with establishing goals for selected tasks whose performance is needed to attain departmental effectiveness in the short run. The MBO process consists of the following explicitly defined steps: a) Set performance goals for a specified period. b) The supervisor and employee participate in goal setting. c) Performance feedback. The MBO process starts with a meeting between the supervisor and each subordinate during which they agree on the major objectives of the employee's job for the next year and the performance outcomes required to achieve those objectives. The participative goal-setting process enables the supervisor to communicate the goals of the department to each employee and to discuss the ways he or she can contribute to departmental goal achievement. The supervisor and employee first assess the degree of success the employee had in achieving previous goals and the reasons for the achievement or lack of achievement thereof. This helps to ensure that the work goals to be agreed upon are challenging but achievable and are integrated with departmental goals and the career goals of the employee. The feedback step of MBO emphasizes the relationship between feedback and performance. Feedback influences performance when it is specific, timely, relevant and accepted by the employee.

Evaluation against others

The evaluation of employees against each other is important for making various decisions, such as who is ready for promotion. This leads to a rank order of employees according to their performance. Ranking is, however, of little use for employee feedback purposes, for compensation decisions and for identifying employee development needs. Ranking tells only who is the best and who is the worst, but it is difficult to determine the performance positions of the people in between.

Figure 11.1 Employees can be evaluated against each other to decide who is ready for promotion.

Source: Glowimages/Getty Images.

Methods that evaluate employees against each other include simple ranking, paired comparison ranking and forced distribution.

■ **Simple ranking**. Simple ranking is done by asking a judge to place a group of individuals in order of merit along some criterion. This process is easy at first, but gets harder. When the appraiser cannot distinguish between employees, a tie rank can be given to both.

■ **Paired comparison ranking**. In the paired comparison method appraisers compare every possible **pair** of individuals on overall performance, or against specific standards. The names of all people to be ranked are written on separate cards. The appraiser selects two names, compares them with the criterion in question, and places the 'loser' in a new pile. The 'winner' and a new person are then compared. The process is repeated until all employees have been ranked from first place to last.

- **Forced distribution**. Forced distribution is a ranking method that requires the appraiser to distribute the employees to be ranked into specified performance categories. The appraiser can place the employees into one of five categories of performance. The proportion of employees to be placed in each category is also decided beforehand.

Selecting a performance appraisal method

All the performance appraisal methods are used regularly. The graphic rating scale is the most widely used technique. Management by objectives is used for managerial, professional and technical employees, not production and office personnel. It seems that the major problems are not with the techniques themselves, but how they are used and by whom. The appraiser is more crucial than the technique in developing effective measurement systems.

Traditionally traits were used to measure the performance of employees. Frequently these traits have no relationship with concrete behaviour. It is difficult to link rewards and development plans to this method. Sometimes a single rating of total job performance is used to measure performance and employees are compared with each other. It is difficult to use this method for feedback, development and goal-setting. Behaviourally anchored rating scales are used to measure observable behaviour, and it leads to an improved task definition. Behavioural observation scales were found to be superior to all other appraisal methods in terms of eliciting favourable reactions (Latham and Mann, 2006). Objective-oriented methods (management by objectives) focus on predetermined goals and improve the objective measurement of results. The emphasis is on performance, not on the individual, and therefore this method is less emotional.

A results-oriented system can encourage behaviour that is functional for evaluation, but dysfunctional for organizational effectiveness. An activity-oriented system motivates activities rather than the accomplishment of results (objectives). A good performance measurement system measures activities (inputs).

Reward for performance

The integration of rewards with the performance management system should take place after 2–3 years of using the system. Compensation should be aimed at the acknowledgement and reward of 'correct behaviour and inputs'. Extrinsic and intrinsic rewards should be used. Non-financial compensation and recognition should form part of the system. The system should measure performance accurately and should lead to fair compensation. The total compensation administration of the organization should be healthy.

Training of appraisers

Training in performance management and appraisal is essential for all managers and supervisors. Studies showed that trained raters were more accurate than untrained raters (Arvey and Murphy, 1998).

Content of appraiser training

Researchers distinguish between training in the mechanics and dynamics of performance appraisal. Training in the mechanics of the performance management system includes the use of performance appraisal forms. Training in the dynamics of performance appraisal includes the establishment and communication of performance standards, writing clear and measurable objectives, interpersonal skills, conflict management, rating errors, observation and measurement of performance, giving feedback, and the performance appraisal interview. Topics that could be included in the training are shown in Focus box 11.4.

Focus 11.4

Content of appraiser training

- The underlying management philosophy of the system.
- The underlying values of the system.
- Techniques used in the system.
- Negotiation of goals and communication of standards.
- Human relations aspects.
- Preparation of employees for performance appraisal.
- Handling of performance appraisal problems.
- Feedback interviews.
- Discussing low performance with workers.
- Observing and recording skills and rating errors.
- Performance dimensions and standards.
- Linking performance with rewards.
- Administrative aspects.

Performance feedback

Appraisers must learn that ongoing feedback is the most important factor in maintaining or improving employee performance. The supervisor has the opportunity to observe the employee's performance, discuss that performance and, if necessary, help the employee to improve that performance.

Rating errors

Appraiser bias is regarded as one of the problems associated with performance appraisal. Latham and Mann (1996) summarize some of the recent research findings regarding appraiser bias as follows: a) Ratings were a stronger reflection of raters' overall biases than true performance factors. b) Supervisors' positive regard for subordinates results in leniency and halo errors, and less inclination to punish poor performance. c) Gender and race bias play a role when ratings are made. Men are rated as more effective than women. Blacks and Asians are rated as less effective than whites.

Ratings errors reduce the reliability, validity and utility of the performance appraisal system (Roberts, 1998). Therefore, raters should be aware of rating errors. The most common appraiser errors are reported in Focus box 11.5.

Focus 11.5

The most common rating errors

- **Halo effect**. An extremely good or poor rating in one performance category induces the appraiser to give correspondingly good or poor ratings on all the other performance categories.
- **Central tendency**. The employee's ratings on all performance standards cluster around the middle point of the rating scale. Although most people are average performers overall, most can also be differentiated along specific performance standards. Giving average ratings can be unfair towards outstanding performers.
- **Leniency rating effects**. The appraiser rates everyone on the positive end of the rating scale regardless of actual levels of performance.
- **Strict rating effects**. The appraiser rates everyone lower than their actual level of performance.
- **Recency effects**. The appraiser is influenced by the employee's most recent positive or negative behaviour.
- **Similar/dissimilar to me effect**. People tend to like others who hold similar opinions, values and attitudes and behave similarly under similar conditions. The appraiser may positively appraise employees who are similar to him or her and negatively appraise those who are different.
- **Initial/first impressions**. An appraiser forms an initially positive or negative impression of the employee and ignores any subsequent information that may distort that first impression.

The ability to identify and define rating errors should minimize their occurrence. Raters should know that they could prevent errors by justifying and recording their ratings (Feldman, 1992). According to Latham and Mann (2006), appraiser bias can be solved by finding ways to increase user acceptance of the appraisal process, basing appraisals on multiple sources, and training observers not only to be objective but also to coach employees throughout the year.

Evaluating performance

Although many organizations say that they teach supervisors and managers in performance appraisal, they usually merely train them on how to fill in the performance appraisal form. Supervisors are instructed to make sure that the appraisals they give to their employees are normally distributed. This type of training is inconsistent with the goals of performance appraisal. Effective training should teach appraisers to increase their rating accuracy and not to distribute the ratings along a normal curve.

The performance appraisal interview

Supervisors and managers must be trained how to conduct the performance appraisal interview.

Methodology of performance appraisal training

Case studies and video material of different jobs must be discussed with managers and supervisors and they must prove that they can assess performance accurately. Adequate opportunities for practice must be given. Frequent discussions of ways to overcome rating errors take place. It is not enough to make trainees aware of rating errors. They must practise ways to overcome rating errors and should receive feedback on their performance. Inter-rater reliability in respect of different case studies should be determined to get the ratings to an acceptable level of accuracy. Special attention must be given to trainees that rate too high or too low.

Training alone will probably not solve performance appraisal problems. Unless raters are motivated to use the system effectively and unless they are given the opportunity for observing their subordinates' performance, performance appraisal errors will not be solved.

Activity 11.1

Performance appraisal training

Why would training in how to conduct performance appraisals be an important issue for organizations to consider?

Sources of appraisal

Supervisors, peers, subordinates and the employees themselves could be involved in the appraisal. Based on the work of Latham and Mann (2006), the research findings regarding the different appraisers can be summarized as follows:

- **Supervisory appraisals**. A subordinate's performance tends to increase in years when performance appraisals take place. However, supervisors spend little time on the appraisals of their subordinates. Poor appraisals result when the supervisor had limited opportunity to observe the behaviour of a subordinate, and when the subordinate is hostile towards the supervisor. The supervisor's role should be to gather data and to make a final decision about the appraisal of a subordinate after gathering data from multiple sources.

- **Peer appraisals**. Peer appraisal is regarded as a reliable source of performance information. Peers tend to place more emphasis on interpersonal relationships and motivation than on task performance. However, inadequate instruments are often used to do appraisals. They are seen as useful when they are done with behaviour observation scales.

- **Self-appraisals**. There is a poor relationship between self-appraisals and appraisals of others. Employees tend to rate their performance more favourably than their supervisors. Cross-cultural differences seem to exist between eastern cultures and western cultures. In eastern cultures, self-criticism is regarded as an important way to improve performance. It seems that individuals with a high self-esteem tend to seek self-verifying feedback, even if it is negative, while individuals with a low self-esteem seek positive feedback.

- **Subordinate appraisals**. Anonymous feedback from subordinates tends to promote positive changes in a supervisor's behaviour and performance. Subordinates who were not allowed to provide anonymous feedback viewed appraisals more negatively than those who were allowed to provide anonymous feedback.

The performance appraisal interview

Effects of the performance appraisal interview

It is a demotivating experience for an employee to receive an unexpected negative appraisal rating (Roberts, 1998). Research has shown that many performance appraisal interviews have the following effects:

- Employees feel more uncertain where they stand after the interview than was the case before the interview.

- Many employees evaluate their supervisors less favourably after the interview (than before it).

- The interview is sometimes conducted in an authoritarian way, which is inconsistent with democratic values.

- The interview does not lead to constructive behaviour change.

Research shows that interview effectiveness will increase when the interview is approached in a problem-solving manner. This includes setting a climate in which the supervisor and subordinate discuss the performance goals and standards and the employee's performance relative to these goals or standards. A problem-solving approach encourages employees to think about their job problems in a non-threatening atmosphere and to provide their own solutions to encountered performance problems. Participation by the employee is one of the most important factors influencing the success of the review.

Preparation for the performance appraisal interview

Evaluation should not be viewed as a once-a-year completion of rating forms. To help with this communication, the manager should hold an appraisal interview with each subordinate to discuss the appraisal and to set objectives for the upcoming appraisal period. Experts advise that employee development and salary action discussions should not occur in the same interview.

The effectiveness of the interview will be increased when the supervisor or manager prepares for the interview. Preparation for the interview includes reviewing:

- The performance appraisal format. He or she must be able to explain the rating scales, how the ratings are derived, and how the numbers on the rating scales are related to performance standards used on the measure.

- The employee's performance. He or she must be able to answer any employee questions and to justify the rating given to the employee.

- Knowledge of the self. The supervisor or manager must review his or her own strengths and weaknesses in interacting with people, in particular the ability to give negative feedback in a constructive manner.

Conducting the performance appraisal interview

There must be active communication between the manager and the subordinate about the performance of the subordinate. The following behaviour may lead to effective performance appraisal interviews:

- **Structure and control the interview**. The purpose of the interview must be stated, control over the interview must be maintained, and an organized and prepared approach must be shown. No interruptions should occur during the interview. The employee should be oriented towards future performance by emphasizing the development of strengths. Ways to accomplish performance improvements should be discussed. At the end of the interview, a summary should be provided of all the major points.

- **Establish and maintain rapport**. An appropriate climate for the interview must be set, the interview must be opened in a warm and non-threatening manner, and the supervisor or manager must be sensitive to the needs and feelings of the employee.

- **Reacting to stress**. The interviewer must remain cool and calm during an employee's outbursts, apologize when appropriate (without retreating unnecessarily) and maintain composure and perspective.

- **Obtain information**. The interviewer must ask appropriate questions, probe to ensure that meaningful issues are discussed, and should seek meaningful information. The interviewer should focus on a limited number of topics so that each topic can be discussed comprehensively. Work goals should be reviewed and attainable objectives should be set.

- **Provide feedback**. The focus should be on facts rather than opinions, and evidence should be available to document the claims. The manager should open with specific positive remarks, be specific regarding performance shortcomings, and orient the discussion to performance comments, not personal criticisms. The manager should guard against overwhelming the employee with information. Too much information can be confusing, while too little information can be frustrating. Probably no more than one or two negative points should be brought up at one evaluation. The handling of negative comments is critical. They should be phrased specifically and be related to performance. Conclude with positive comments and total evaluation results.

- **Resolve conflict**. The interviewer should manage the conflict in the interview, make appropriate commitments and set realistic goals to ensure conflict resolution.

- **Develop the employee**. The interviewer should offer to help the employee develop his or her career plans, specify development needs and recommend sound developmental actions.

- **Motivate the employee**. The interviewer should provide incentives for the employee to stay with the organization and perform effectively, provide commitments to the employee to encourage high performance levels and support the employee's excellent performance.

Maier (1976) describes three generally used approaches to these interview situations: tell and sell, tell and listen, and problem solving. The tell-and-sell approach is best for new and inexperienced employees, while the problem solving approach, which encourages employee participation, is useful for more experienced employees.

Performance management

In the past, organizations focused on performance appraisal. Currently, the focus is shifting to performance management (Cederblom and Pemerl, 2002). Performance management is a planned, systematic management system, which can be divided into a few integrated subsystems, directed at the improvement of individual, group and organizational effectiveness. The subsystems include the determination of performance objectives and standards, performance measurement, feedback and development of employees.

Performance management starts with the question, 'Which performance must be managed?'. This has to do with where and what the organization wants to be and what it wants to achieve in the coming years. The long-term strategic plan is used to select the specific goals of the organization, and the behaviour that should be reinforced and rewarded to achieve the goals. Performance objectives, linked to the business plan, should be decided for each department and individual. Performance must be managed to bridge the gap between the current position (as shown by diagnosis) and desired position (as shown by the strategic plan) through the management of resistance to change.

Coaching and feedback form part of performance management (Latham and Mann, 2006). Feedback and coaching result in improved supervisor and employee relationships, increased commitment to the organization and reduced intentions to quit.

Activity 11.2

Forced ranking: Friend or foe?

Jack Welch, retired Chief Executive Officer of General Electric (GE), is associated with forced ranking. GE annually used this performance management tool to eliminate the bottom 10 per cent of employees that were rated as poor/low performers by means of the forced ranking system.

Forced ranking systems are performance evaluation programmes under which managers rank employees against each other and then use the rankings to determine who receives raises, rewards, bonuses, promotions, and, in some instances, who is terminated (AARP, 2007). Predetermined percentages of employees are forced into categories, sometimes designated by letter grades such as A, B and C; in other cases the categories are numerical, and in others there are labels such as 'superior' and 'needs improvement'. The distribution typically follows a bell-shaped curve with 10 or 20 per cent in the top category, 70 or 80 per cent in the middle, and 10 per cent in the bottom. The top-ranked employees are considered 'high-potential' employees and are often targeted for a more rapid career path and leadership development programmes. In stark contrast, those ranked at the bottom are denied bonuses and increases. They may be given a probationary period to improve their performance but are often terminated if they fail to show improvement.

Fans of forced ranking argue that ranking employees enables companies to reward top performers, eliminate unproductive workers and raise the overall level of productivity. On the other hand, its critics assert that forced ranking creates an overly competitive workplace where employee cooperation and teamwork are replaced with ruthless competition to outrank and outlast co-workers.

The AARP (2007) argues that one of the most common criticisms of forced ranking systems is that the criteria used to rank employees are not objective and, consequently, are subject to bias. The forced ranking systems adopted by Ford, Goodyear, General Electric, Conoco, Microsoft, Capital One and Sprint all have been challenged as being designed to get rid of workers of a specific race, age or gender rather than poor performers.

Debate the pro's and con's of forced ranking as a performance evaluation system

Which ethical challenges might be inflicted by this method?

For more opinions and information visit:

www.aarp.org/money/careers/employerresourcecenter/law/forced_ranking
AARP (2007)

www.businessweek.com/careers/content/feb2007/ca20070212_272450.htm

Why 'Forced' Job Rankings Don't Work by Liz Ryan

http://edweb.sdsu.edu/people/ARossett/pie/Interventions/forcedranking_1.htm

Performance Management: Forced Ranking by Charlotte A. Donaldson

Summary

- Performance appraisal is a human resource management activity that is used to determine the extent to which an employee is performing the job effectively.

- A well-designed performance appraisal system can serve various purposes, namely developmental, reward, motivational, human resource planning, communication and human resource management research purposes.

- The successful implementation of performance appraisal is affected by the philosophy and strategy of management, performance criteria and standards, the way in which the system is established, the methods used to appraise performance, the link between rewards and performance, and the training of appraisers.

- Training in performance management and appraisal is essential for all managers and supervisors. Trained raters are more accurate than untrained raters.

- Supervisors, peers, subordinates and the employees themselves could be involved in the appraisal.

- It is a demotivating experience for an employee to receive an unexpected negative appraisal rating. It seems that interview effectiveness will increase when the interview is approached in a problem-solving manner. Participation by the employee is one of the most important factors influencing the success thereof.

- Performance appraisal should not be viewed as a once-a-year completion of rating forms. The manager should hold an appraisal interview with each subordinate to discuss his or her appraisal and to set objectives for the upcoming appraisal period. Employee development and salary action discussions should not occur in the same interview.

- Performance management is a planned, systematic management system that can be divided into a few integrated subsystems, directed at the improvement of individual, group and organizational effectiveness. The subsystems include the determination of performance objectives and standards, performance measurement, feedback and development of employees. Coaching and feedback form part of performance management.

Key concepts and terms

Appraiser training	Peer appraisal
Behavioural criteria	Performance appraisal
Behavioural rating scale	Performance appraisal interview
Central tendency	Performance criteria
Checklist	Performance management
Coaching	Rating errors
Direct index method	Recency effects
First impression	Self-appraisal
Forced distribution	Simple ranking
Graphic rating scale	Strict rating
Halo effect	Subordinate appraisal
Management by objectives	Supervisory appraisal
Output criteria	Trait criteria
Paired comparison ranking	

Sample essay titles

- What are the content and methodology of a training programme in performance appraisal for managers?
- What are the advantages and disadvantages of the different performance appraisal methods?
- Which method could be used for the appraisal of performance of sales staff?

Further reading

Books

Armstrong, M. (2004). *Performance Management: Key Strategies and Practical Guidelines*. London: Kogan Page.

Grote, R.C. (2002). *The Performance Appraisal Question and Answer Book: A Survival Guide for Managers*. New York: American Management Association.

Journal articles

Den Hartog, D.N., Boselie, P., and Paauwe, J. (2004). Performance management: A model and research agenda. *Applied Psychology: An International Review*, 53, 556–569.

Loveday, B. (2006). Policing performance: The impact of performance measures and targets on police forces in England and Wales. *International Journal of Police Science and Management*, 8, 282–293.

12 Career development

This chapter introduces the reader to the topic of **career development.** The first section focuses on the definition of terms such as career development, career planning and **career management.** The chapter then proceeds to the importance of career development. We also look at career theories, and the role of life and **career stages** in career development. The third section looks at **career success.** This is followed by a discussion of **career planning** and career management as components of career development. Lastly, we focus on the evaluation of career management.

Learning outcomes	

When you have completed this chapter you should be able to:

1. Define career, career development, career planning and career management and discuss the importance of career development.
2. Evaluate theories of career development.
3. Define life stages, career stages and career success and the role it plays in career development.
4. Discuss career planning as a component of career development.
5. Discuss career management as a component of career development.
6. Point out the importance of evaluating career development.

Definition of terms

A career is a sequence of positions/jobs/occupations held by one person over his or her entire working life. The word 'career' comes from the Latin for 'carriageway' or roadway on which the Roman charioteers drove their chariots. Hall (1976) defines a career as follows: '... the individually perceived sequence of attitudes and behaviours associated with work-related experiences over the span of the person's work life'. The term *career* is also associated with paid employment, or at the least self-employment. If we take this view, then you might very well think of other types of careers. What about the career of a house-person, who does not work outside the home, but who is in charge of the smooth running of a household? Is this a case of paid employment or not? What about the career of the professional criminal or thief? Does such a person really have a career?

Career development encompasses career planning and the implementation of career plans by means of education, training, job search and acquisition, and work experiences. From the perspective of the *organization*, career development is the process of guiding the placement, movement and growth of employees through **assessment,** planned training activities and planned job assignments. Therefore, career development includes both personal career planning and organizational career management (Beach, 1985; Milkovich and Boudreau, 1994).

Career planning is a personal process through which workers plan their work life by identifying and implementing steps to attain career goals. Career planning includes evaluating one's own abilities and interests, examining career opportunities, setting career goals and planning appropriate developmental activities. Career planning is mainly an individual process, but the employing organization can assist through career counselling offered by the organizational and work psychologists and supervisors. More specifically, organizations can present workshops to assist workers in evaluating themselves and in deciding upon developmental programmes, by making career planning workbooks available to interested workers, and by disseminating information about jobs within and outside the organization.

Career management, the other subset of career development, focuses upon plans and activities of the organization (Beach, 1985). In career management the management of the organization matches individual employee career plans with organizational needs and implements programmes to accomplish these joint objectives.

Activity 12.1

Relationship between human resource planning and career development

What is the relationship between human resource planning, career development, personal career planning and organizational career planning?

The importance of career development

Recent changes in career patterns are mainly because of external factors, such as globalization, rapid technological changes, labour market deregulation and changes in organizational structures (Kidd, 2002: 179). Often skilled workers have been displaced because of automation. Deregulation in the UK and USA reduced job security and increased the need to adapt to more flexible forms of working. In addition, employability (regularly updating knowledge and skills) became important, because life-long employment is no longer guaranteed.

In general, workers want interesting and meaningful work and they want to utilize and develop their skills and abilities. Career development actions enable both an individual and the organization that employs him or her to meet these expectations. Depending on the state of the economy, many workers change organizations quite a few times during their working lives. This emphasizes the important role that career planning plays in an individual's life.

The importance of career development can also be deduced from other reasons for career development in organizations. If an organization pays the necessary attention to the career development of employees, it will be able to attract the required qualified workers because the word quickly travels around. Many qualified people would like to be employed by such organizations. It also leads to lower turnover among employees, because they now see that their expectations are being met. Employees tend to be more productive and to perform better when their abilities are being utilized more fully.

Career theory

Person–environment fit

Person–environment fit refers to the degree of congruence between workers and their environments. Applying this perspective to career planning implies that reliable and valid data should be gathered regarding individual differences (such as abilities, interests, personality and values) and jobs. Person–environment fit is positively related to employee well-being and negatively related to employee discontent (Tinsley, 2000). Person–environment fit is measured in terms of rewards sought by the individual and satisfaction offered, as well as between individual abilities and the demands of the work. The following theories focus on person–environment fit:

- **The Minnesota theory of work adjustment** (Dawis and Lofquist, 1984). Work adjustment refers to the process by which an individual seeks to achieve and maintain correspondence with the work environment. This model focuses on rewards sought and abilities used.

- **The attraction–selection–attrition (ASA) model** (Schneider et al, 1995). The ASA model suggests that organizational homogeneity increases over time through three stages. In the first stage, called 'attraction', people who hold values similar to those espoused by the organization are attracted towards the organization as potential employees. In the second stage, called 'selection', the organization actively chooses the applicants that are perceived to be most similar to the employees already in the organization. Finally, the third stage, called 'attrition', occurs when employees realize that they are not as similar to the organization as was once believed. The result of these three stages is that the personal values and preferences of the people within an organization should grow more similar over time. Fit, according to this theory, is a result of recruitment and selection of limited people.

- **The theory of vocational choice** (Holland, 1997). Holland's theory proposed that individuals seek occupational environments that are congruent with their vocational interests. Individuals can be classified in terms of six personality types, namely realistic, investigative, artistic, social, enterprising and conventional. Work settings can also be categorized according to this model.

Because individuals search for environments that allow them to express their interests, skills, attitudes and values, and take on interesting problems and agreeable roles, work environments become populated by individuals with related occupational personality types.

The role of life stages in career development

The term 'career development' implies a developmental process. It is a fact that developmental psychology and individual differences form two of the three bases of career development. The third basis is the fact that positions/jobs/occupations also differ from one another, because they place different demands on people and they 'compensate' people in different ways.

A few years back, developmental psychology did not play a major role in career development. There were two reasons for this. First, much emphasis in developmental psychology was placed on the development of children and adolescents. It was only later that researchers also started looking into the development of adults. Second, researchers concentrated to a large degree on the matching of individual differences with the differences between jobs. However, it is obvious that both individuals and jobs change over time.

Developmental psychologists have established that most people move through a sequence of 'orderly' life stages. There are different ways of describing these life stages. One way to classify life stages is in terms of stages such as early childhood, middle childhood, late childhood, early adolescence, middle adolescence, late adolescence, the youth stage, early adulthood, middle adulthood and late adulthood. Daniel Levinson (1978) also identified transition stages or life structures, which can be found when one for instance moves from early adulthood to middle adulthood (or midlife). It is important to take note of these life stages because each stage brings its own issues that an individual has to face and tasks that have to be carried out.

Even though many of the tasks and issues that an individual has to face have to do with one's own development (for instance partaking in sporting activities or hobbies) and with family issues, these tasks and issues are often intertwined with career tasks and issues. This is because every person is a 'whole' person. The main implication of viewing an employee as a 'whole' person is that organizations should take note of the fact that much of what happens at work influences the family and personal life of an employee. This, for instance, means that if an organization deems it necessary to transfer an employee to another town or city, the management should consider what the influence of such a relocation will be on the employee's family, and on the employee's personal adjustment.

The role of career stages in career development

Running parallel to life stages, but not quite identical to them, are different career stages. As in the case of life stages, there are models or approaches to identifying and describing these career stages. Even more than in the case of life stages, not every person's career stages perfectly fit the different career stages one supposedly moves through. An individual has to a certain degree more 'influence' over his or her career than over his or her life stages. One's career is also more open to influences such as the state of the economy and the profitability of the organization for which one works.

Career choice

Career choice is a developmental process. This means that there may even be sub-stages in occupational choice. This is not hard to understand. Take for instance a young boy who wishes to be a fire-fighter because he sees it as an exciting job, or the young girl who wishes to be a nurse at all costs. Once they start growing older, they realize that these jobs may not be as glamorous as they first thought them to be. They also start to notice that they are better at certain tasks than at others. A little later they realize that they need to look earnestly at an occupation that matches their skills, abilities and personality characteristics. In the occupational choice stage a person moves through the sub-stages of fantasy, realism and specification.

The individual should understand him or herself as well as the world of work very well to make a meaningful occupational choice. This means that he or she should have self-insight regarding his or her needs, abilities, interests and personality characteristics. Such an individual should also have knowledge of different occupations and the requirements that one should meet to successfully practise those occupations.

Once an occupational choice is made, preparation to enter that occupation is needed. This may take on many different forms. One of these forms can be the choice of specific school/college/university subjects. It can be in the form of doing some kind of apprenticeship. Some people view occupational choice and preparing for the world of work as one big career stage.

The next (sub-)career stage may be that of finding a position/job and entering the world of work by joining an organization or by becoming self-employed. This has become one of the major tasks young people have to accomplish considering the loose labour market that exists. The individual should have qualified himself or herself to enter the chosen occupation. Such an individual should also know where to look for possible job openings and how to write a letter of application, complete an application form, compile a curriculum vitae and act during a selection interview.

The early career

The next big career stage is that of the **early career**. Some people view this stage as consisting of two main sub-stages, namely the stage of becoming established in the world of work and the achievement stage. This early career runs somewhat parallel to that of the life stage of early adulthood. It is important to note that the time that an individual has to establish him or herself in the world of work roughly corresponds with the time the person in early adulthood is likely to get married and start a family. This places quite a burden on a person. Most people at that stage of life also have the energy, vigour and enthusiasm that it takes to accomplish these tasks.

An individual who finds him or herself in the establishment stage should show willingness to learn and to work hard. Such a person should try to fit into the organization and into the way things are done. At the same time he or she should also show initiative and a willingness to make a contribution to the organization. He or she should also keep in mind that in the beginning he or she is in a certain sense 'on probation' and that other organizational members are busy trying to decide whether he or she will be a worthy member of the organization.

One of the most important things an organization can do is to present the newcomer with challenging work as soon as it is possible. In this way the new employee can test him or herself. At the same time the organization can get an indication of whether the new employee will be able to make a contribution to the organization in the long run. It is also important that the organization gives the individual some feedback on performance.

Note that we talk about the sub-stage of achievement, rather than the sub-stage of advancement. Achievement might lead to advancement, but sometimes this is not the case. A person might perform in such a way that he or she is eligible for promotion, but it is not forthcoming because the promotional channels might be blocked or clogged by more senior personnel. This condition is aggravated by the processes of downsizing and rightsizing, and by the fact that organizational structures nowadays tend to be much 'flatter' than in previous times. If a person at this stage does not want to leave the organization, other ways will have to be found to keep him or her interested and productive.

Midcareer

The next career stage is that of **midcareer**, which roughly corresponds with the life stage of middle adulthood. Some people especially find moving from the last part of early adulthood to the first part of middle adulthood a very trying time. Some people call this the midlife transition or even the midlife crisis. A person facing a midlife crisis is likely to ask him or herself a lot of questions. Some of these questions might be: 'Why am I working so hard?'; 'Is there more to life than work?'; 'Have I been neglecting my family?'. The person in midcareer starts to question things again. Not every person experiences a midlife crisis. This means that there is nothing wrong with one if one does not experience a midlife crisis. On the other hand there is nothing 'abnormal' about experiencing a midlife crisis either.

Many persons at this stage ask themselves questions that are associated with work/careers. This is the time for a person to do some stocktaking concerning the career goals that he or she set him or herself at the start of his or her career. A person in this stage realizes that there is only so much time left to accomplish certain tasks or to reach certain goals. For the first time many people really become aware of the fact that they are mortal beings, whose life might end sooner than they might think. No wonder then that some people talk about people experiencing a midcareer crisis. The organization can make counselling facilities available to employees who wish to use such a service.

One of the main tasks of the midcareer stage is to stay productive in a job, and to strive to update skills. If the latter does not happen, a person's skills become obsolete. An individual should always try to keep up with developments and changes in his or her field of specialization or employment. An organization could assist workers to upgrade their knowledge and skills on a continuous basis. Another task is to handle the reaching of a possible plateau in a career. When a worker reaches a plateau, it means that he or she cannot advance further in the organization. It may be due to changes in the person, such as the lack of (updated) skills or the loss of speed and the like. Sometimes the plateau is caused by organizational factors, such as a lack of promotional opportunities.

The late career

The final career stage is that of the **late career.** Because more people opt for early retirement or receive severance packages before reaching retirement age, many people do not really reach this stage in organizations. For those who do, there are two main tasks to be accomplished in this stage. The one task is basically the same as that of the middle career stage, namely to still be productive in one's work. This again implies that one needs to ensure that one's skills remain up to date. The other main task is that of adequately preparing for retirement.

Adequate preparation for retirement takes on many forms. Financial planning for retirement should actually start in the early career. If one leaves it until late career, it is usually too late to really do anything about it. When preparing to retire, the worker should look into aspects such as housing, medical care, relations with friends and relatives and one's state of health. Psychological preparation for retirement is perhaps one of the most important, but often also one of the most neglected aspects.

When thinking about psychologically preparing oneself for retirement, one must remember that work plays an important role in the lives of most people. By working, one ensures a livelihood for oneself and for one's dependants. But work also fulfils other needs. Here one can think of such needs as the need for social interaction, the need to make a meaningful contribution to society, the need to keep busy and to make use of one's abilities and skills and perhaps even to fill the time one has available. When one retires, work ceases to fulfil these needs. Something else will then have to fulfil these needs, and one will have to reorientate oneself to the new situation.

Career success

In the past it was assumed that a person was successful in his or her career when he or she had a job that was paying a good salary and having a high status (Beach, 1985). Other signs of career success were the fact that a person was moving upwards to positions of greater responsibility. At the same time the person was a loyal employee and the organization rewarded the person in different ways for his or her hard work and dedication. In some instances, this scene has drastically changed. The changing nature of the workforce can also be seen in a difference in orientation in regard to career success. Nowadays, people place much more emphasis upon personal freedom, self-determination and a personal view of career success.

This new orientation regarding career success manifests itself in the following ways:

- The individual wants to control his or her own career development, by deciding when or whether to undergo additional training/acquire additional skills, to apply for particular positions/jobs and when to leave the organization.

- Personal values, such as freedom, growth and self-determination, play an important role in any career decision that an individual makes.

- The individual wants to maintain a healthy balance between involvement in work/career, with family and friends and his or her own developmental activities (such as the practising of sport or hobbies).

- Each individual has his or her own view of what it takes and what it means to be successful. This means that career success is a very personal thing. It might still be the attainment of a senior position in an organization or receiving a fat pay cheque. On the other hand, it might be something like experiencing personal freedom, experiencing self-respect or being heavily involved in non-work activities.

All that has been said so far implies that the person who wishes to experience career success will have to play an important and active role in his or her own career planning and personal career management. Such a person does not wait for the organization to do something about his or her career development, but assumes full responsibility for his or her destiny, as far as it is under his or her own control.

Career planning as a component of career development

Career planning is defined as the personal process of planning one's own work life. It was also pointed out, however, that an organization can, in different ways, assist an individual with personal career planning. If one keeps in mind that it is important to match an individual's personal career planning with the career management efforts of the organization, the way in which this assistance is presented plays an important role in career development.

The primary responsibility for career planning lies with the individual concerned. Only the individual can know what he or she wants out of his or her career. This means that career planning is to a large degree an individualized and personalized process and that each employee should develop his or her own career plan. An individual should take the necessary time and put in the necessary effort to develop a sound career plan. An organization can and actually should assist an individual in career planning. There are different ways of going about this. Another party that plays an important role in an individual's career planning is the immediate supervisor or manager of the particular individual. It is suggested that an organization should prepare a supervisor/manager to efficiently play this role.

The individual should develop a personal career plan. This involves four steps, namely: a) an assessment by the individual of his or her other abilities, interests and career goals; b) an assessment by the organization of the individual's abilities and potential; c) communication of career options and opportunities within the organization; and d) career counselling to set realistic goals and plans for their accomplishment (Bryars and Rue, 1994). When an individual engages in career self-management, he or she usually has some decision to make regarding his or her career. In order to make this decision, he or she should first do some career exploration. This means that he or she should find out more about him or herself and about the opportunities and demands presented by the world of work. On the basis of this, the individual should set career goals and identify different strategies that can be followed to reach these goals.

Once a decision has been made on strategies, these strategies should be implemented. One such strategy might be to perform as best as one can in one's present job. Once a strategy is implemented, the individual must use the feedback received from work and non-work sources to make the necessary adjustments in the strategy being followed. For instance, the individual's supervisor might be pleased that the individual puts in a lot of overtime and rewards him or her for doing this. On the other hand the individual's family, at the same time, may rebuke him or her for not spending enough time with them.

An organization could play the following roles in assisting an employee with career planning:

- Assisting the individual in appraising him or herself. Individuals can be assisted in appraising themselves by providing them with different career planning workbooks. The purpose of these workbooks is to let the individual engage in self-exploration and self-assessment. The individual should be assisted in identifying his or her own strengths and weaknesses, abilities, skills and interests. Besides completing the workbooks, the individual might also be assisted in taking aptitude, interest and personality tests in order to learn more about him or herself. Sometimes individuals can take part in assessment centres, and receive feedback on their performance in these centres. Sometimes organizations may organize career planning workshops.

- Assisting the individual in identifying different career opportunities. Once an individual has identified his or her abilities, interests and other career-related characteristics, the individual should be assisted in identifying jobs/occupations where these characteristics can be put to use. An individual should be encouraged to make use of these opportunities. Sometimes it might mean that a particular individual might be encouraged to look outside the organization for possible job openings. If an organization encourages an individual to look for career opportunities outside the organization, then the possibility exists that the individual might leave the organization.

- Assisting the individual in setting personal career goals. The individual should set operational and conceptual goals. An operational goal is usually seen as one that is tied to the attainment of a specific position. A conceptual goal is one in which the values that one wishes to attain in one's career are found. Such a value might, for instance, be to render service to people in need of assistance. Because goal setting in general enhances the likelihood of an individual reaching a certain point, it is very important to pay close attention to the way in which career goals are set. For instance, they should not be too easy or too difficult to reach, but should at the same time be challenging enough to the individual, so that he or she needs to utilize his or her abilities in order to reach the goals. The goals should also be specific enough, so that one is able to tell if one has reached one's goals.

- Assisting the individual in planning career strategies. Sometimes these strategies are called career plans.

- Assisting the individual in implementing career strategies. Once an individual has decided on strategies, he or she should be encouraged to implement it/them. Here an organization should see to it that the necessary developmental or training opportunities are made available to the individual.

Career management as a component of career development

Integrating career management with human resource planning

Human resource planning is the basis of human resource management. In this case it is important to remember that through human resource planning, the future demand and supply of human resources is determined. The present employees form part of the supply of human resources. Through the process of human resource planning one can determine in what developmental and training activities present employees should partake in order to prepare them for future job openings. That is why it is important to integrate human resource planning with career management

Identifying career paths/ladders

The process of human resource planning should help to identify the different ways in which individuals can progress through the ranks of an organization. This is depicted by means of career paths or career ladders that individuals can follow. It also shows what training and developmental activities an individual needs to undergo, as well as the skills needed to fill these jobs. Sometimes this is called the traditional approach to career pathing. A typical traditional career path is depicted in Figure 12.1.

Because of changing circumstances, organizations need to look at the traditional career paths that have been identified. Organizations need to ensure that a realistic approach to career pathing is followed. This approach is

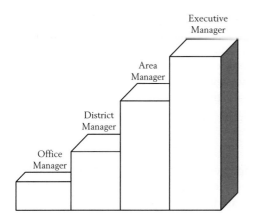

Figure 12.1 An example of a 'traditional' career path.

not an easy one to follow, because of the characteristics of these realistic career paths. Ivancevich and Glueck (1989) describe these characteristics as follows:

- They would include lateral and downward possibilities, as well as upward possibilities, and they would not be tied to 'normal' rates of progress.

- They would be tentative and responsive to changes in organizational needs.

- They would be flexible enough to take into account the qualities of individuals.

- Each job along the paths would be specified in terms of acquirable skills, knowledge and other specific attributes, not merely in terms of educational credentials, age or work experience.

An example of a realistic career path is given in Figure 12.2.

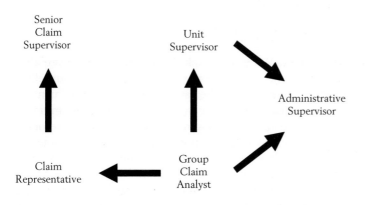

Figure 12.2 Example of a realistic career path.

Informing employees of career paths/ladders

Once career paths have been identified, employees should be informed of these paths. This will enable them to engage in realistic personal career planning that is integrated with the career management efforts of the organization. Employees should also be informed of the results of the human resource planning forecasts that have been done.

Doing job posting

Once vacancies become available, employees should be informed of them. They must then be allowed to 'bid' or apply for these vacancies. It can thus be seen that career management should also be integrated with the recruitment effort.

Assessing employees

The assessment of employees should be done in an ongoing way in organizations, and should not be left until vacancies occur. Through the process of performance appraisal, information on the potential of each employee should be available on a continuous basis. Usually an employee's immediate supervisor/manager is responsible for keeping the performance appraisal up to date. Because of the fact that performance appraisals are to a large degree based upon the judgement and views of one person (the supervisor/manager), organizations sometimes use assessment centres to assess employees. Although an assessment centre is a rather costly method, it does have the advantage of resulting in judgements of different observers about the performance and potential of a particular employee being pooled. Especially if an assessment centre is geared towards development, these pooled judgements can be of tremendous value when used to give feedback to participants in an assessment centre. In this way their own career planning can be enhanced. At the same time the organization can utilize the information gained at the assessment centre for organizational career management. The information on each employee contained in the human resource information system can also be used in the assessment process, especially if this information is continually being updated.

Offering career counselling

Although counselling is, strictly speaking, the domain of counselling psychologists, it often happens that counselling aspects come into play when undertaking career management. When feedback is given to an employee after attending an assessment centre, one can well argue that an element of counselling was present in that situation. The same can be said when a supervisor/manager discusses an employee's performance appraisal with him or her. If an employee talks to his or her supervisor/manager or to someone in the human resource department about the availability of career opportunities inside or outside the organization, elements of counselling are again present. Earlier on we mentioned the possibility of offering career planning workshops to employees for doing their personal career planning. During such workshops one will usually find that some career counselling takes place.

When an employee talks to his or her supervisor/manager about a career problem he or she experiences, elements of counselling are again present. That is why it is important to train supervisors/managers in basic counselling skills. This does not mean that they can fulfil the role of a counselling or a clinical psychologist. It does mean, however, that they will be in a position to decide when to refer a person experiencing career or personal problems to an expert, such as a organizational and work, a counselling or a clinical psychologist.

Career counselling is in order when employees experience career problems such as plateauing and obsolescence. It is also appropriate when there is a mismatch between an individual's personal career planning and the career management actions that the organization wishes to carry out. Sometimes individuals also face career related problems when they move from one life or career stage to the next. In this regard one can think about the problems faced by a person experiencing a midlife or midcareer crisis.

Using work experiences

Sometimes people tend to forget that one of the best methods of career management that can be utilized by an organization is the type of work experiences the employee is subjected to. It does imply, however, that these experiences are structured in a meaningful, planned and coordinated way. As Beach (1985) points out, these work experiences can take on different forms, such as having (a) challenging job(s), being rotated from one job to another, being assigned to a temporary task force, receiving a promotion or being transferred sideways.

The one person who plays a very important role in the utilization of work experiences as a career management tool is the immediate manager of the employee concerned. The manager must be able and willing to expose an employee to these work experiences. If a manager is not trained and rewarded for these actions, very little will become of this type of career management tool. Sometimes managers spend much time and effort on developing employees. It is then understandable why they are reluctant to 'let go' of these employees, once promotional opportunities become available.

Sometimes it becomes clear that work experiences alone will not adequately prepare an employee for future advancement. It may be necessary for the employee to receive further off-the-job training or education.

Adjusting human resource policies and practices

From what has been said thus far, it is clear that if an organization wishes to have a well-functioning career management system in place, it may be necessary to make some adjustments in its personnel policies and practices. In the past, the spouse or other family members of an employee had no role to play when it came to matters such as promotions or relocations. Because much emphasis nowadays is placed on the importance of managing the 'whole' person, organizations might find it necessary, if not beneficial, to involve or consult family members on certain career issues.

Another interesting aspect that comes to mind is the possibility of installing a 'fall-back' system that allows for a person who is promoted, but who does not make the grade in the new position/job, to move back to the previous position/job, or one similar to it.

Job rotation (being moved from one job to another in order to gain experience) has been mentioned previously as a method of career management. Sometimes employees who are rotated experience anxiety as they are constantly being moved from job to job and are unable to settle down. In order to build their sense of job security, they need to be given the assurance of being permanently employed.

Evaluation of career management

As is the case with all human resource management activities, the career development actions of an organization should be constantly monitored and evaluated. Heneman et al (1989) point out that an organization may ask the following questions when it wants to determine whether its career management system really works:

- Do the employees make use of the facilities offered by the system?

- Does the system provide accurate and useful information?

- Do employees undergo the developmental activities/experiences they need?

- Are employees able to realize their career plans?

- Are promotion and transfer decisions being improved?

- Do employees experience fewer or less severe career related problems than they did before?

- Do employees who participate in the career management activities provided have more 'successful' careers than those who do not?

- How do the results of the career management system compare with the cost of the system?

The answers to these and other questions about the effectiveness of an organization's career development efforts can be used as feedback to make the necessary adjustments in the career management system. In this way one can ensure that the career development of employees in an organization is optimized.

Summary

- A career is defined as the sequence of positions/jobs/occupations a person holds during the course of his or her work life.

- Career development can be viewed from two perspectives, namely that of the individual, who plans his career and implements the career plan, and that of the organization that manages the individual's career. Thus career development can be viewed as having two components, namely personal career planning and organizational career management.

- Career development is an important human resource activity, because it ensures the quality of the work life of employees, while at the same time supplying the organization with qualified employees.

- Person-environment refers to the degree of congruence between workers and their environments. Applying this perspective to career planning implies that reliable and valid data should be gathered regarding individual differences (such as abilities, interest, personality and values) and jobs.

- When doing career management, one should keep in mind that employees move through different life and career stages. Employees also tend to have their own views regarding career success. If career planning is viewed from the perspective of an organization, it consists of assisting the individual in the following actions: appraising him or herself, identifying different career opportunities, setting personal career goals and planning and implementing different career strategies.

- Career management, when viewed from an organization's perspective, consists of the following actions: integrating career management with human resource planning, identifying and providing career paths/ladders, adjusting labour policies and practices to fit in with the career development perspective, doing job posting, assessing employees, offering career counselling to employees and using work experiences of employees to develop their careers. Keep in mind that career planning is a highly individualized process. It is also important to evaluate the career development actions of an organization.

Key concepts and terms

Assessment	Early career
Career	Job posting
Career choice	Late career
Career counselling	Midcareer
Career development	Person–environment fit
Career management	Minnesota theory of work
Career path	adjustment
Career planning	Attraction – selection – attrition
Career stage	Model
Career success	

Sample essay titles

- What are the implications of the midcareer crisis for organizational career management?
- What are the implications of person–environment fit for career development?

Further reading

Books

Brown, S.D., and Lent, R.W. (2005). *Career Development and Counseling: Putting Theory and Research to Work*. Hoboken, NJ: John Wiley.

Gibson, R.L., and Mitchell, M.H. (2006). *Introduction to Career Counseling for the 21st Century*. New Jersey: Merrill Prentice Hall.

Journal articles

Reese, R.J. (2006). Effects of a university career development course or career decision-making self-efficacy. *Journal of Career Assessment*, 14, 252–266.

Warr, P., and Pearce, A. (2004). Preferences for careers and organisational cultures as a function of logically related personality traits. *Applied Psychology: An International Review*, 53, 423–435.

3 | Further aspects of organizational psychology

13 Well-being and dysfunctional behaviour at work

This chapter introduces the reader to work-related well-being and **dysfunctional behaviour** in organizations. The first section focuses on **work-related well-being**. Work-related well-being is conceptualized in terms of positive and negative aspects. The importance, causes, effects and management of work-related well-being are discussed. The chapter then proceeds to dysfunctional behaviour. For the purposes of this chapter, various types of dysfunctional behaviours are discussed, including **absenteeism, presenteeism, theft, sexual harassment, bullying,** and **alcohol** and drug misuse.

Learning outcomes

When you have completed this chapter you should be able to:

1. Define work-related well-being in terms of negative aspects (e.g. distress) and positive aspects (e.g. **eustress**).
2. Describe the causes of work-related well-being.
3. Discuss the effects of distress and eustress, and moderators thereof.
4. Identify interventions which could be used to manage work-related well-being.
5. Describe various forms of dysfunctional behaviour and make recommendations on the best ways to deal with these behaviours.

Work-related well-being

Definition of terms

In order to prosper and to survive in a continuously changing environment, organizations need *healthy and motivated employees* (Weinberg and Cooper, 2007) Individuals' experiences at work, be they physical, emotional or social in nature, affect them while they are in the workplace. In addition, these experiences spill over into non-work domains. Researchers and managers have generally recognized that a lack of health and well-being can potentially affect workers and their organizations in negative ways.

Ryff and Singer (1998) define human well-being as a multi-dimensional process that involves intellectual, social, emotional and physical health. This definition implies that health is regarded as the presence of the positive in the mind as well as in the body. This view is also consistent with the holistic model of health, which posits six dimensions of wellness, namely emotional, intellectual, spiritual, occupational, social and physical (Quick and Tetrick, 2003). Well-being goes beyond the fixed idea of health as an absence of illness. It implies a proactive stance towards achieving optimal physical, mental and emotional well-being. Complete health is the absence of physical and mental morbidity and the presence of sufficient levels of physical and mental well-being. Incomplete health or unwellness reflects either high levels of physical health and well-being but poor mental health (high morbidity or low well-being), or high levels of mental health and well-being but poor physical health (high morbidity or low well-being); being completely unhealthy reflects high physical and mental morbidity and low physical and mental well-being (Keyes, 2002).

Keyes (2002) hypothesized complete mental health to be a bipolar continuum, varying from flourishing to languishing. In *flourishing*, an individual experiences high levels of positive emotion and also functions well both psychologically and socially. *Languishing* refers to emptiness, stagnation and a life of despair. Keyes (2002) operationalized this continuum by means of questions on psychological, social and emotional well-being. Psychological well-being includes self-acceptance, personal growth, purpose in life, environmental mastery, autonomy and positive relations with others. Social well-being refers to social acceptance, social actualization, social contribution, social coherence and social integration. Emotional well-being includes positive affect, negative affect, life satisfaction and happiness.

Focus 13.1

Concepts of well-being in Africa

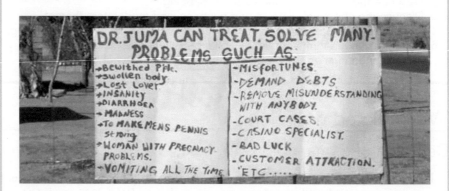

In the past, attention to the health of employees in the work situation was mainly directed at working conditions that were physically too aggravating. In recent years the human factor has become more and more important. This is the reason why attention has come to be focused on the total well-being of people. This refers not only to the absence of health problems, but also to the promotion of well-being of the total human being. However, it is not easy to define well-being and to distinguish it from health. The ambiguity about what well-being really is can be illustrated by this advertisement of a traditional healer in South Africa.

In line with the above-mentioned definitions and holistically seen, work-related well-being consists of two states, namely distress and eustress (Nelson and Simmons, 2003). These terms are defined in Focus box 13.2.

Focus 13.2

Distress versus eustress

Distress is defined as a negative psychological response to a stressor, as indicated by the presence of negative psychological states.

Eustress is defined as a positive psychological response to a stressor, as indicated by the presence of positive psychological states. Eustress reflects the extent to which cognitive appraisal of the situation is seen to benefit or enhance an individual's well-being.

When assessing eustress, the indicators thereof should be positive psychological states, such as attitudes or emotions. Stable dispositional variables are not acceptable indicators of eustress, which must be subject to change according to cognitive appraisals of stressors. The work attitudes positive affect, meaningfulness and manageability may be good indicators of eustress (Nelson and Simmons, 2003). Positive affect is a state of pleasurable engagement and reflects the extent to which a person feels enthusiastic, active and alert (Watson et al, 1988). Positive affect can be measured as a state or trait, with state positive affect capturing how one feels at given points in time, whereas the trait represents stable individual differences in the level of affect generally experienced. State positive affect is a separate factor from negative affect (George and Brief, 1992). Meaningfulness is the extent to which one feels that work makes sense emotionally, and that problems and demands are worth investing energy in, are worthy of commitment and engagement, and are challenges that are welcome. Manageability is the extent to which one perceives that resources are at one's disposal that are adequate to meet the demands posed by the work situation.

Work engagement can be regarded as a form of occupational eustress. Schaufeli and Bakker (2004: 295) define work engagement as 'a positive, fulfilling, work-related state of mind that is characterized by vigour, dedication, and absorption'. Vigour represents a positive affective response to one's ongoing interactions with significant elements in one's job and work environment that comprises the interconnected feelings of physical strength, emotional energy and cognitive liveliness. Dedication is characterized by deriving a sense of significance from one's work, by feeling enthusiastic, proud of one's job, and by feeling inspired and challenged by it. Absorption is characterized by being totally and happily immersed in one's work and having difficulty detaching oneself from it.

The importance of work-related well-being

Remarkable changes have occurred in the world of work over the last few decades. Specific changes include the increased utilization of information and communication technology, the rapid expansion of the service sector, the globalization of the economy, the changing structure of the workforce, the increasing flexibilization of work, the creation of the 24-hour economy, and the utilization of new production concepts (e.g. team-based work, tele-work, downsizing, outsourcing and subcontracting). Modern employees increasingly work in offices (and less in agriculture or industry) with information or clients (and less with tangible objects), in teams (and less in isolation), and with less job security (Turner et al, 2002). These changes might result in distress or eustress. In addition, many organizations have implemented practices that attempt to reduce costs and increase productivity, which often leads to a mentality that favours profitability over the *welfare of people*.

During 2005/2006 a total of 2 million people in the UK were suffering from illness they believed was caused or made worse by their current or past work. Almost 75 per cent of the cases were musculoskeletal disorders, stress, depression or anxiety. A total of 523,000 of these were new cases in the last 12 months. A total of 1969 people died of mesothelioma (a type of cancer). Overall, 24 million days were lost due to work-related ill health. It seems that one in five workers report that they find their work either very or extremely stressful. Each case of stress-related ill health leads to an average of 29 working days lost. A total of 13.4 million working days were lost due to stress, depression and anxiety. Work-related stress costs society about 4 billion pounds in the UK (1996 prices). Research in one organization showed that a stress management programme reduced the sickness absence from 10.75 to 8.29 days over one year, which represents a £1.9 million saving over two years. Cost-benefit analysis showed a net saving of £1.57 million (Tasho et al, 2005).

Studies have confirmed relationships between safety attitudes and occupational injuries, psychological distress and accident rates (Siu et al, 2004), job dissatisfaction and work-related accidents and incidents (Hoffmann and Stetzer, 1996), poor safety performance and anxiety and depression (Dunbar, 1993). A perception of high job overload is associated with an increased tendency to engage in unsafe acts (Hoffmann and Stetzer, 1998).

Causes of work-related well-being

The work-related well-being of individuals could be affected by outside forces, organizational factors and individual factors.

Outside forces

Forces outside the organization such as the following could affect the work-related well-being of individuals (Luthans, 1992):

■ **The rate of social and technological change**. Employees are constantly subjected to various changes, including new value systems in society and developments in information technology. Technological changes and innovations can make a person's skills and knowledge obsolete. Such innovations include the use of automated production processes, the use of robots in production processes, and the use of computers and computer technology. These changes might lead to the fear of losing one's job, which in turn might lead to distress.

- **The family**. The family situation of employees may also affect their well-being in a positive or negative way, resulting in either eustress or distress. Relocation of the family and changes in the financial situation of the family can act as significant stressors for employees.

- **Race, sex, social class and community**. Sometimes minority groups are subjected to more stressors than majority groups. It seems as if women experience more psychological distress than men. Especially in the case of professional women, the sources of stress are located in discrimination, stereotyping, balancing the demands of work/career and family and experiencing social isolation. Men, again, are more likely to suffer from severe physical illness due to stress. It may also be that people in different socio-economic classes are exposed to different groups of stressors. Community stressors include bad housing conditions, lack of services, and noise and air pollution.

- **Environmental factors**. Environmental factors such as economic and political factors might impact on the well-being of an individual. During times of economic uncertainty people tend to become worried about their work security, which might lead to feelings of stress. Political uncertainty may have much the same effect.

Organizational forces

Job and organizational demands and resources might result in either **occupational distress** or **eustress.** In general, it seems that **job demands** and a lack of **job resources** result in distress, while the availability of job resources might result in eustress (Schaufeli and Bakker, 2004).

Job demands refer to those physical, psychological, social or organizational aspects of the job that require sustained physical and/or psychological effort and are therefore associated with certain physiological and/or psychological costs. Job demands include the following (Baron and Greenberg, 1990; Robbins, 1996):

- **Role demands**. Role demands relate to pressures which are placed on a person because of the particular role he or she plays. Role demands include role conflict, role ambiguity and role overload/underload.

- **Responsibility for others.** Individuals who are responsible for other people and who must motivate them, reward or punish them and communicate with them, are more likely to experience higher levels of stress than people that are responsible for the other functions.

- **Interpersonal demands**. Interpersonal demands are pressures which are created by other employees. These pressures can develop out of poor interpersonal relationships and a lack of social support.

- **Organizational structure**. In an organization which is characterized by a high degree of differentiation, different sections or departments sometimes tend to function on their own. If there is no efficient way in which the efforts of the different departments or sections can be integrated, people who function in jobs which depend on this integration might experience the situation as stressful. When there is excessive dependence on rules and regulations, and when individuals have no participation in decisions which affect them, it might be a source of stress.

- **The nature of specific jobs**. Some jobs, for example emergency room physician, fire-fighter, airline pilot, production manager and foreman, are more stressful than others. It seems that these jobs require of the people who hold them to a great extent to make decisions, to constantly monitor devices or materials, to repeatedly exchange information with others, to work in unpleasant physical working conditions and to perform unstructured rather than structured tasks.

- **Physical job conditions**. Excessive heat, cold, humidity, dryness in the air, and noise can also increase stress.

Job resources are those physical, psychological, social or organizational aspects of the job that may be functional in achieving work goals, reducing job demands and stimulating personal growth and development (Schaufeli and Bakker, 2004). Job resources include the following:

- **Organizational support** (including the nature of relationships with managers/supervisor, ambiguities regarding work, availability of information, communication and participation). If employees perceive a lack of organizational support, they may experience distress. However, if they perceive support from the organization, they will tend to experience eustress.

- **Growth opportunities** in the job (including variety, challenge, opportunities to learn and/or independence). When an employee perceives that a job lacks variety, learning opportunities and autonomy, distress might result. Most people like to have some variety in their work, but sometimes people experience too much variety in their tasks as being stressful. When there is great interdependence between the person's tasks and the tasks of others, the person is likely to experience stress.

- **Social support** in the job (including support from colleagues and contact possibilities with co-workers).

- **Advancement opportunities** at work (including advancement in terms of remuneration and career opportunities). Remuneration refers to being paid adequately for the work that you do. Career opportunities include being able to progress financially, having opportunities to follow training courses and having opportunities for promotion.

- **Job security** (e.g. security in terms of a job in the immediate future, and staying on the same job level).

Moderators of work-related well-being

Different people react differently to the same stressor. It is also true that some people seem to thrive on stressful situations, while others are unable to cope. It thus seems as if there are certain factors which determine the relationship between potential sources of stress and the way in which different people experience these stressful situations.

- **Perception**. A person reacts in response to his or her perception of reality rather than to reality itself. To one person a challenging assignment means that he or she is able to make use of his or her potential and abilities, while to another person the same assignment might be interpreted as being a threat to his or her well-being.

- **Job experience**. For many people the newness of a situation poses a threat. At the same time, once these people get used to a particular situation, the situation seems to become less threatening. The same goes for the work situation: the more one is exposed to it, the less stressful it becomes. Therefore, job experience tends to be negatively related to work stress. Employees who have been with an organization for a long time will tend to experience less stress.

- **Social support**. Social support is the support which is given by colleagues, supervisors and family members with whom a person shares particular relationships. It seems that contact with others, especially significant others, helps one to cope with stressors.

- **Sense of coherence**. Sense of coherence refers to a global orientation that expresses the extent to which one has a pervasive though dynamic feeling of confidence that the stimuli deriving from one's internal and external environments in the course of living are structured, predictable and explicable; the resources are available to one to meet the demands posed by these stimuli; and these demands are challenges, worthy of investment and engagement.

- **Self-efficacy**. Self-efficacy is defined as '... beliefs in one's capabilities to mobilise the motivation, cognitive resources, and courses of action needed to meet given organizational demands' (Wood and Bandura, 1989: 408). Task-specific self-efficacy is a state-based expectation or judgement about the likelihood of successful task performance measured immediately before any effort is expended on the task. It is a powerful motivator of behaviour because efficacy expectations at a given point in time determine the initial decision to perform a task, the effort expended and the level of persistence that emerges in the face of adversity.

- **Locus of control**. Rotter (1966) proposed the concept of locus of control as the perception by the individual of his or her ability to exercise control over the environment. Those characterized by an internal locus of control believe they have control over their environment and their personal successes, whereas those with an external locus of control view their lives as controlled by external factors such as chance or powerful others. Compared to individuals with an external locus of control, individuals with an internal locus of control will be less inclined to cope with frustrations in organizations by withdrawing or by reacting aggressively (Rahim and Psenicka, 1996).

- **Optimism**. Nelson and Simmons (2003) distinguish between two conceptualizations of optimism, namely dispositional optimism (Carver and Scheier, 2007) and learned optimism (Seligman, 2002). Learned optimism relates to an optimistic explanatory style. Dispositional optimism is defined as a global expectation that good things will be plentiful in the future and that bad things will be scarce. Optimists seem to use more problem-focused **coping** strategies than do pessimists. Optimists are less likely to accept the reality of a challenge to their current lives. They are less likely to display signs of disengagement. Optimists experience less distress than pessimists when dealing with difficulties in their lives.

- **Psychological hardiness**. Kobasa (1982) studied executives who were under considerable stress and who were both hardy and non-hardy. The researchers found that the hardy executives had a lower rate of stress-related illness and were characterized as having commitment (they became very involved in what they were doing); challenge (they believed that change rather than stability was normal); and control (they felt they could influence the events around them).

- **Coping**. The level of stress an individual experiences in his or her organizational context, and the extent to which adverse effects such as psychological and other strains occur, depend on how effectively he or she copes with stressful organizational situations. Coping refers to perceptual, cognitive or behavioural responses that are used to manage, avoid or control situations that could be regarded as difficult (Lazarus and Folkman, 1984). Workers could use problem-focused and/or emotion-focused coping styles.

The effects of work-related well-being

High levels of occupational distress and low levels of eustress could lead to physical, psychological and/or behavioural effects.

Physical effects

Physical effects of stress include headaches, spastic colon, indigestion, ulcers, high blood pressure, palpitations, hyperventilation, asthma, stiff and sore muscles, trouble with sleeping, change in appetite, change in sexual drive and decreased immunity.

Psychological effects

The experiencing of high levels of stress may lead to feelings of anger, anxiety, depression, nervousness, irritability, tension and boredom. This may lead to lower job performance, lower self-esteem, resentment of supervision, inability to concentrate and make decisions, and job dissatisfaction (Luthans, 1992).

Behavioural effects

Behaviours which are directly related to job stress include the following: undereating or overeating, sleeplessness, increased smoking and drinking, and drug abuse. There also seems to be a relationship between stress and absenteeism, and between stress and labour turnover. One can imagine that these symptoms are very costly to organizations. Absenteeism and labour turnover have direct cost implications for organizations. A person who is suffering from sleeplessness is unable to perform up to standard. Drinking and drug abuse lead to people being unable to concentrate on the task at hand, which might lead to industrial accidents. Drinking and drug abuse may also contribute to absenteeism.

Work performance effects

Sometimes mention is made of the so-called 'inverted-U' relationship between stress and performance (Robbins, 1996). Low levels of performance accompany low levels of stress. As the level of stress increases, the level of performance also increases, until it reaches an optimum point. If the level of stress increases beyond this point, the level of performance goes down again.

There are exceptions to the general rule that stress seems to lower job performance (Robbins, 1996). There are some people who are able to turn out exceptional performance at times of experiencing high stress, perhaps because they have become experts in the task(s) being performed. Perhaps these 'experts' view high levels of stress as challenges rather than threats. In many situations, stress can indeed interfere with performance (Baron and Greenberg, 1990). However, its precise effects depend on several different factors (e.g. complexity of the task being performed, personal characteristics of the individuals involved, their previous experience with this task).

Managing work-related well-being

The following general guidelines are provided regarding the role of the organization in ensuring well-being at work (Barling et al, 2002):

- **Ergonomics**. Ergonomics is concerned with the design of a work system in which work methods, machines, layout, equipment and physical environment (e.g. lighting, heat, noise and vibration) are compatible with the physical and behavioural characteristics of the worker. Physical ergonomics focuses on the design of the physical workplace. Cognitive ergonomics focuses on the fit between mental requirements of a job and human abilities. Organizational ergonomics focuses on system risks.

- **Assessment and evaluation of employees**. Personnel assessment and evaluation should be used to ensure an optimal fit between the values and goals of the employee and those of the organization. Wellness audits which focus on both positive and negative aspects of work-related well-being should be implemented and feedback should be given on individual, group and organizational levels.

- **Job redesign and work changes**. The redesigning of jobs could reduce the exposure to psychosocial risks and increase employee motivation. Jobs could be designed to reduce exposure to stressors such as work overload, role demands and conflicts. Furthermore, lacking job resources such as job control and support from co-workers and supervisors should be addressed. Repetitive tasks could be reduced through the technique of job enlargement.

- **Leadership**. A 'good' leader is able not only to prevent job stress and **burnout** among his or her followers, but also to enhance motivation and engagement. Leaders should: a) acknowledge and reward good performance instead of exclusively correcting substandard performance; b) be fair; c) put problems on the agenda and discuss these in an open, constructive and problem-solving way, both in work meetings and in individual talks; d) inform employees on a regular basis and as early and completely as possible in face-to-face meetings about important issues; e) coach employees by helping them with setting goals, planning their work, pointing out pitfalls and giving advice as necessary; f) interview employees on a regular basis about their personal functioning, professional development and career development. Leaders should express their commitment by giving high priority to safety matters at meetings, allowing high status for safety officers and emphasizing safety training,

- **Training**. In addition to being purely directed at the job content, training programmes that promote employee health and well-being should also be directed at personal growth and development. For instance, they should include time-management, stress management, personal effectiveness and self-management. Work training is a learning process across the entire lifespan that is ultimately related to the employee's job performance. This could be achieved by increasing employees' efficacy beliefs through mastery experiences, vicarious experience, verbal persuasion and positive emotional states.

- **Organizational structure and climate**. Changing the organizational structure and creating a supportive organizational climate can be implemented by decentralizing functions, and by moving the responsibility for decision-making to the levels where people are able to make decisions regarding their own work. If employees see the appraising of performance and the subsequent rewards they receive as being fair, they will tend to experience less stress.

- **Job security**. Especially during hard economic times, job security is high on the priority list of employees. Job security lessens the stress generated by the possibility of unemployment caused by lay-offs or retrenchments.

- **Career development**. By attending to the career development of employees, organizations show that they care about the needs and aspirations of their employees. Career development provides employees with the opportunity to develop their skills and abilities, and to reach their career goals.

- **Organizational roles**. It is management's responsibility to reduce conflict by clarifying organizational roles. Each employee should know what is expected of him or her, and should also have the necessary means for carrying out his or her responsibilities.

■ **Employee wellness programmes**. Employee wellness programmes focus on physical and mental wellness. Regarding physical wellness, services can be provided for people to take part in fitness programmes, to lose weight, to control their diets, to quit smoking and to control their intake of alcohol and drugs. Regarding mental wellness, counselling services and access to the services of clinical psychologists and psychiatrists can be provided.

Dysfunctional behaviour at work

Next, various types of dysfunctional behaviour are discussed, including absenteeism, presenteeism, theft, sexual harassment, bullying, and alcohol and drug misuse (Langan-Fox et al, 2007).

Absenteeism

Absenteeism is used as a mechanism to withdraw from aversive situations at work (Hulin, 1991). Absenteeism could be divided into two types, namely absence for medical and non-medical reasons. Sickness absenteeism is defined as absence attributed by the employee to illness or injury and accepted as such by the employer (Searle, 1997).

Absence levels in the UK are measured in two main ways. The first comprises periodic surveys by bodies including the Confederation of British Industry and the Chartered Institute of Personnel and Development (CIPD). The mean absence rate for 2002 was reported as 3.9 per cent, down from 4.4 per cent in 2001 and roughly similar to the two previous years' surveys. The rate was higher in the public sector than the private (4.6 per cent against 3.1 per cent). The second method thus uses questions to individual employees through the General Household Survey and the Labour Force Survey. Estimates from the latter put the average absence rate at only 2 per cent, while figures from the former indicate little in the way of an overall trend since the 1970s. Higher rates in the public sector are confirmed (www.eiro.eurofound.ie). The costs of absence are estimated at an average of GBP 567 per employee per year. However, studies over many years show that rigorous measurement remains very rare, so that these estimates are really averages of guesses. A study in Europe showed that about 60 per cent of the hours lost due to absenteeism were lost because of illness (Ilgen 1990).

In the UK, 177 million days were lost in 1994, which represented a cost of GBP 11 million. Absenteeism leads to both direct costs (such as sick pay, overtime, costs of overstaffing, management and administration costs and loss of service provision) and indirect costs (such as disruption to service provision, reduced patient care quality, costs of recruitment, selection and training of replacement staff, lower morale and pain and suffering for those who are absent). Absence is a problem related to a minority of employees. However it seems that certain groups within a workforce, such as young people and women, are major contributors to absenteeism rates (Kristensen, 1991).

Long-term absence is likely to be associated with medical problems, while short-term absence is likely to be caused by social and personal factors rather than illness (Searle, 1997). The factors listed in Focus box 13.3 might cause absenteeism (Labriola et al, 2006).

Focus 13.3

Causes of absenteeism

- Work and role design. Absenteeism is likely to be higher in contexts where work is boring or roles are unclear.
- Workload and stress. Absenteeism is likely to be higher where workload is excessive or where people experience job insecurity and occupational stress.
- Organization and team size. Absenteeism tends to be higher in larger organizations and teams.
- Organizational culture and climate. Absenteeism tends to be higher if the management style is perceived as aggressive or uncaring.
- Physical demands. Absenteeism tends to be higher when a job involves physical demands such as lifting objects and pushing heavy loads.
- Injuries at work. A high incidence of work-related injuries may result in absenteeism.
- Lifestyle factors. Alcohol and drug-related problems may result in absenteeism.
- Persistent or recurrent conditions. Health conditions which are persistent or recurrent may result in absenteeism.
- Family or domestic commitments. Employees often experience domestic difficulties which may result in absenteeism.
- Travel difficulties. Workers will tend to be more absent when the work location is not easily accessible.

Organizations could do the following to manage the problem of absenteeism: a) communicate the absenteeism policy to all employees; b) optimize recruitment, selection and induction; c) maintain an effective performance management system, rewards and incentives; d) optimize the design of jobs and the organization; and e) implement **occupational health** initiatives.

Presenteeism

Presenteeism is defined as the practice of coming to work when the individual should not, which results in physically being present at work, but functionally absent (Middaugh, 2006). Presenteeism is less apparent than absenteeism and results because an employee is distracted, tired, depressed or ill (Aronsson and Gustafsson, 2005). Presenteeism is regarded as a measure of lost productivity cost due to employees actually showing up for work, but not being fully engaged and productive mainly because of personal health and life distractions. Three types of presenteeism are shown in Focus box 13.4 (Aronsson et al, 2000; Aronsson and Gustafsson, 2005).

Focus 13.4

Types of presenteeism

- **Sickness presenteeism**. Employees go to work despite complaints and ill health. It does not entail that the employee pretends to be ill to avoid job duties or misusing company time at work. Sickness presenteeism is expected to be related to increased risk of ill health because it restricts opportunities for recuperation (McEwen, 1998).
- **Insecurity-commitment presenteeism**. Employees put in excessive work hours as an expression of commitment or a way of coping with job insecurity.
- **Disengagement presenteeism**. Employees do not invest energy in a focused way in their work, mainly because they face demands and lack personal and/or job resources.

Regarding the prevalence of sickness presenteeism, it was shown that up to one-third of employees go back to work without sufficient recovery. Aronsson et al (2003) found that sickness presenteeism was higher in human service professions, including teachers, nurses and social workers, especially when people found it difficult to wind down after work. Kivimaki et al (2005) found that 17 per cent of unhealthy employees in British public service took no sick leave during a 3-year follow-up period. The incidence of serious coronary events in that group was, after correction for conventional risk factors, twice as high as that of unhealthy employees with moderate levels of sickness-absence.

Studies showed that presenteeism has negative effects in terms of productivity and economic outcomes, happiness levels of employees, and ill health. Employees who work at diminished capacity cost their employers an estimated $180 to $250 billion each year. Presenteeism accounts for 61 per cent of an employee's total lost productivity and medical costs. Loss of productivity is significantly greater from days being at work while sick compared to missed work days due to illness (Middaugh, 2006) ($180 billion of $250 billion of productivity loss due to presenteeism). Presenteeism accounts for between 18 and 61 per cent of the total cost of worker illness (Goetzel et al, 2004).

Presenteeism is caused by high work load, time pressure, work/home interference, low replaceability, understaffing, conflicting demands, lack of resources and low control over pace of work (Aronsson and Gustafsson, 2005).

Presenteeism can be managed by focusing on individual attitude and behavioural changes, as well as organizational interventions (see Focus box 13.5).

Theft

There are as many signs of theft as there are ways to steal. Certain conditions or incidents may not be the result of carelessness or incompetence but indications that theft is in progress. Inventory or product found near employee

Focus 13.5

Dealing with presenteeism

- Conduct anonymous wellness surveys and ask employees to offer suggestions for improvement.
- Present health and wellness awareness training to supervisors and employees.
- Create access to physical fitness facilities.
- Direct employees to utilize confidential employee assistance programmes.
- Use the services of disability specialists to assist employees with chronic injuries to modify their work techniques.
- Include a disease management specialist to support individuals who are experiencing a chronic condition.
- Discourage overtime and promote the importance of lunch breaks and annual holidays.
- Attend to work/life balance programmes.
- Explore community resources to provide support (e.g. sick child care).
- Consider work from home as an option.
- Provide the necessary job resources (e.g. an interesting and meaningful job, a clear role and responsibilities, fair pay and security, interpersonal contact and supportive supervision).

exits, sensitive documents discovered in copying machines, and employees in key positions who refuse to take time off have been signs of past theft and may be indications of existing dishonesty.

All organizations are probably experiencing some degree of employee theft. The list of items workers steal from their employers is endless and includes such items as inventory, money, parts, components, supplies, information and customers. It is estimated that 95 per cent of all businesses experience employee theft, and management is seldom aware of the actual extent of losses or even the existence of theft.

It is very difficult for a manager to accept the possibility that workers that he or she hired, trusts and works beside are capable of engaging in theft. Consequently, various misconceptions about the problem exist, for example: a) Most theft is caused by non-employees. b) Well-paid and/or senior employees are trustworthy/loyal and do not steal. c) Honest employees can be counted on to report employee theft. d) Employee theft is conspicuous and can be detected in its early stages and it is not necessary to formally inform employees that theft will not be tolerated.

Reasons for theft which are reported by employees include the following: a) The opportunity of theft presented itself through lax policies and controls and management indifference. b) Management (rather than employees financial needs) created opportunities for theft. c) Management was stealing so it is acceptable for employees to steal as well. d) Employees are underpaid and are only taking what they deserve. e) Everybody does it. f) The organization makes a large profit and workers deserve some of it. g) The organization angered the worker.

It is crucial to understand the reasons for worker theft and to initiate sound loss prevention measures. The following steps should be taken:

- Identify possible existing theft and potential opportunities or risks to potential theft. Immediately develop a plan to eliminate or reduce exposure to these risks.

- Educate supervisors, managers and the general employee population as to the impact employee theft has on them and how they are the key to solving the problem.

- Develop a loss prevention programme that ensures an ongoing effort to prevent and detect dishonest activity.

Sexual harassment

Sexual harassment is defined as any sexually-based behaviour that is knowingly unwanted and 1) has an adverse effect on a person's employment status, 2) interferes with a person's job performance, or 3) creates a hostile or intimidating work environment. This definition is drawn from laws that were written to protect victims of sexual harassment. Points one and two are known as 'quid pro quo' sexual harassment, which means that the victim is punished somehow as a result of saying no. The third point refers to situations in which either the direct behaviour or surrounding behaviour of perpetrators creates personal stress or a situation in which one would not want to work. Sexual harassment consists of three components, namely: a) gender harassment, i.e. hostile or insulting attitudes or behaviour; b) unwanted sexual attention; c) sexual coercion, i.e. sexual cooperation linked to job outcomes (Gelfand et al, 1995).

Sexual harassment is a widespread problem in the workplace. The numbers of 28 per cent and 90 per cent reflect the ends of a range of the percentage of women reporting being sexually harassed. The percentage of men reporting being harassed in the workplace is between 14 and 18 per cent (Fitzgerald, 1995; Schneider et al, 1997). Harassment is more likely to be perceived when: a) the target is female and the perpetrator is male; b) the target has less power than the perpetrator; c) the behaviour is repeated; d) the target has requested for the behaviour to stop; d) negative consequences follow; e) the target suffers emotional or stress-related symptoms; and f) the organization has been 'soft' on perpetrators in the past.

Although both men and women are reporting that sexual harassment is less likely today than it was 5 or 10 years ago, the number of lawsuits being filed for harassment is increasing. One reason for this is that people's perceptions of what harassment is have changed. As public awareness of sexual harassment increases, more and more people are likely to interpret a broader range of behaviours as offensive or illegal. For example, in the late 1970s, a female worker was repeatedly threatened with rape and even grabbed in the crotch by male co-workers. But when she sued, a judge at that time ruled that it was not sexual harassment because it was simply part of the regular horseplay that went on between co-workers. In the 1990s, a male graduate student had to remove a picture of his wife in a bikini from his desk because the placement of the picture there offended female office mates.

Self-reported sexual harassment is related to headaches, sleep disturbances and psychosomatic symptoms such as reduced self-esteem, increased anger, stress, anxiety, fear and depression (Fitzgerald et al, 1997).

The role of organizational and work psychologists is to help organizations to develop effective policies and procedures on sexual harassment. They should also be instrumental in designing training programmes to promote: a) a general awareness of sexual harassment; b) communication skills so that sexual harassment could be avoided before it happens; and c) conflict resolution skills to address harassment when it occurs.

Bullying

Bullying is defined as '... those repeated actions and practices that are directed to one or more workers, which are all unwanted by the victim, which may be done deliberately or unconsciously, but clearly cause humiliation, offence, and distress, and that may interfere with job performance and/or cause an unpleasant working environment' (Einarsen, 1999: 17). According to Einarsen et al (2003), bullying at work means:

harassing, offending, socially excluding someone of negatively affecting someone's work tasks. In order for the label of bullying (or mobbing) to be applied to a particular activity, interaction or process it has to occur repeatedly and regularly (e.g., weekly) and over a period of time (e.g., six months). Bullying is an escalating process in the course of which the person confronted ends up in an inferior position and becomes the target of negative social acts. A conflict cannot be called bullying if the incident is an isolated event or if two parties of approximately equal 'strength' are in conflict.

The incidence of bullying varies depending on the country and the definition of the frequency of bullying. Leymann (1990) reported that 25 per cent of Swedish workers experienced 'mobbing' at some point in their lives, while Rayner (1997) found that 50 per cent of UK workers have experienced mobbing at some point in their lives. Leymann (1990) reported an incidence of 3.5 per cent in Sweden (measured as once a week for six months). Jennifer, Cowie, and Ananiadou (2003) found that 33.7 per cent of a sample of employees in Europe reported that they were bullied at work, although only 20 per cent identified themselves as victims.

Focus box 13.6 provides explanations for bullying.

Focus 13.6

Explanations for bullying

- **Bullying as a personal phenomenon**. Personal factors of victims and perpetrators have been related to bullying. Victims might be targeted because they have high self-esteem or because they are overachievers (Brodsky, 1976). The personality (e.g. aggression) of a bully is also regarded as a reason for bullying (Randall, 1997).
- **Bullying as an interpersonal phenomenon**. Social factors have been related to bullying. Victims perceive envy as one of the reasons why they were bullied (Einarsen, 1997).
- **Bullying as an organizational phenomenon**. Organizational factors could explain why bullying occurs. Work situations characterized by uncertainty, authoritarian situations, role ambiguity and poor work relationships seem to contribute to bullying (Leymann, 1990; Zapf, 1999).

Bullying may result in (Hoel et al, 2004): a) physical symptoms (e.g. sweating, shaking and feeling sick), and b) psychological symptoms (e.g. anxiety, panic attacks, depression, anger and loss of self-confidence). Victims of bullying experience symptoms of post-traumatic stress disorder (Mikkelsen and Einarsen, 2002).

Organizations need to be proactive in dealing with bullying. Employers should put in place policies emphasizing that bullying will not be allowed. Such policies should detail the possible consequences of bullying (e.g. disciplinary action) and should be communicated to the entire workforce. Organizations should also provide training to managers, human resources staff and workers on identifying and managing bullying. Workers who complain about bullying should be treated in a sensitive way and supported by the organization. A measure of bullying should be developed and validated. Causes of bullying in workers who obtain high scores on this measure should be carefully analysed and it could then be dealt with (Notelaers et al, 2006).

Alcohol and drug misuse

All over the world substances such as alcohol and other drugs are often used by people of working age. The misuse of two substances, namely alcohol and nicotine, is often associated with negative health effects. However, both prescription drugs (e.g. morphine, anxiolytics, painkillers) and illegal drugs (e.g. cocaine, heroine and amphetamines) are also often misused.

Alcohol dependence and abuse

Alcohol abuse occurs in all societies. Alcohol is a central nervous system depressant and intoxicant. Its use and abuse is one of the major sources of health and socialization problems (Snyman and Sommers, 1999). Alcoholism is a syndrome consisting of two phases, namely problem drinking and alcohol addiction. Problem drinking is the repetitive use of alcohol, often to alleviate emotional problems, such as anxiety. Alcohol addiction is a true addiction similar to that which occurs following the repeated use of other sedative-hypnotics (Tierney et al, 1999). Drinking more than two drinks per day for men (more than 15 drinks per week) or one drink per day for women (more than 12 drinks per week) increases the risk of developing dependence on alcohol.

Complications of alcoholism include liver disorders, gastrointestinal problems, cardiovascular problems, diabetes complications, hormonal disturbances, birth defects, bone loss, neurological complications and an increased risk of cancer. Other complications of alcoholism and alcohol abuse may include domestic abuse and divorce, poor performance at work, increased likelihood of motor vehicle fatalities and arrest for drunken driving, greater susceptibility to accidental injuries from other causes, and higher incidence of suicide and crime (Snyman and Sommers, 1999; Tierney et al, 1999).

Substance and drug abuse

Two general aspects are common to most types of drug dependence, namely psychological dependence and physical dependence. Psychological dependence involves feelings of satisfaction and a desire to repeat the administration of the drug to produce pleasure or avoid discomfort. This mental state is a powerful factor involved in chronic use of psychotropic drugs, and with some drugs psychological dependence may be the only factor involved in intense craving and compulsive use. Physical dependence is defined as a state of adaptation to a drug, accompanied by development of tolerance and manifested by a withdrawal syndrome.

The development of drug dependence is complex and unclear. The psychology of the individual and drug availability determine the choice of addicting drug and the pattern and frequency of use. Drug dependency is partly related to cultural patterns and socio-economic classes. Factors involved in the mechanisms leading to drug abuse include sadness, low self-esteem, social alienation and environmental stress, particularly if accompanied by feelings of impotence to effect change or to accomplish goals.

Other psychoactive substances

Two other commonly used substances, namely nicotine and caffeine, may cause physical dependence. Withdrawal from caffeine (more than 250 mg/day) can produce headaches, irritability, lethargy and occasionally nausea. Abstinence symptoms from nicotine include irritability, anxiety, craving, insomnia, tremor and lethargy. Withdrawal symptoms may continue for four to six weeks, and craving may persist for many months.

Summary

- Human well-being is a multi-dimensional process that involves intellectual, social, emotional and physical health.

- Work-related well-being consists of two states, namely distress and eustress. Distress is defined as a negative psychological response to a stressor, as indicated by the presence of negative psychological states. Eustress is defined as a positive psychological response to a stressor, as indicated by the presence of positive psychological states.

- Remarkable changes have occurred in the world of work over the last few decades, which might result in distress or eustress.

- The work-related well-being of individuals could be affected by outside forces (e.g. the rate of social and technological change, the family, race, sex, social class and community and environmental factors), organizational factors (e.g. role demands, responsibility for others, interpersonal demands, organizational structure, the nature of specific jobs, physical job conditions, organizational support, growth opportunities, social support, advancement opportunities, and job security) and individual factors (e.g. perception, job experience, sense of coherence, self-efficacy, locus of control, optimism, hardiness and coping).

- High levels of occupational distress and low levels of eustress could lead to physical, psychological, behavioural and/or work performance effects.

- Guidelines to ensure well-being at work include attention to ergonomics, assessment and evaluation of employees, job redesign and work changes, implementing effective leadership, providing training, changing the organizational structure and climate, job security, attending to career development, clarifying roles and implementing employee wellness programmes. Employee wellness programmes focus on physical and mental wellness. Regarding physical wellness, services can be provided for people to take part in fitness programmes, to lose weight, to control their diets, to quit smoking and to control their intake of alcohol and drugs. Regarding mental wellness, counselling services and access to the services of clinical psychologists and psychiatrists can be provided.

- Various types of dysfunctional behaviour are distinguished, including absenteeism, presenteeism, theft, sexual harassment, bullying, and alcohol and drug misuse.

Key concepts and terms

Absenteeism	Occupational eustress
Alcohol abuse	Occupational health
Bullying	Optimism
Burnout	Presenteeism
Coping	Psychological hardiness
Dysfunctional behaviour	Self-efficacy
Ergonomics	Sexual harassment
Eustress	Social support
Job demands	Theft
Job resources	Work engagement
Locus of control	Work-related well- being
Occupational distress	

Sample essay titles

- Is all (work) stress necessarily bad?
- What (potential) sources of distress and eustress are associated with the fact that an organization is an open system?
- What role do job demands and job resources play in occupational distress and eustress?
- What are the most important effects of distress?

Further reading

Books

Antonio, A., and Cooper, C. (2005). *Research Companion to Organizational Health Psychology*. Cheltenham: Edward Elgar Publishing.

Nelson, D.L., and Simmons, B.L. (2003). 'Health psychology and work stress: A more positive approach.' In: J.C. Quick and L.E. Tetrick (Eds), *Handbook of Occupational Health Psychology*. Washington, DC: American Psychological Association, 97–119.

Schabracq, M.J., Winnubst, J.A.M., and Cooper, C.L. (2003). *The Handbook of Work and Health Psychology*. Chichester: John Wiley.

Seligman, M.E.P. (2002). *Authentic Happiness: Using the New Positive Psychology to Realize Your Potential for Lasting Fulfillment*. London: Nicholas Brealey.

Journal articles

May, D.R., Gilson, R.L., and Harter, L.M. (2004). The psychological conditions of meaningfulness, safety, and availability and the engagement of the human spirit at work. *Journal of Occupational and Organizational Psychology*, 77, 11–37.

Schaufeli, W.B., and Bakker, A.B. (2004). Job demands, job resources and their relationship with burnout and engagement: A multi-sample study. *Journal of Organizational Behavior*, 25, 293–315.

14 Organizational design, development and culture

This chapter introduces the reader to organizational design, development and culture. The first section focuses on organizational design. The term is defined and the dimensions of organizational design are discussed. Furthermore, types of organizational structures are distinguished. The consequences of a poor organizational structure are also shown. The chapter then proceeds to organization development. The importance and characteristics of **organization development** are discussed. We look at the stages in organization development. We focus on the management of **change** in terms of three steps, namely unfreezing, movement and refreezing. The last section focuses on organizational culture. The concept is defined, and the components and a typology thereof are described. Lastly, the development and change of organizational culture are summarized.

Learning outcomes

When you have completed this chapter you should be able to:

1. Define the terms organizational design, organization development and organizational culture.
2. Describe the dimensions of organizational design, the types of structures and the consequences of a poor structure.
3. Motivate the importance of organization development.
4. Identify the characteristics of organization development and the different subsystems in organizations.
5. Discuss the stages in organization development.
6. Apply a three-phase model (**unfreezing**–change–**refreezing**) to change in organizations.
7. Define organizational culture by referring to the components thereof.
8. Explain a typology of organizational culture.
9. Summarize how organizational culture develops and changes.

Organizational design

The terms organization and **organizational design** will be defined, and the principles of organizational design will be reviewed (Galbraith et al, 2002).

Definition of terms

An organization can be defined as 'a **system** of consciously coordinated activities or forces of two or more persons' (Barnard, 1938: 73). All organizations have four characteristics, namely: a) a common goal; b) **coordination** of effort, which is achieved through formulation and enforcement of policies, rules and regulations; c) division of labour so that workers perform separate but related tasks; and d) a hierarchy of authority, which is a control mechanism to make sure that the right people are doing the right things at the right time (Schein, 1980).

Organizational design is defined as the formal system of communication, authority and responsibility adopted by an organization which constitutes its internal structure (Baron and Greenberg, 1990). All organizations have an internal structure by which they operate in order to reach their goals. This structure varies from organization to organization.

The dimensions of organizational design

An organization chart (indicating the organizational structure) is a graphic representation of formal authority and the division of labour. The organizational chart (referred to as an organogram) provides a pictorial representation of the structural framework of an organization.

Terms that are relevant for the structuring of organizations include authority, responsibility and accountability. a) Authority is a form of power that orders the actions of others through commands. b) Responsibility is an obligation placed on a person who occupies a certain position. c) Accountability is the subordinate's acceptance of a given task to perform because he or she is a member of the organization (Furnham, 1997). Authority relationships can be traced on an organizational chart by following the lines downwards. Responsibility relationships can be traced by following the same lines upwards.

Organizational structure is characterized by four dimensions, namely a) hierarchy of authority, b) division of labour, c) spans of control, and d) line and **staff positions** (Furnham, 1997).

- **Hierarchy of authority**. The organizational chart specifies who reports to whom in the organization. In this regard it is necessary to consider the appropriate levels of responsibility and authority to be delegated. **Centralization** versus **decentralization** refers to the degree to which authority is retained by higher-level managers in the organization. In a decentralized organization a significant amount of authority and decision-making is delegated to lower levels, while in a centralized organization a limited amount of authority and decision-making is delegated to lower levels. Decentralization is advocated by those who believe in the empowerment of people. If most decisions are made by managers, employees tend to act as unthinking executors of their commands. The amount of centralization will depend on the size and **complexity** of the organization, geographical dispersion of activities and competence of staff. Managers in large organizations are forced to delegate more authority. Decentralization of authority is also necessary when the activities of the organization are geographically dispersed. However, the degree of competence (abilities, skills and motivation) of employees might make it difficult to decentralize authority.

- **Division of labour**. The organizational chart indicates who is responsible for what activities. Departmentalization is used to group related work activities into manageable units. Functional similarity can be used as a basis to divide labour. Jobs with similar objectives and requirements are grouped to form a section. The achievement of functional similarity depends on various factors, including the volume of work, traditions, preferences and work rules, the nature of departments and the possibility of conflict of interest. If the organization is large, more specialization occurs. Although tasks may be similar, traditions, preferences and work rules might prevent their assignment to one individual. Similar functions may also occur in different departments. Separation of functions may occur to prevent conflict of interest. Departmentalization can be done based on function, customer, geographical territory or project.

- **Spans of control**. The **span of control** refers to the number of people reporting to a specific manager. The span of control can vary from narrow to wide. The narrower the span of control, the closer the supervision and the higher the administrative costs as a result of a higher manager-to-worker ratio. Leanness and administrative efficiency dictate wide spans of control. There is no hard and fast rule regarding the optimum span of control. A narrow span of control is applicable when the work is complex, if jobs are interdependent and if the organization is operating in an unstable environment. A narrow span of control does, however, have some disadvantages. It is expensive, because it adds levels of management. It makes vertical communication more complex and slows down decision-making. It discourages employees from acting autonomously. To a great degree the span of control depends on the nature of the tasks which are being performed. If the task is of a routine and repetitive nature, employees need less supervision than in the case of highly complex tasks being carried out. Also, when employees have the necessary training for and experience of carrying out tasks (perhaps even complex tasks) they need less supervision. In such cases the span of control can be widened.

- **Line and staff positions**. Line managers occupy formal decision-making positions within the chain of command. Staff managers do background research and provide technical advice and recommendations to line managers, who have the authority to make decisions. Line people, who are directly involved in the production of goods and services, often feel that they are the experts in their own fields and that they do not need or want advice from staff departments. People in staff departments might feel that the people in line departments have too narrow a focus, and that they actually need the advice and input from staff departments. Often, top management accepts the advice from staff departments over that of the line departments. It is obvious that the line–staff relationship can be a difficult one, and one which should certainly be taken into consideration when thinking about organizational structures and organizational design.

Types of organizational structures
Mechanistic versus organic structures

Mechanistic organizations are characterized by less flexible and more stable organizational structures (Gordon, 2002). Activities are specialized into clearly defined jobs and tasks (e.g. in an assembly line). Workers of high rank typically have greater knowledge of the problems facing the organization than those at lower levels. Policies, procedures and rules guide much of the decision-making in the organization. Rewards are mainly obtained through obedience to the directions of supervisors and managers.

Organic organizations have flexible organizational designs and can adjust rapidly to change (Gordon, 2002). These organizations put less emphasis on job description and specialization. Workers become involved in decision-making when they have the knowledge or skills that will help to solve the problem. Workers holding higher positions are not necessarily assumed to be better informed than workers on lower levels. Horizontal relationships are considered as important as vertical relationships. Status and rank differences are de-emphasized, and the structure of the organization is less permanent.

The choice between mechanistic and **organic structures** depends on various factors, including the culture in a country and organization, and the personality and values of workers.

Matrix organizations

The **matrix organizational** design is characterized by dual hierarchies (a functional hierarchy and a product hierarchy) and a balance of power between these two hierarchies. The responsibilities of the functional manager include recruiting and hiring functional specialists, maintaining their expertise by training, and ensuring that products meet technical specifications. Product managers recruit specialists for each product, ensure that each product is completed on time and within budget, and ensure that functional specialists comply with the product goals.

Matrix organizations allow for the good use of limited resources since resources can be shifted between products or projects. Workers gain experience from both a functional and general management perspective. However, the dual lines of authority lead to conflicts, which may result in frustration, anxiety and stress. This type of structure requires that workers spend more time in meetings. Matrix managers also need to have particular skills (Furnham, 1997).

The consequences of a poor structure

The business environment and the organization's product should in part determine the structure of an organization. Therefore, there are no good or bad structures. A poor structure is one which is inappropriate for the specific goal that the organization wants to achieve.

A poorly designed organizational structure might have the following outcomes:

- It may suit the aims and personality of powerful individuals who created them rather than the needs of the organization. The structure should not follow the skills profile available but rather a comprehensive analysis of the task and organization.

- It can lead to stress for workers, especially if duties are not clearly described.

Structural deficiencies may result in low motivation and morale (because of insufficient delegation, unclear roles, overload and inadequate support systems), late and inappropriate decisions (because of poor coordination and delegation), conflict and poor response to change.

Organization development

Definition of organization development

Harvey and Brown (1996) define organization development (OD) as a long-range effort to improve an organization's ability to cope with change and its problem-solving and renewal processes through effective management of the organizational culture. It is a planned, systematic approach to change and involves changes to the whole organization or important segments of it. The purpose of OD is to increase the effectiveness of the system, and also to develop the potential of all individual members. It makes use of planned behavioural science interventions which are carried out in collaboration with organization members to help find improved ways of working together towards individual and organizational goals. OD is a discipline applying behavioural science to help organizations adapt to changes. It is aimed not only at improving the organization's effectiveness, but also at enhancing the effectiveness of organization members (Harvey and Brown, 1996).

The importance of organization development

Organization development is aimed at improving the effectiveness of the organization and its members by means of a systematic change programme (Palmer et al, 2006). An effective organization is one in which both the individual and organization can develop. Healthy organizations' strengths lie in change – the ability to transform their products and organization in response to changes in the economy. Organizations find themselves in a changing environment, and the only thing which is constant is change. Most people are unprepared to cope with it. Organizations are never completely static. They are in continuous interaction with external forces. Focus box 14.1 summarizes the external forces that lead to a need for OD.

These changes imply that organizations should focus on adding value. This manifests in a tendency to move from autocracy to democracy in organizations, flatter organization structures, a focus on core business, a tendency to split up into business units and the use of self-regulating work groups.

Characteristics of organization development

Organization development has the following characteristics (Harvey and Brown, 1996; French and Bell, 1999):

- **Planned change**. OD is a planned strategy to bring about organizational change. The change effort aims at specific objectives and is based on a diagnosis of problem areas.

- **Collaboration**. OD involves a collaborative approach to change, which includes the involvement and participation of those organization members most affected by the changes.

- **Performance**. OD programmes include an emphasis on ways to improve and enhance performance and quality.

- **Humanistic values**. OD relies on a set of humanistic values about people and organizations which aims at gaining more effective organizations by opening up new opportunities for increased use of human potential.

- **Systems**. OD represents a systems approach concerned with the interrelationship of various divisions, departments, groups and individuals as interdependent subsystems of the total organization.

- **Scientific approaches**. OD is based upon scientific approaches to increase organizational effectiveness.

The organization as a socio-technical system

Organization development may be referred to as a systems approach to change (Weick, 2000). An organization is viewed as an open socio-technical system of coordinated human and technical activities. The various organizational processes and functions are not considered as isolated elements, but as parts reacting to and influencing other system elements. According to Harvey and Brown (1996), an organization is an open system consisting of five components (see Focus box 14.2)

Focus 14.2

Characteristics of an open system

1. **The structural subsystem**. The structural subsystem includes the formal design, policies and procedures of the organization. It is usually set forth by the organization chart and includes the division of work and patterns of authority.
2. **The technical subsystem**. The technical subsystem includes the primary functions, activities and operations, including the techniques and equipment used to produce the outputs of the system.
3. **The psychosocial subsystem**. The psychosocial subsystem includes the network of social relationships and behavioural patterns of members, such as norms, roles and communications. It is referred to as the culture of the organization.
4. **The goals and values subsystem**. The goals and values subsystem includes the vision and mission of the organization. Such goals might include profits, growth and survival and are often taken from the larger environment.
5. **The managerial subsystem**. The managerial subsystem spans the entire organization by directing, organizing and coordinating all activities towards the basic mission. The managerial subsystem is important in integrating the activities of the other subsystems.

Stages in organization development

Organization development programmes are based on a systematic analysis of problems and a top management actively committed to the change effort. Many organization development programmes use the action research model (Cummings and Worley, 2005). Action research involves collecting information about the organization, feeding this information back to the client system and developing and implementing change programmes to improve system performance.

Action research provides at least two benefits for organizations. First, it is problem focused. The change agent objectively looks for problems and the type of problem determines the type of change action. A lot of change activities are solution-centred rather than problem-centred. The change agent has a favourite solution – for example implementing teams or management by objectives – and then seeks out problems his or her solution fits. Second, because action research so heavily involves employees in the process, resistance to change is reduced. Once employees have actively participated in the feedback stage, the change process takes on a momentum of its own. The employees and groups who have been involved become an internal source of sustained pressure to bring about change.

Stage 1: Anticipating change

Before an OD programme can be implemented, the organization must anticipate the need for change. The first step is the manager's perception that the organization is somehow in a state of disequilibrium or needs improvement. The state of disequilibrium may result from growth or decline or from competitive, technological, legal or social changes in the external environment. There must be a felt need, since only felt needs convince individuals to adopt new ways. Managers must be sensitive to changes in the external environment.

Stage 2: Developing the consultant–client relationship

After an organization recognizes a need for change and a consultant contacts the system, a relationship begins to develop between the consultant and the client system. The development of this relationship is an important determinant of the probable success or failure of the OD programme. As with many interpersonal relationships, the exchange of expectations and obligations (the formation of a psychological contract) depends to a high degree upon a good first impression or match between consultant and the client system. The consultant may be a manager or other member of the organization, referred to as an internal consultant, or an outside source referred to as an external consultant. The consultant attempts to establish a pattern of open communication, a relationship of trust and an atmosphere of shared responsibility. Issues dealing with responsibility, rewards and objectives must be clarified, defined or worked through at this point.

The consultant must decide at what point to enter the system and what his or her role should be. The consultant may intervene with the sanction and support of top management and either with or without the sanction and support of the members in the lower levels of the organization. Upon first entering the client system, the OD consultant begins evaluating its readiness for organization development. It is a mistake to assume that because most organizations can benefit greatly from an OD programme, they must have one. Answers to the following questions will help to assess the client's readiness for OD (French and Bell, 1996; Harvey and Brown, 1996): a) Are the learning goals of OD appropriate? b) Is the cultural system of the client ready for OD? c) Are the key people involved? d) Are members of the client system adequately prepared and oriented to OD?

Stage 3: Organizational diagnosis

After the consultant has intervened and developed a working relationship with the client, the consultant and the client begin to gather data about the client system. The collection of data is an important activity providing the organization and the client with a better understanding of client system problems.

Diagnosis is a systematic approach to understanding and describing the present state of the organization. The purpose of the diagnostic phase is to specify the nature of the exact problem requiring solution, to identify the underlying causal forces and to provide a basis for selecting effective change strategies and techniques. Focus box 14.3 shows the issues which are critical in **organizational diagnosis** (Harvey and Brown, 1996).

Focus 14.3

Critical issues in organizational diagnosis

- **Simplicity**: Keep data as simple as possible and use simplicity in presentation.
- **Visibility**: Use visible measures of what is happening.
- **Involvement**: Emphasize participation and involvement of organization members in diagnosis.
- **Primary factors**: Use undistorted collection of primary operating variables in diagnosis.
- **Measure what is important**: Pursue the straightforward assessment of variables which are critical to success.
- **Sense of urgency**: During diagnosis, gain an overall sense of urgency for change.

One rule for the consultant is to question the client's diagnosis of the problem, because the client may be biased. After acquiring data relevant to the situation which is perceived to be in disequilibrium, the consultant and client analyse the data together to identify problem areas and causal relationships. A weak, inaccurate or faulty diagnosis can lead to a costly and ineffective change programme. The objective of the diagnostic phase is to determine the exact problem that needs solution, to identify the causal forces in the situation and to provide a basis for selecting effective change strategies and techniques.

Two other concerns are important in organizational diagnosis. First, it is important to use a **diagnostic model** when diagnosing organizations. A diagnostic model is a representation of how organizations function, and is crucial in understanding organizations. Diagnostic models include the analytical model of Lawrence and Lorsch (1986), the socio-technical systems model, and the force-field analysis model. Although these models are not discussed here, they are important and should be kept in mind when approaching an organization for a diagnosis. Second, the **data collection** process should be considered. The most obvious step in data collection is defining the goals and objectives of the change programme. This step is necessary to determine which information is relevant. The next step is to identify the central variables involved in the situation (e.g. production, turnover, culture and values). The last step is to select a data-gathering method. Although organizations generate a large amount of 'hard' data, it may present an incomplete picture of organizational performance. The consultant and client may decide to increase the range and depth of the available data by using interviews, direct observation and/or questionnaires as a basis for further action programmes.

Stage 4: Interventions

The diagnostic phase leads to a series of interventions, activities or programmes aimed at resolving problems and increasing organization effectiveness. An intervention is defined as an instrument or tool that will enact and accomplish a state or goal (Burke, 2005). Intervention is regarded as part of the implementation phase of an organization change, which is the core of an organization change effort. Interventions aim to change some aspects of an organization (e.g. its climate, employees, structure or procedures) to improve the health or functioning of the client system.

The definition of an intervention includes various important elements (French and Bell, 1999). First, an intervention refers to something that happens in an organization's life. Interventions include educational activities, methods, techniques observations, interviews and questionnaires which are used to bring about organizational improvements. Second, an intervention refers to different levels of activities, e.g. a single task, a sequence of related tasks, activities that are related but also different, and an overall plan for the improvement of the organization. Third, an intervention implies joint collaboration between an organization and a client. For organization development interventions to be successful, the interdependencies between various sub-elements of the organization must be considered.

Argyris (1970) distinguished between three tasks of an intervener, namely to generate valid and useful information, to help the client to make free and informed choices, and to assure the client's internal commitment to choices made:

- **Generating valid and useful information**. Valid and useful information refers to the factors and their interrelationships that create problems for the client system.

- **Helping the client to make free and informed choices**. The second task of the intervener is to help the client system to make free, informed choices and to provide the client with alternatives for action.

- **Assuring the client's internal commitment to choices**. The third task of the intervener is to assure that the client is committed to choices made.

Interventions can be categorized based on the target group, namely a) personal and interpersonal interventions, b) team interventions, c) **inter-group interventions,** and d) organizational interventions.

a. Personal and interpersonal interventions

The central theme of personal and interpersonal interventions is learning through the examination of underlying processes. These interventions also focus on individuals and their development and growth within the organization.

- **Sensitivity training laboratories**. Sensitivity training groups are also known as training groups (T-groups). T-Groups is an approach to human relations training which provides individuals with the opportunity to learn more about themselves and their impact on others, in particular to learn how to function more effectively in face-to-face situations.

- **Transactional analysis**. **Transactional analysis** involves a system of interaction analysis, which assists people to understand their feelings and behaviour and which helps them to form satisfactory interpersonal relationships.

- **Behaviour modelling**. Behaviour modelling is a structured, effective and reliable method that can be used to train people in interpersonal skills. The rationale of behaviour modelling is that behaviour is shaped by external stimuli, that behaviour is learned through the observation of other persons (models), that behaviour is shaped and maintained by the consequences thereof, and that behaviour is repeated because of the reinforcement of similar behaviour in the past.

- **Life and career planning interventions**. Life and career planning interventions are used to assist individuals to focus on their life and career goals so that they can be empowered to exert better control over their own destinies.

- **Wellness promotion and stress management interventions**. Stress management interventions have embedded a range of practices that offer opportunities for individual development and employee well-being.

- **Counselling and coaching**. Counselling is used to help employees cope with personal problems which are interfering with their work. Coaching is used to help employees perform new tasks and/or improve their performance of old tasks or skills.

b. Team/group interventions

Team/group interventions are focused on group development and the interaction between individuals within groups or teams. Team interventions can be applied to family groups (i.e. intact work teams) and special groups (i.e. special project teams). The following team building designs are applicable to work teams (Dyer, 1995; French and Bell, 1999):

- **The family group diagnostic meeting**. This type of team intervention is used to analyse and evaluate the current functioning of the team and to identify problems that the team should work on.

- **The family group team building meeting**. The family group team building meeting is used to improve the effectiveness of the group by focusing on task accomplishment, relationships in the team, and group processes.

- **Process consultation interventions**. Process consultation is a philosophy of helping which involves joined diagnosis by client and consultant. Schein (1969) defines process consultation as a '... set of activities on the part of the consultant that help the client to perceive, understand, and act upon the process events that occur in the client's environment in order to improve the situation as defined by the client'. A process consultant helps the client to become aware of and improve group and interpersonal processes.

- **Role analysis team building**. Role analysis team building is used to clarify roles in a team when a unit is newly organized and team members do not know what others do and what others expect of them, changes and reassignments have been made in the team and members are no longer sure how functions fit together, job descriptions are outdated, conflict and interpersonal disruptions in the team are increasing, and the manager engages primarily in one-to-one management.

- **Role negotiation team building**. Role negotiation team building is used when the causes of a team's effectiveness are based on people's behaviour that they are unwilling to change. Using this technique, team members ask each other to change behaviours that will make it possible for the other person to do his or her job more effectively.

c. Inter-group interventions

Inter-group interventions are necessitated because of interdependency between teams and groups in organizations, conflicting objectives of teams, perceived power imbalance between groups, role conflict and role ambiguity and personality conflict.

- **Inter-group team building interventions**. In inter-group team building interventions, key members work on issues of interface. The meeting typically involves five steps, namely: a) Working separately, the two work groups make lists of how they see themselves, how they think the other group sees them, and how they see the other group. b) The two groups meet and a person from each group presents their lists. c) The two groups meet separately to discuss. d) Subgroups are formed by mixing members of the two groups and these groups develop action plans. e) A follow-up evaluation meeting is held.

- **Organizational mirror interventions**. These give feedback to teams on how other elements of organization view them. Units meet together to process data with the objectives of identifying problems and formulating solutions.

- **Third-party peacemaking interventions**. A third-party peacemaking intervention is a technique that can be used to resolve the conflict between two or more people. Confrontation is an essential feature of third-party peacemaking (French and Bell, 1999). The parties involved in the conflict must be willing to confront the fact that conflict exists and should realize that it has implications for their effectiveness.

d. Organizational interventions

- **Confrontation meeting**. The confrontation meeting as an organizational development intervention was developed by Richard Beckhard as a one-day meeting of the entire management of an organization in which they take a reading of their own organizational health.

- **Strategic planning intervention**. Cummings and Worley (2005) state that strategic interventions link the internal functioning of the organization to the larger environment and transform the organization to keep pace with changing conditions. According to French and Bell (1999), organization development practitioners should become experts in strategic management processes and need to have thorough knowledge of strategic management content.

- **Survey feedback**. **Survey feedback** intervention is the most effective if the organization wants to include a large group of people. This type of intervention is mostly used in diagnosing situations that need attention within the organization and to plan and implement organizational improvements. This approach of organization development surveys the unit of analysis through questionnaires and feedback to all the relevant role-players.

- **Grid OD**. According to French and Bell (1999), the Grid was designed by Robert R. Blake and Jane S. Mouton as a six-phase programme which will last about three to five years. The programme utilizes a considerable number of instruments, enabling individuals and groups to assess their own strengths and weaknesses; it focuses on skills, knowledge and processes necessary for effectiveness at the individual, group, inter-group and total-organization levels. The Grid OD programme is effective because it showed greater profits, lower costs and less waste.

- **Job design**. Job design is the process of incorporating tasks and responsibilities into jobs to make them more meaningful, productive and satisfying. Various models can be followed in redesigning jobs, including the job characteristics model (Hackman and Oldham, 1976), the job demand-control model (Karasek, 1979) and the interdisciplinary approach of Campion and Berger (1990).

- **Quality circles**. Quality circles are focused on customer satisfaction through continuous improvement and teamwork.

- **Management by objectives**. Management by objectives is based on the philosophy that the manager and employee ought to negotiate or collaborate on defining the objectives that the worker is to pursue over the next time period (Drucker, 1954; Odiorne, 1965).

- **Socio-technical systems**. According to Trist et al (1963), a socio-technical system design is based on the premise that an organization or a work unit is a combination of social and technical parts that is open to its environment. A **socio-technical system** focuses on the interdependencies between and among people, technology and environment in order to optimize both social and technical elements in organizations. The social system aims to design a work structure that is responsive to the psychological needs of employees.

The OD consultant should consider the following three aspects in selecting the appropriate intervention (French and Bell, 1996; Harvey and Brown, 1996). First, the potential results of the technique of the intervention should be considered. The interventions should solve the intended 'problems' and result in positive outcomes. Second, the possibility to implement the interventions should be considered. The expected costs of interventions should be weighed against the potential benefits thereof. Last, it is important to assess clients' willingness to participate in the interventions beforehand.

Stage 5: Self-renewal, monitoring and stabilizing action programmes

Once an OD programme is implemented, the next step is to monitor the results and stabilize the desired changes. This stage concerns the assessment of the effectiveness of change strategies in attaining stated objectives. Each stage of an OD programme needs to be monitored to gain feedback on member reactions to change efforts. The system members need to know the results of change efforts in order to determine whether they ought to modify, continue or discontinue the activities.

Once a problem has been corrected and a change programme implemented and monitored, means must be devised to make sure that the new behaviour is stabilized and internalized. If this is not done, the system tends to regress to previous ineffective modes or states. The client system needs to develop the capability to maintain innovation without outside support.

Management of change

According to Kurt Lewin (1952), any change process consists of three phases, namely unfreezing the status quo, movement to a new state (change), and refreezing the new change to make it permanent (see Figure 14.1).

Figure 14.1 Lewin's Three-Step Change Model.

The status quo can be considered to be an equilibrium state. To move from this equilibrium – to overcome the pressures of both individual resistance and group conformity – unfreezing is necessary. It can be achieved in three ways (see Figure 14.2). The driving forces, which direct behaviour away from the status quo, can be increased. The restraining forces, which hinder movement from the existing equilibrium, can be decreased. A third alternative is to combine the two approaches.

Unfreezing

Organization members should be unfrozen to overcome resistance to change. Individuals must be prepared for change and must release physical and psychic energy for it (Burke, 1996). Dissatisfaction with the status quo can be created to encourage employees to experiment with new behavioural forms. Focus box 14.4 shows that dissatisfaction can be generated by engaging in specific behaviours (Beer and Walton, 1990; Burke, 1994).

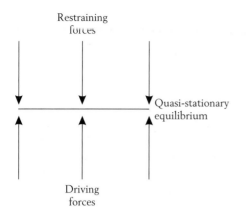

Figure 14.2 Force field analysis (Kurt Lewin).

Focus 14.4

Creating dissatisfaction with the status quo

■ Make employees aware of the need for change by presenting the reality of the situation to them (e.g. a decrease in sales figures, an increase in costs, high labour turnover and rate of absenteeism). It is easier to generate motivation for change if a competitive crisis is present.
■ Disclose the differences between the present and the desired situation.
■ Describe a more desirable future situation, i.e. develop a vision of a future state that could energize people. Leaders should be more concerned about the determination of a desired state than how to get there.
■ Communicate positive expectations regarding the change.
Expectations of employees may serve as a self-fulfilling prophecy and encourage them to invest energy in change programmes which they expect to succeed.
■ Inform employees about the expected advantages of changes for them.

As soon as employees understand the necessity of change, they must be convinced that the proposed changes are workable. This can be facilitated by pilot projects which involve employees, which may indicate that the assumptions underlying changes are valid. Pilot projects will promote feelings of security, which will help employees to change.

Manage the change process

Change implies the learning of new attitudes and/or behaviour by making the person aware of new sources of information, or by helping him or her to look at old information in a new way. Change can take place in two ways, namely a) by identifying with a role model, mentor, friend or other person and by learning to see things from his or her frame of reference, and b) by scanning the environment to find a specific problem. It is difficult to manage the change process because people seldom react as was planned. Organizational politics are also involved and people's perceptions, emotions and behaviour are affected by changes.

Stabilizing the change ('refreezing')

Refreezing involves the stabilizing of changes by helping the person to integrate the new activities in his or her routine activities. Various mechanisms can be used to stabilize changes (Burke, 1994), namely: a) The individual should be given the opportunity to determine if the new attitudes and/or behaviour really fit his or her self-concept, are congruent with other parts of his or her personality and if they can be integrated comfortably. b) The individual should be given the opportunity to test if others will accept and confirm the new attitudes and behaviour. It is important to tell people which things would not change. The latter serves as an anchor to provide stability to manage changes. The reward system can be used to reinforce behaviour. Formal and public acknowledgement of employees who help to move the organization in the desired direction may help to specify what acceptable behaviour is. Guardians may be employed to serve as role models and norm carriers of the new culture and changes.

Organizational culture

Definition of organizational culture

Organizational culture is defined as 'how things are done around here' (Drennan, 1992: 1). As employees work together, specific procedures or ways in which work is done, problems are handled and decisions are made become established, and in time these procedures and ways become the accepted way in which such actions are performed (Cartwright et al, 2001). Schein (1990: 111) defined organizational culture as follows: '... a pattern of basic assumptions, invented, discovered, or developed by a given group, as it learns to cope with its problems of external adaptation and internal integration, that has worked well enough to be considered valid and therefore is to be taught to new members as the correct way to perceive, think and feel in relation to those problems'.

Organizational culture is not necessarily the overt behaviour which can be observed when visiting an organization. It is not only the written policy or values, but also the basic assumptions which influence the behaviour, architecture and layout of offices (Schein, 1983). Organizational culture includes traditions, events and established practices which created patterns of relating and problem solving in the organization. It is the rules and guidelines prescribing to participants how they should participate, how they should act and what they should not do.

Organizational culture should not be confused with organizational climate. Organizational climate can be observed and measured more directly and has a longer research history than organizational culture (Schein, 1990). Organizational climate can be described as a psychological state which is strongly influenced by organizational factors such as systems, structures and management behaviour.

Components of organizational culture

Organizational culture consists of the following four components (Cummings and Huse, 1989):

- **Assumptions**. Assumptions describe what is important and how problems in the organization are solved. These assumptions could be studied through intensive observation, focused questions and intensive self-analysis. People are normally unaware of these assumptions.

- **Values and beliefs**. People cannot easily become aware of their values and beliefs. Values describe the things which are important for organization members. Values can be studied by using interviews, observation and questionnaires. A questionnaire is normally less useful in measuring values, because it makes assumptions about the dimensions which should be studied.

- **Behavioural norms**. Behavioural norms are unwritten behavioural rules of which people can be aware. These norms prescribe how people should behave in specific situations.

- **Artefacts**. Artefacts are the highest level of cultural awareness and refer to creations which are visual manifestations of other cultural levels. It includes the observable behaviour of employees, dress, structures, systems, policies, procedures, rules, records, annual reports and physical layout of the organization. It is, however, difficult to judge artefacts accurately – they are not necessarily a reliable indicator of how people behave.

The development of organizational culture

Organizational culture develops as a result of previous crises, achievements, successes and failures in an organization. These aspects lead to the formation of assumptions regarding the following aspects: reality, truth, time, human nature and human relations (Schein, 1990). The founders of an organization traditionally have a major impact on the organization's culture (Schein, 1985). They are unconstrained by previous customs or ideologies. The culture develops as employees identify with the leader as role model. Once an organization's culture is started and begins to develop, there are a number of practices which can help solidify the acceptance of core values and ensure that the culture maintains itself. These practices include:

- **Selection of entry-level personnel**. The first step is to select candidates whose characteristics and values fit those of the organization. Evidence indicates that those candidates who have a realistic job preview of the culture will turn out better.

- **Placement in the job**. New personnel are subjected to a series of different experiences, the purpose of which is to enable them to question the organization's norms and values and to decide whether or not they can accept them.

- **Job mastery**. Once the initial cultural shock is over, the next step is that the employee should master his or her job.

- **Measuring and rewarding performance**. The next step of the socialization process consists of meticulous attention to measuring operational results and to rewarding individual performance.

- **Adherence to important values**. The next step involves careful adherence to the organization's most important values. Identification with these values helps employees reconcile personal sacrifices brought about by their membership of the organization.

- **Reinforcing the stories and folklore**. The next step involves reinforcing organizational folklore. This entails keeping alive stories which validate the organization's culture and way of doing things. The folklore helps to explain why the organization does things in a particular way.

- **Recognition and promotion**. The final step is the recognition and promotion of individuals who have done their jobs well and who can serve as role models to new people in the organization.

Changing organizational culture

Before an organization can change its culture, it should become aware of the current culture. Organizations which do not have knowledge of their culture are vulnerable, especially because of the covert nature of organizational culture. Awareness could be regarded as the first step which is necessary to facilitate change. Outsiders can play an important role in helping organizations to become aware of their culture.

Harvey and Brown (1996) point out that culture change requires a change in the hearts and beliefs of employees. Motivation to change can be enhanced by creating dissatisfaction with the status quo, and by encouraging employees to believe that the change is possible and wanted. Cultural change should not be forced on people. A participative approach is required to influence the deepest level of culture. A top-down approach to change may be used when a single culture exists or when the focus is on changing norms rather than assumptions. Strategies which could be implemented to change organizational culture include developing a shared vision and mission, defining objectives and target behaviour, and the implementation and evaluation of interventions. The proactive involvement of the manager and management staff is crucial for cultural change. Employees should be encouraged to change, and a fair performance appraisal and reward system should be used to recognize performance.

Summary

- Organizational structure is characterized by four dimensions, namely hierarchy of authority, division of labour, spans of control, and line and staff positions.

- Types of organizational structures include mechanistic versus organic structures and matrix organizations.

- There are no good or bad structures. A poor structure is one which is inappropriate for the specific goal that the organization wants to achieve.

- Organization development is a long-range effort to improve an organization's ability to cope with change and its problem solving and renewal processes through effective management of the organizational culture.

- Organization development is aimed at improving the effectiveness of the organization and its members by means of a systematic change programme.

- Forces that lead to a need for organization development include socio-economic factors, customer expectations, government factors such as laws and regulations, technological advancements, stakeholders' expectations, the changing nature of expectations of employees and unions, and globalization and increased competition. Organization development has six characteristics, namely planned change, collaboration, performance, humanistic values, a systems approach and a scientific approach.

- The stages in organization development are anticipating change, developing the consultant–client relationship, organizational diagnosis, interventions, self-renewal, monitoring and stabilizing action programmes, and the management of change.

- Organizational culture includes traditions, events and established practices which created patterns of relating and problem solving in the organization. It is the rules and guidelines prescribing to participants how they should participate, how they should act and what they should not do. It consists of four components, namely assumptions, values and beliefs, norms and artefacts.

- Organizational culture develops as a result of previous crises, achievements, successes and failures in an organization.

- Before an organization can change its culture, it should become aware of the current culture. Motivation to change can be enhanced by creating dissatisfaction with the status quo, and by encouraging employees to believe that the change is possible and wanted. A participative approach is required to influence the deepest level of culture.

Key concepts and terms

Anticipating change
Behaviour modelling
Centralization
Change
Coaching
Collaboration
Complexity
Confrontation meeting
Consultant–client relationship
Coordination
Counselling
Division of labour
Hierarchy of authority
Humanistic value
Inter-group interventions
Intervention
Life and career planning
Management by objectives
Matrix organization
Organic structure

Organization
Organizational design
Organization development
Organizational diagnosis
Performance
Planned change
Quality circle
Refreezing
Scientific approach
Sensitivity training laboratories
Socio-technical system
Span of control
Staff positions
Strategic planning
Survey feedback
System
Transactional analysis
Unfreezing
Wellness promotion

Sample essay titles

- Which changes necessitate organization development?
- How can organizational change be effectively managed?
- What are the differences between organizational climate and culture?
- What are the dimensions of organizational culture? How can organizational culture be studied?

Further reading

Books

Burke, W.W. (2005). 'Implementation and continuing the change effort'. In: W.J. Rothwell and R.L. Sullivan (Eds), *Practicing Organization Development*, (2nd Ed.). San Francisco: Pfeiffer, 313–326.

Cummings, T.G., and Worley, C.G. (2005). *Organization Development and Change*, (8th Ed.). Cincinnati: South-Western College Publishing.

Journal articles

De Caluwé, L., and Vermaak, H. (2004). Change paradigms: An overview. *Organization Development Journal*, 22, 9–18.

Rushmer, R.K. (1997). How do we measure the effectiveness of team building? Is it good enough? Team management systems: A case study. *Journal of Management Development*, 16, 93–110.

References

Adams, J.S. (1963). Toward an understanding of equity. *Journal of Abnormal and Social Psychology*, 67, 422–436.

Aft, L.S. (1985). *Wage and Salary Administration: A Guide to Job Evaluation*. Reston, VA: Reston Publishing Company.

Agars, M., and Kotke, J. (2005). 'Innovations in diversity management.' In: R. Burke and C. Cooper (Eds), *Reinventing Human Resource Management*. London: Routledge.

Ajzen, I. (2001). Nature and operation of attitudes. *Annual Review of Psychology*, 52, 27–58.

Ajzen I., and Fishbein, M. (1977). Attitude-behavior relations: A theoretical analysis and review of empirical literature. *Psychological Bulletin*, 84, 888–918.

Ajzen, I., and Fishbein, M. (1980). *Understanding Attitudes and Predicting Social Behaviour*. Upper Saddle River, NJ: Prentice Hall.

Alderfer, C. (1969). An empirical test of a new theory of human needs. *Organizational Behavior and Human Performance*, 4, 142–175.

Allport, G.W. (1961). *Pattern and Growth in Personality*. London: Holt, Rinehart and Winston.

Antonio, A., and Cooper, C. (2005). *Research Companion to Organizational Health Psychology*. Cheltenham: Edward Elgar Publishing.

Antonovsky, A. (1987). *Unraveling the Mystery of Health: How People Manage Stress and Stay Well*. San Francisco: Jossey-Bass.

Argyris, C. (1970). *Intervention Theory and Method: A Behavioral Science View*. Reading, MA: Addison-Wesley.

Argyris, C. (1990) *Overcoming Organizational Defenses: Facilitating Organizational Learning*. Boston: Allyn and Bacon.

Argyris, C., and Schön, D.A. (1978). *Organizational Learning: A Theory of Action Perspective*. Reading, MA: Addison-Wesley.

Argyris, C., Putnam, R., and Smith, D.M. (1985). *Action Science*. San Francisco, CA: Jossey-Bass.

Armstrong, M. (2004). *Performance Management: Key Strategies and Practical Guidelines*. London: Kogan Page.

Armstrong, M. (2006). *A Handbook of Human Resource Management Practice*. London: Kogan Page.

Armstrong, M., Cummins, A., Hastings, S., and Wood, W. (2003). *Job Evaluation: A Guide to Achieving Equal Pay*. London: Kogan Page.

Arnold, J., Cooper, C.L., and Robinson, I.T. (1995). *Work Psychology: Understanding Human Behaviour in the Workplace*, (2nd Ed.). London: Pitman Publishing.

Aronsson, G., and Gustafsson, K. (2005). Sickness presenteeism: Prevalence, attendance-pressure factors, and an outline of a model for research. *Journal of Occupational and Environmental Medicine*, 47, 958–966.

Aronsson, G., Gustafson, K., and Dallner, M. (2000). Sick but yet at work: An empirical study of sickness presenteeism. *Journal of Epidemiological Health*, 54, 502–509.

Aronsson, G., Svensson, L., and Gusstafson, K. (2003). Unwinding, recuperation, and health among compulsory school and high school teachers in Sweden. *International Journal of Stress Management*, 10, 217–234.

Arthur, D. (1995). The importance of body language. *HR Focus*, 72, 22–23.

Arvey, R.D., and Faley, R.A. (1988). *Fairness in Selecting Employees*, (2nd Ed.). Reading, MA: Addison-Wesley.

Arvey, R.D., and Murphy, K.R. (1998). Performance evaluation in work settings. *Annual Review of Psychology*, 49, 141–168.

Axtell, R.E. (1991). *The Do's and Taboos of Body Language Around the World*. New York: Wiley.

Azar, B. (1996). People are becoming smarter: Why? *APA Monitor*, 27, 20.

Bales, R.F. (1953). 'The equilibrium problem in small groups.' In: T. Parsons, R.F. Bales and E.A. Shils (Eds), *Working Papers in the Theory of Action*. Glencoe, IL: Free Press, 111–161.

Bandura, A. (1977). Self-efficacy: Toward a unifying theory of behaviour change. *Psychological Review*, 84, 191–215.

Bandura, A. (1982). Self-efficacy mechanism in human agency. *American Psychologist*, 37, 122–147.

Bandura, A. (1989). Human agency in social cognitive theory. *American Psychologist*, 44, 1175–1184.

Barker, R.T., Johnson, I.W., and Pearce, G. (1995). Enhancing the student listening skills and environment. *Business Communication Quarterly*, 58, 28–33.

Barling, J., Kelloway, K., and Zacharatos, A. (2002). 'Occupational safety.' In: P. Warr (Ed.), *Psychology at Work*, (5th Ed.). London: Penguin Books, 253–275.

Barnard, C.I. (1938). *The Functions of the Executive*. Cambridge, MA: Harvard University Press.

Barnes-Farrell, J. (2001). 'Performance appraisal.' In: M. London (Ed.), *How People Evaluate Others in Organizations*. London: LEA, 135–150.

Bar-On, R. (1997). *BarOn Emotional Quotient Inventory*. Toronto: Multi-Health Systems.

Baron, R.A., and Greenberg, J. (1990). *Behavior in Organisations: Understanding and Managing the Human Side of Work*, (3rd Ed.). Boston, MA: Allyn and Bacon.

Barrick, M.R. (2001). *Personality Testing: Controversial No More*. Paper presented at the 4th Annual Conference of the Society for Industrial Psychology, Pretoria, South Africa, June 2001.

Barrick, M.B., and Mount, M.K. (2005). Yes, personality matters: Moving on to more important matters. *Human Performance*, 18, 359–372.

Barrick, M.R., and Mount, M.K. (1991). The big five personality dimensions and job performance: A meta-analysis. *Personnel Psychology*, 44, 1–26.

Barrick, M.R., Mount, M.K., and Judge, T.A. (2001). Personality and performance at the beginning of the new millenium: What do we know and where do we go next? *International Journal of Selection and Assessment*, 9, 9–30.

Barry, B., and Stewart, G.L. (1997). Composition, process and performance in self-managed groups: the role of personality. *Journal of Applied Psychology*, 82, 62–78.

Bass, B.M. (1981). *Stogdill's Handbook of Leadership: A Survey of Theory and Research*. New York: The Free Press.

Bass, B.M. (1985). *Leadership and Performance Beyond Expectation*. New York: Free Press.

Bass, B.M. (1990). From transactional to transformational leadership: Learning to share the vision. *Organizational Dynamics*, 18, 19–31.

Bass, B.M. (1997). 'Concepts of leadership.' In: R.P. Vecchio (Ed.), Leadership: *Understanding the Dynamics of Power and Influence in Organizations*. Notre Dame, IN: University of Notre Dame Press, 3–23.

Bass, B.M. (1998). *Transformational Leadership: Industrial, Military, and Educational Impact*. Mahwah, NJ: Erlbaum.

Baumeister, R.F. (1982). A self-presentational view of social phenomena. *Psychological Bulletin*, 91, 3–26.

Beach, D.S. (1985). *Personnel: The Management of People at Work*, (5th Ed.). London: Macmillan.

Beckhard, R. (1967). The confrontation meeting. *Harvard Business Review*, 45(2), 149–155.

Beehr, T., and Bowling, N. (2005). 'Hardy personality, stress and health.' In: C. Cooper (Ed.), *Handbook of Stress Medicine and Health*. Boca Raton, Fl: CRC Press.

Beer, M., and Walton, E. (1990). Developing the competitive organization: Interventions and strategies. *American Psychologist*, 45, 154–161.

Berger, L.A., and Berger, D.R. (2000). *The Compensation Handbook*, (4th Ed.). New York: McGraw-Hill.

Berry, J.W. (1989). Imposed etics-emics-derived etics: The operationalizations of a compelling idea. *International Journal of Psychology*, 24, 721–735.

Bertua, C., Anderson, N., and Salgado, J.F. (2005). The predictive validity of cognitive ability tests: A UK meta-analysis. *Journal of Occupational and Organizational Psychology*, 78, 387–409.

Blake, R.R., and Mouton, J.S. (1964). *The Managerial Grid*. Houston, TX: Gulf.

Block, J. (1995). A contrarian view of the five factor approach to personality description. *Psychological Bulletin*, 117, 187–213.

Borman, W.C., and Motowidlo, S.J. (1997). Task performance and contextual performance: The meaning for personnel selection research. *Human Performance*, 10, 99–109.

Bormann, E.G., and Bormann, N.C. (1988). *Effective Small Group Communication*. Minneapolis, MN: Burgess.

Brannick, M.T., and Levine, E.L. (2002). *Job Analysis: Methods, Research, and Applications for Human Resource Management in the New Millennium*. Thousand Oaks, CA: Sage Publications.

Brayfield, A.H. and Crockett, W.H. (1955). Employee attitudes and employee performance. *Psychological Bulletin*, 52, 396–424.

Breckler, S.J. (1984). Empirical validation of affect, behavior, and cognition as distinct components of attitude. *Journal of Personality and Social Psychology*, 47, 1191–1205.

Brewerton, P., and Millward, L. (2004). *Organisational Research Methods*. London: Sage.

Brodsky, C. (1976). The Harassed Worker. Lexington, MA: D.C. Heath and Company.

Brown, S.D., and Lent, R.W. (2005). *Career Development and Counseling: Putting Theory and Research to Work*. Hoboken, NJ: Wiley.

Bryars, L.L., and Rue, L.W. (1991). *Human Resource Management*, (3rd Ed.). Homewood, IL: Irwin.

Bryars, L.L., and Rue, L.W. (1994). *Human Resource Management*, (4th Ed.). Burr Ridge, IL: Irwin.

Bryson, J., and Hosken, C. (2005). What does it mean to be a culturally competent I/O psychologist in New Zealand? *New Zealand Journal of Psychology*, 34, 69–76.

Bundel, T. (2004). *Effective Organizational Communications*. London: Prentice-Hall.

Burke, R., and Cooper, C. (2004). *Leading in Turbulent Times*. Oxford: Oxford University Press.

Burke, R., and Cooper, C. (2006). *Inspiring Leaders*. London: Routledge.

Burke, W.W. (1994). *Organizational Development: A Normative View*, (2nd Ed.). Reading, MA: Addison-Wesley.

Burke, W.W. (2005). 'Implementation and continuing the change effort.' In: W.J. Rothwell and R.L. Sullivan (Eds), *Practicing Organization Development*, (2nd Ed.). San Francisco, CA: Pfeiffer, 313–326.

Burns, T., and Stalker, G.M. (1961). *The Management of Innovation*. London: Tavistock.

Campion, M.A., and Berger, C.J. (1990). Conceptual integration and empirical test of job design and compensation relationships. *Personnel Psychology*, 43, 525–553.

Caprara, G.V., Barbaranelli, C., Hahn, R., and Comrey, A.L. (2001). Factor analysis of the NEO PI-R inventory and the Comrey Personality Scales in Italy and the United States. *Personality and Individual Differences*, 30, 217–228.

Carr, A. (2004). *Positive Psychology: The Science of Happiness and Human Strengths*. Hove: Brunner-Routledge.

Cartwright, S., Cooper, C., and Earley, C. (2001). *International Handbook of Organizational Culture and Climate*. New York: Wiley.

Carver, C.S., and Scheier, M.F. (2002). 'Optimism.' In: C.R. Snyder and S.J. Lopez (Eds). *Handbook of Positive Psychology*. Oxford: Oxford University Press, 231–243.

Cascio, W.F. (2001). Knowledge creation for practical solutions appropriate to a changing world of work. *South African Journal of Industrial Psychology*, 27, 14–16.

Cattell, R.B. (1965). *The Scientific Analysis of Personality*. London: Penguin Books.

Cederblom, D., and Pemerl, D.E. (2002). From performance appraisal to performance management: One agency's experience. *Public Personnel Management*, 31, 131–140.

Chamorro-Premuzic, T. (2007). *Personality and Individual Differences*. London: Blackwell.

Chen, C., Gostafson, D., and Lee, Y. (2002). The effect of a qualitative decision aid on group polarization. *Group Decision and Negotiation*, 11, 329–344.

Cheung, F.M. (2004). Use of western and indigenously developed personality tests in Asia. *Applied Psychology: An International Review*, 53, 173–191.

Cheung, F.M., Leung, K., Zhang, J.X., Sun, H.F., Gun, Y.G., Song, W.Z., and Xie, D. (2001). Indigenous Chinese personality constructs: Is the five-factor model complete? *Journal of Cross-Cultural Psychology*, 32, 407–433.

Church, A.T., and Lonner, W.J. (1998). The cross-cultural perspective in the study of personality: Rationale and current research. *Journal of Cross-Cultural Psychology*, 29, 32–62.

Church, A.T., Katigbak, M.S., and Reyes, J.A.S. (1996). Toward a taxonomy of trait adjectives in Filipino: Comparing personality lexicons across cultures. *European Journal of Personality*, 10, 3–24.

Clarke, S., and Robertson, I. (2005). A meta analytic review of the big five personality factors and accident involvement in occupational settings. *Journal of Occupational and Organizational Psychology*, 78, 355–376.

Clawson, J. (2006). 'The inspirational nature of level three leadership.' In: R. Burke and C. Cooper (Eds), *Inspiring Leaders*. London: Routledge, 105–116.

Clegg, S., Kornberger, M., and Pitsis, T. (2005). *Managing and Organizations*. London: Sage.

Conger, J.A., and Kanungo, R.N. (1987). Toward a behavioral theory of charismatic leadership in organizational settings. *The Academy of Management Review*, 12, 637–647.

Conger, J.A., and Kanungo, R.N. (1998). *Charismatic Leadership in Organizations*. Thousand Oaks, CA: Sage Publishers.

Conner, M., and Clawson, J. (2004). *Creating a Learning Culture*. Cambridge: Cambridge University Press.

Conte, J.M., Dean, M.A., Ringenbach, K.L., Moran, S.K., and Landy, F.J. (2005). The relationship between work attitudes and job analysis ratings: Do rating scale type and task discretion matter. *Human Performance*, 18, 1–21.

Cooper, C. (2005). *Leadership and Management in the 21st Century*. Oxford: Oxford University Press.

Cooper, D., Robertson, I., and Tinline, G. (2003). *The Psychology of Personnel Selection*. London: Routledge.

Costa, P.T., and McCrae, R.R. (1988). Personality in adulthood: A six-year longitudinal study of self-reports and spouse ratings on the NEO Personality Inventory. *Journal of Personality and Social Psychology*, 54, 853–863.

Coyle-Shapiro, J., Shore, L., Taylor, S., and Tetrick, L. (2004). *The Employment Relationship*. Oxford: Oxford University Press.

Cummings, T.G., and Huse, E.F. (1989). *Organization Development and Change*, (4th Ed.). St. Paul: West.

Cummings, T.G., and Worley, C.G. (2005). *Organization Development and Change*, (8th Ed.). Cincinnati, OH: South-Western College Publishing.

Dawis, R.V., and Lofquist, L.H. (1984). *A Psychological Theory of Work Adjustment: An Individual Differences Model and its Applications*. Minneapolis, University of Minnesota Press.

De Caluwé, L., and Vermaak, H. (2004). Change paradigms: An overview. *Organization Development Journal*, 22, 9–18.

DeGroot, T., and Kluemper, D. (2007). Evidence of predictive and incremental validity of personality factors, vocal attractiveness, and the situational interview. *International Journal of Selection and Assessment*, 15, 30–39.

Den Hartog, D.N., Boselie, P., and Paauwe, J. (2004). Performance management: A model and research agenda. *Applied Psychology: An International Review*, 53, 556–569.

Derlega, V.J., Winstead, B.A., and Jones, W.H. (2005). *Personality: Contemporary Theory*, (3rd Ed.). Belmont, CA: Wadsworth.

Dienesch, R.M. and Liden, R.E. (1986). Leader-member exchange model of leadership: A critique and further development. *The Academy of Management Review*, 11, 618–634.

Digman, J.M. (1989). Five robust trait dimensions: Development, stability, and utility. *Journal of Personality*, 57, 195–214.

Digman, J.M. (1997). Higher-order factors of the Big Five. *Journal of Personality and Social Psychology*, 73, 1246–1256.

Dimock, H.G. (1987). *Groups: Leadership and Group Development*. San Diego, CA: University Associates.

Dobbins, G.H., Cardy, R.L., and Platz-Vieno, S.J. (1990). A contingency approach to appraisal satisfaction: An initial investigation of the joint effects of organizational variables and appraisal characteristics. *Journal of Management*, 16, 619–632.

Drennan, D. (1992). *Transforming Company Culture*. Berkshire: McGraw-Hill.

Drucker, P.F. (1954). *The Practice of Management*. New York: Harper and Row.

Duckitt, J. and Foster, D. (1991). Introduction to the special issue: Race, social attitudes, prejudice. *South African Journal of Psychology*, 21, 199–202.

Dunbar, E. (1993). The role of psychological stress and prior experience in the use of personal protective equipment. *Journal of Safety Research*, 24, 181–187.

Dunette, M. (1976). *Handbook of industrial and organizational psychology*. Chicago: Rand McNally College Publishing Company.

Dyer, W.G. (1995). *Team Building: Current Issues and New Alternatives*, (3rd Ed.). Reading, MA: AddisonWesley.

Edenborough, R. (2007). *Assessment Methods in Recruitment Selection and Performance: A Manager's Guide to Psychometric Testing, Interviews and Assessment Centers*. London: Kogan Page.

Einarsen, S. (1999). The nature and causes of bullying at work. *International Journal of Manpower*, 20, 16–27.

Einarsen, S., Hoel, H., Zapf, D., and Cooper, C.L. (2003). 'The concept of bullying at work: The European tradition.' In: S. Einarsen, H. Hoel, D. Zapf, and C.L. Cooper (Eds), *Bullying and Emotional Abuse in the Workplace: International Perspectives in Research and Practice*. London: Taylor and Francis, 3–30.

Elliot, C., and Turnbull, S. (2005). *Critical Thinking in Human Resource Development*. London: Routledge.

Eysenck, H.J. (1992). Four ways five factors are not basic. *Personality and Individual Differences*, 6, 667–673.

Faragher, E.B., Cass, M., and Cooper, C. (2005). The relationship between job satisfaction and health: A meta-analysis. *Occupational Environmental Medicine*, 62, 105–112.

Feldman, D.C. (1984). The development and enforcement of group norms. *Academy of Management Review*, 9, 47–53.

Feldman, J. (1992). The case for non-analytic performance appraisal. *Human Resource Management Review*, 2, 9–35.

Festinger, L. (1957). *A Theory of Cognitive Dissonance*. Evanston, IL: Row, Perterson and Company.

Fiedler, F.E. (1967). *A Theory of Leadership Effectiveness*. New York: McGraw-Hill.

Fishbein, M. (Ed.). (1967). *Readings in Attitude Theory and Measurement*. New York: Wiley.

Fishbein, M., and Ajzen, J. (1975). *Belief, Attitude, Intention and Behaviour: An Introduction to Theory and Research.* Reading, MA: Addison-Wesley.

Fiske, D.W. (1949). Consistency of factorial structures of personality ratings from different sources. *Journal of Abnormal and Social Psychology*, 44, 329–344.

Fitzgerald, L.E. (1995). Sexual harassment: Violence against women in the workplace. *American Psychologist*, 48, 1070–1076.

Fitzgerald, L.E., Drasgow, F., Hulin, C.L., Gelfand, M.J., and Magley, V.J. (1997). Antecedents and consequences of sexual harassment in organizations: A test of an integrated model. *Journal of Applied Psychology*, 82, 578–589.

Fogli, L., and Whitney, K. (1991). ServiceFirst: A Test to Select Service Oriented Personnel. Symposium conducted at the Annual Meeting of the American Psychological Association, San Francisco.

French, J.R.P., and Raven, B. (1959). 'The bases of social power.' In: D. Cartwright (Ed.), *Studies in Social Power.* Ann Arbor, MI: Institute for Social Research, 150–167.

French, W.L., and Bell, C.H. (1999). *Organizational Development: Behavioral Science Interventions for Organization Improvement*, (5th Ed.). Englewood Cliffs, NJ: Prentice Hall.

Furnham, A. (1997). *The Psychology of Behaviour at Work: The Individual in the Organization.* Sussex, UK: Psychology Press.

Galbraith, J., Downey, D., and Kates, A. (2002). *Designing Dynamic Organizations.* New York: AMACOM.

Gelfand, M.J., Fitzgerald, L.F., and Drasgow, F. (1995). The structure of sexual harassment: A confirmatory analysis across cultures and settings. *Journal of Vocational Behavior*, 47, 164–177.

Gelfand, M.J., Erez, M., and Aycan, Z. (2007). Cross-cultural organizational behaviour. *Annual Review of Psychology*, 58, 479–514.

George, J.M., and Brief, A.P. (1992). Feeling good – doing good: A conceptual analysis of the mood at work – organizational spontaneity relationship. *Psychological Bulletin*, 112, 310–329.

Gerber, P.D., Nel, P.S., and Van Dyk, P.S. (1995). *Human Resources Management*, (3rd Ed.). Halfway House: Southern Book Publishers.

Gerhart, B., and Milkovich, G. (1992). 'Employee compensation: research and practice.' In: M.D. Dunnette and L.M. Hough (Eds), *Handbook of Industrial and Organizational Psychology.* CA: Psychological Press.

Gersick, C.J.G. (1988). Time and transition in work teams: Toward a new model of group development. *Academy of Management Journal*, 31, 9–41.

Gibson, R.L., and Mitchell, M.H. (2006). *Introduction to Career Counseling for the 21st Century.* New Jersey: Merrill Prentice Hall.

Goetzel, R.Z., Long, S.R., Ozminkowski, R.J., Hawkins, K., Wang, S., and Lynch, W.D. (2004). Health, absence, disability, and presenteeism: Cost estimates of certain physical and mental health conditions affecting U.S. employers. *Journal of Occupational and Environmental Medicine*, 48, 398–412.

Goffman, E. (1959). *The Presentation of Self in Everyday Life.* New York: Doubleday.

Goldberg, L.R. (1990). An alternative 'description of personality': The big five factor structure. *Journal of Personality and Social Psychology*, 59, 1216–1229.

Goldberg, L.R. (1993). The structure of phenotypic personality traits. *American Psychologist*, 48, 26–34.

Goleman, D. (1995). *Emotional Intelligence.* New York: Bantam Books.

Gordon, J.R. (2002). A diagnostic approach to organizational behavior. Boston, MA: Allyn & Bacon.

Graen, G.B., and Uhl-Bien, M. (1995). Relationship-based approach to leadership: Development of leader-member exchange (LMX) theory of leadership over 25 years: Applying a multi-level multi-domain perspective. *Leadership Quarterly*, 6, 219–247.

Gray, J.L., and Starke, F.A. (1980). *Organizational Behavior: Concepts and Applications*, (2nd Ed.). Columbus, OH: Charles E. Merril Publishing Company.

Grote, R.C. (2002). *The Performance Appraisal Question and Answer Book: A Survival Guide for Managers.* New York: American Management Association.

Hackman, J.R. (1987). 'The design of work teams.' In: J.W. Lorsch (Ed.), *Handbook of Organizational Behavior.* Englewood Cliffs, NJ: Prentice Hall, 315–339.

Hackman, J.R., and Oldham, G.R. (1976). Motivation through the design of work: Test of a theory. *Organizational Behaviour and Human Performance*, 16, 250–279.

Hall, J.A. (1985). 'Male and female nonverbal behaviour.' In: A.W. Siegman and S. Feldstein (Eds), *Multichannel Integrations of Nonverbal Behavior.* Hillsdale, NJ: Lawrence Erlbaum, 195–226.

Hall, D. T. (1976). *Careers in organizations.* Glenview, IL: Scott, Foresman.

Halpin, A.W., and Winer, B.J. (1957). 'A factorial study of the leader behavior descriptions.' In: R.M. Stogdill and A.E. Coons (Eds), *Leader Behavior: Its Description and Measurement*. Columbus, OH: Bureau of Business Research, Ohio State University.

Hambleton, R.K., and Oakland, T. (2004). Advances, issues and research in testing practices around the world. *Applied Psychology: An International Review*, 53, 155–156.

Hart, P.M. (1999). Predicting employee life satisfaction: A coherent model of personality, work and non-work experiences, and domain satisfaction. *Journal of Applied Psychology*, 84, 564–584.

Harvey, D.F., and Brown, D.R. (1996). *An Experiential Approach to Organization Development*, (5th Ed.). Upper Saddle River, NJ: Prentice Hall.

Heneman, H.G., Schwab, D.P., Fossum, J.A., and Dyer, L.D. (1989). Personnel/human resource management (4th Ed.). Homewood, IL: Irwin.

Hersey, P., and Blanchard, K.H. (1982). *Management of Organizational Behavior: Utilizing Human Resources*, (4th Ed.). Englewood Cliffs, NJ: Prentice Hall.

Herzberg, F., Mausner, B., and Snyderman, B.B. (1959). *The Motivation to Work*, (2nd Ed.). New York: Wiley.

Hoag, B., and Cooper, C. (2006). *Managing Value-Based Organizations*. Cheltenham: Edward Elgar Publications.

Hoel, H., Faragher, B., and Cooper, C.L. (2004). Bullying is detrimental to health, but all bullying behaviours are not necessarily equally damaging. *British Journal of Guidance and Counselling*, 32, 367–387.

Hoffmann, D., and Stetzer, A. (1998). The role of safety climate and communication in accident interpretation: Implications of learning from negative events. *Academy of Management Journal*, 41, 644–657.

Hoffmann, D.A., and Stetzer, A. (1996). A cross-level investigation of factors influencing unsafe behavior and accidents. *Personnel Psychology*, 49, 307–339.

Hofstede, G. (1980). *Culture's Consequences: International Differences in Work-Related Values*. Beverly Hills, CA: Sage.

Hogan, R., and Kaiser, R.B. (2005). What we know about leadership. Review of General Psychology.

Holland, J.L. (1997). *Making Vocational Choices*, (3rd Ed.). Odessa, FL: Psychological Assessment Resources.

Hough, L., and Furnham, A. (2003). 'Use of personality variables in work settings.' In: W. Borman, D. Ilgen, and R. Klimoski, (Eds), *Handbook of Psychology*. New York: Wiley, 131–169.

Hough, L.M., and Oswald, F.L. (2000). Personnel selection: Looking toward the future – remembering the past. *Annual Review of Psychology*, 51, 631–664.

Hulin, C.L. (1991). 'Adaptation, persistence and commitment in organisations.' In: M.D. Dunette and L.M. Hough (Eds), *Handbook of Industrial and Organizational Psychology*, (2nd Ed.). Palo Alto, CA: Consulting Psychologists Press, 445–507.

Ilgen, D.R. (1990). Health issues at work. *American Psychologist*, 45, 273–283.

Infante, D.A., and Gorden, W.I. (1985). Superiors' argumentativeness and verbal aggression as predictors of subordinates' satisfaction. *Human Communication Research*, 12, 117–125.

Ivancevich, J.M., and Glueck, W.G. (1989). *Foundations of Personnel: Human Resource Management*, (4th Ed.). Homewood, IL: Irwin.

Ivey, A.E. (1988). *Intentional Interviewing and Counseling: Facilitating Client Development*. Pacific Grove, CA: Brooks/Cole.

Jang, K.L., Livesley, W.J., and Vernon, P.A. (1996). Hereditability of the big five personality dimensions and their facets: A twin study. *Journal of Personality*, 64, 577–591.

Janis, I. (1972). *Victims of group think*. Boston: Houghton-Mifflin.

Jennifer, D., Cowie, H., and Ananiadou, K. (2003). Perceptions and experience of workplace bullying in five different working populations. *Aggressive Behavior*, 29, 489–496.

Jewell, L.N., and Reitz, H.J. (1981). *Group Effectiveness in Organisations*. Glenview, IL: Scott Foresman.

John, O.P. (1990). 'The "Big Five" factor taxonomy: Dimensions of personality in the natural language and in questionnaires.' In: L. Pervin (Ed.), *Handbook of Personality: Theory and Research*. New York: Guilford Press, 66–100.

Johnson, D.W. (1997). *Reaching Out: Interpersonal Effectiveness and Self-Actualisation*, (4th Ed.). Englewood Cliffs, NJ: Prentice Hall.

Johnson, D.W., and Johnson, F.P. (1994). *Joining Together Groups: Group Theory and Skills*, (5th Ed.). Englewood Cliffs, NJ: Prentice Hall.

Judge, T.A., and Ilies, R. (2002). Relationship of personality to performance motivation: A meta-analytic review. *Journal of Applied Psychology*, 87, 797–807.

Judge, T.A., and Watanabe, S. (1993). Another look at the job satisfaction–life satisfaction relationship. *Journal of Applied Psychology*, 78, 939–948.

Judge, T.A., Thoresen, C.J., Bono, J.E., and Patton, G.K. (2001) The job satisfaction–job performance relationship: A qualitative and quantitative review. *Psychological Bulletin*, 127, 376–407.

Kahya, E. (2006). A revision of a job evaluation system. *Journal of Advanced Nursing*, 56, 314–324.

Karasek, R.A. (1979). Job demands, job decision latitude and mental strain: Implications for job redesign. *Administrative Science Quarterly*, 24, 285–308.

Katz, D., and Kahn, R.L. (1978). *The Social Psychology of Organizations*, (2nd Ed.). New York: Wiley.

Kauffeld, S. (2006). Self-directed work groups and team competence. *Journal of Occupational and Organizational Psychology*, 79, 1–21.

Kelloway, E.K., and Barling, J. (1991). Job characteristics, role stress and mental health. *Journal of Occupational Psychology*, 64, 291–304.

Kepes, S., and Delery, J. (2006). 'Designing effective HRM systems.' In: R. Burke and C. Cooper (Eds), *The HR Revolution: Why Putting People First Matters*. Oxford: Elsevier, 55–78.

Keyes, C.L.M. (2002). The mental health continuum: From languishing to flourishing in life. *Journal of Health and Social Behavior*, 43, 207–222.

Kidd, J.M. (2002). 'Careers and career management.' In: P. Warr (Ed.), *Psychology at Work*, (5th Ed.). London: Penguin Books, 178–202.

Kirkpatrick, D.L. (1959). Techniques for evaluating training programs. *Journal of the American Society of Training Directors*, 13, 3–26.

Kivimaki, M., Head, J., and Ferrie, J.E. (2005). Working while ill as a risk factor for serious coronary events: The Whitehall II studies. *American Journal of Public Health*, 95, 98–102.

Klein, C., Derouin, R.E. and Salas, E. (2006). Uncovering workplace interpersonal skills: A review, framework, and research agenda In G.P. Hodgkinson & J.K. Ford (Eds.), *International review of industrial and organizational psychology: Volume 21*. Chichester: John Wiley and Sons.

Klikauer, T. (2007). *Communications and Management at Work*. London: Palgrave.

Kluckhohn, F., and Strodtbeck, F. (1961). *Variation in Value Orientations*. Evanston, IL: Row, Peterson.

Kobasa, S.C. (1982). 'The hardy personality: towards a social psychology of stress and health.' In: G.S. Sanders and J. Suls (Eds), *Social Psychology of Health and Illness*. Hillsdale, NJ: Erlbaum, 3–32.

Kompier, M., and Cooper, C. (1999). *Preventing Stress, Improving Productivity*. London: Routledge.

Kozlowski, S.W., and Bell, B.S. (2003). 'Work groups and teams in organizations.' In: W. Borman, D. Ilgen and R. Klimoski (Eds), *Handbook of Psychology*. New York: Wiley, 333–375.

Kraiger, K., Ford, J., and Salas, E. (1993). Application of cognitive skill based and affective theories of learning comes in new methods of training evaluation. *Journal of Applied Psychology*, 78, 311–28.

Kraut, A.I. (1976). 'New frontiers for assessment centres.' In: K.M. Rowland, M. London, G.R. Ferris, and J.L. Sherman (Eds), *Current Issues in Personnel Management*. Boston, MA: Allyn and Bacon.

Kristensen, T.S. (1991). Sickness absenteeism and work strain among Danish slaughterhouse workers: An analysis of absence from work regarded as coping behaviour. *Social Science and Medicine*, 32, 15–27.

Labriola, M., Christensen, K.B., Lund, T., Nielsen, M.L., and Diderichsen, F. (2006). Multilevel analysis of workplace and individual risk factors for long-term sickness absence. *Journal of Occupational and Environmental Medicine*, 48, 923–928.

Lacoursiere, R.B. (1980). *The Life Cycle of Groups*. New York: Human Sciences Press.

Landy, F.J. (2005). Some historical and scientific issues related to research on emotional intelligence. *Journal of Organizational Behavior*, 26, 411–424.

Langan-Fox, J., Cooper, C., and Klimoski, R. (2007). *Research Companion to the Dysfunctional Workplace*. Cheltenham, Glos: Edward Elgar.

Latham, G.P. (2007). *Work Motivation: History, Theory, Research, and Practice*. Thousand Oaks, CA: Sage.

Latham, G.P., and Mann, S. (2006). 'Advances in the science of performance appraisal: Implications for practice.' In: G.P. Hodgkinson and J.K. Ford (Eds), *International Review of Industrial and Organizational Psychology*. Chichester: Wiley, Volume 21, 295–337.

Latham, G.P., and Pinder, C.C. (2005). Work motivation theory and research at the dawn of the twenty-first century. *Annual Review of Psychology*, 56, 485–516.

Lawrence, K.A. (2004). Why be creative? Motivation and copyright law in a digital era. *IP Central Review*, 1, 2. (http://ipcentral.info/review/v1n2lawrence.pdf.)

Lawrence, P.R., and Lorsch, J.W. (1986). *Organization and Environment*. Boston, MA: Harvard Business School Press.

Lazarus, R.S., and Folkman, S. (1984). *Stress, Appraisal, and Coping*. New York: Springer.

Levi, D. (2001). *Group Dynamics for Teams*. Thousand Oaks, CA: Sage.

Levinson, D.J. (1978). *The Seasons of a Man's Life*. New York: Ballantine Books.

Lewin, K. (1952). *Field Theory in Social Science*. New York: Harper and Row.

Leymann, H. (1990). Mobbing and psychological terror at workplaces. *Violence and Victims*, 5, 119–126.

Liden, R.C., Martin, C.L., and Parsons, C.K. (1993). Interviewer and applicant behaviours in employment interviews. *Academy of Management Journal*, 36, 372–386.

Locke, E.A. (1976). 'The nature and causes of job satisfaction.' In: M.D. Dunette (Ed.), *Handbook of Industrial and Organizational Psychology*. Chicago: Rand McNally, 1297–1349.

Locke, E.A. (2005). Why emotional intelligence is an invalid concept. *Journal of Organizational Behavior*, 26, 425–431.

Locke, E.A., and Latham, G.P. (1984). *Goal Setting: A Motivational Technique That Works?* Englewood Cliffs, NJ: Prentice Hall.

Locke, E.A., and Latham, G.P. (2002). Building a practically useful theory of goal setting and task motivation: A 35-year Odyssey. *American Psychologist*, 57, 705–717.

Loden, M. (1996). *Implementing Diversity*. Chicago, IL: Irwin.

Lombardo, M.M., and Eichinger, R.W. (2000). For Your Improvement: A Development and Coaching Guide, (3rd Ed.), 389. Lominger Ltd., Inc.

Lonner, W.J., and Malpass, R.S. (1994). *Psychology and Culture*. Boston, MA: Allyn and Bacon.

Loveday, B. (2006). Policing performance: The impact of performance measures and targets on police forces in England and Wales. *International Journal of Police Science and Management*, 8, 282–293.

Luft, J. (1984). *Group Processes: An Introduction to Group Dynamics*. Palo Alto, CA: Mayfield.

Luthans, F. (1992). *Organizational Behavior*, (6th Ed.). New York: McGraw-Hill.

Luthans, F. (2002a). Positive organizational behavior: Developing and maintaining psychological strengths. *Academy of Management Executive*, 16, 57–72.

Luthans, F. (2002b). The need for and meaning of positive organizational behavior. *Journal of Organizational Behavior*, 23, 695–706.

Mabey, C., and Iles, P. (2001). *Managing Learning*. London: Thompson Learning.

Macfarlane, D., Fortin, P., Fox, J., Gundry, S. Oshry, J., and Warren, E. (1997). Clinical and human resource planning for the downsizing of psychiatric hospitals: The British Columbia experience. *Psychiatric Quarterly*, 68, 25–42.

McAdams, D.P., and Pals, J.L. (2006). A new big five: Fundamental principles for an integrative science of personality. *American Psychologist*, 61, 204–217.

Maier, N.R.F. (1976). *The Appraisal Interview: Three Basic Approaches*. La Jolla, CA: University Associates.

Mani, B.G. (2002). Performance appraisal systems, productivity, and motivation: A case study. *Public Personnel Management*, 31, 141–159.

Mann, R. (1959). A review of the relationship between personality and performance in small groups. *Psychological Bulletin*, 56, 241–270.

Margerison, C.J., and McCann, D.J. (1990). *Team Management: Practical New Approaches*. London: Mercury Press.

Martin, D.C., Bartol, K.M., and Kehoe, P.E. (2000). The legal ramifications of performance appraisal: The growing significance. *Public Personnel Management*, 29, 379–405.

Maslow, A.H. (1970). *Motivation and Personality*, (2nd Ed.). New York: Harper.

Maslow, A.H. (1971). *The Farther Reaches of Human Nature*. New York: Viking.

May, D.R., Gilson, R.L., and Harter, L.M. (2004). The psychological conditions of meaningfulness, safety, and availability and the engagement of the human spirit at work. *Journal of Occupational and Organizational Psychology*, 77, 11–37.

Mayer, J.D., Caruso, D.R., and Salovey, P. (1999) Emotional intelligence meets traditional standards for an intelligence. *Intelligence*, 27, 267–298.

Mayer, J.D., Salovey, P., and Caruso, D. (2000). 'Competing models of emotional intelligence.' In: R.J. Sternberg (Ed.), *Handbook of Human Intelligence*. New York: Cambridge University Press, 396–420.

Mayer, R.C., Davis, J.H., and Schoorman, F.D. (1995). An integrative model of organizational trust. *Academy of Management Review*, 20, 709–732.

McClelland, D. (1955). *Studies in Motivation*. New York: Appleton-Century-Crofts.

McClelland, D. (1984). *Motives, Personality, and Society*. Now York: Praeger

McClelland, D. (1987). *Human Motivation*. Cambridge: Cambridge University Press.

McCrae, R.R., and Costa, P.T. (1997). Personality trait structure as human universal. *American Psychologist*, 52, 509–516.

McCrae, R.R. and Costa, P.T. Jr. (1995). Trait explanations in personality psychology. *European Journal of Personality*, 9, 231–252.

McEwen, B.S. (1998). Protecting and damaging effects of stress mediators. *New England Journal of Medicine*, 338, 171–179.

McGregor, D. (1960). *The Human side of Enterprise*. New York: McGraw Hill.

Middaugh, D.J. (2006). Presenteeism: Sick and tired at work. *Medsurg Nursing*, 15, 103–105.

Mikkelsen, G.E., and Einarsen, S. (2002). Basic assumptions and symptoms of post-traumatic stress among victims of bullying at work. *European Journal of Organizational and work psychology*, 11, 87–111.

Milkovich, G.T., and Boudreau, J.W. (1994). *Human Resource Management*, (7th Ed.). Burr Ridge, Illinois: Irwin.

Mintzberg, H. (1983). *Structure in Fives: Designing Effective Organizations*. Englewood Cliffs, NJ: Prentice Hall.

Moorhead, G., and Griffin, R.W. (1989). *Organizational Behaviour*, (2nd Ed.). Boston, MA: Houghton Mifflin.

Napier, R.W., and Gershenfeld, M.K. (1987). *Groups: Theory and Experience*. Boston, MA: Houghton-Mifflin.

Nelson, D., and Cooper, C. (2007). *Positive Organizational Behaviour*. London: Sage.

Nelson, D.L., and Simmons, B.L. (2003). 'Health psychology and work stress: A more positive approach.' In: J.C. Quick and L.E. Tetrick (Eds), *Handbook of Occupational Health Psychology*. Washington, DC: American Psychological Association, 97–119.

Nemetz, P.L., and Christensen, L. (1996). The challenge of cultural diversity: Harnessing a diversity of views to understand multiculturalism. *Academy of Management Review*, 21, 434–462.

Norman, W.T. (1963). Toward an adequate taxonomy of personality attributes. *Journal of Abnormal and Social Psychology*, 66, 574–583.

Northouse, P. (2001). *Leadership: Theory and Practice*, (2nd Ed.). London: Sage.

Notelaers, G., Einarsen, S., De Witte, H., and Vermunt, J.K. (2006). Measuring exposure to bullying at work: The validity and advantages of the latent class cluster approach. *Work and Stress*, 20, 289–302.

Oakland, T. (2004). Use of educational and psychological tests internationally. *Applied Psychology: An International Review*, 53, 157–172.

Odiorne, G.S. (1965). *Management by Objectives*. New York: Pitman.

Palmer, I., Dunford, R., and Akin, G. (2006). *Managing Organizational Change*. New York: McGraw Hill.

Paterson, T.T. (1972). *Job Evaluation*. London: Business Books, Volumes 1 and 2.

Pendry, L.F., Driscoll, D.M., and Field, S.C.T. (2007). Diversity training: Putting theory into practice. *Journal of Occupational and Organizational Psychology*, 80, 27–50.

Pervin, L., and Cooper, C. (1999). *Personality: Critical Concepts in Psychology*. London: Routledge.

Pervin, L.A., and John, O.P. (2001). *Personality: Theory and Research*, (8th Ed.). New York: Wiley.

Porter, L., and Lawler, E. (1968). *Managerial attitudes and performance*, Homewood, IL: Dorsey Press.

Putnam, L.L. (1988). 'Understanding the unique characteristics of groups within organizations.' In: R.S. Cathcart, and L.A. Samovar (Eds), *Small Group Communication*. Dubuque, Iowa: Wm. C. Brown, 76–85.

Quick, J.C., and Tetrick, L.E. (2003). *Handbook of Occupational Health Psychology*. Washington, DC: American Psychological Association.

Rahim, A.M. and Psenicka C. (1996). A structural equations model of stress, locus of control, social support, psychiatric symptoms, and propensity to leave a job. *The Journal of Social Psychology, 136*(1), 69–84.

Randall, P. (1997). *Adult Bullying: Perpetrators and Victims*. London: Routledge.

Raudsepp, E. (1992). Are you properly assertive? *Supervision*, 53, 17–18.

Rayner, C. (1997). The incidence of workplace bullying. *Journal of Community and Applied Social Psychology*, 7, 199–208.

Reese, R.J. (2006). Effects of a university career development course or career decision-making self-efficacy. *Journal of Career Assessment*, 14, 252–266.

Reynolds, P.D. (1984). Leaders never quit: Talking, silence and influence in interpersonal groups. *Small Group Behaviour*, 15, 404–413.

Robbins, S.P. (1996). *Organizational Behavior: Concepts, Controversies and Applications*, (7th Ed.). Englewood Cliffs, NJ: Prentice Hall.

Roberts, G.E. (1998). Perspectives in enduring and emerging issues in performance appraisal. *Public Personnel Management*, 27, 301–320.

Roe, R.A., and Ester, P. (1999). Values and work: Empirical findings and theoretical perspective. *Applied Psychology: An International Review*, 48(1), 1–21.

Roe, R.A., Zinovieva, R.A.R., Dienes, E., and Ten Horn, L.A. (2000). A comparison of work motivation in Bulgaria, Hungary, and the Netherlands. *Applied Psychology: An International Journal*, 49, 658–687.

Rokeach, M. (1973). *The Nature of Human Values*. New York: Free Press.

Rosenfeld, P., Giacolone, R., and Riordan, C. (2002). *Impression Management*. London: Thomson Publishing.

Rotter, J.B. (1966). Generalised expectancies for internal versus external control of reinforcement. *Psychological Monographs*, 80, 1–28.

Rushmer, R.K. (1997). How do we measure the effectiveness of team building? Is it good enough? Team management systems: A case study. *Journal of Management Development*, 16, 93–110.

Russell, J.A., Bachorowski, J., and Fernandez-Dols, J. (2003). Facial and vocal expressions of emotion. *Annual Review of Psychology*, 54, 329–349.

Ryan, A.M. (2003). Defining ourselves: I/O psychology's identity quest. *The Industrial–Organizational Psychologist*, 41, 21–33.

Ryff, C.D., and Singer, B. (1998). The contours of positive human health. *Psychological Inquiry*, 9, 1–28.

Rynes, S.L., Gerhart, B., and Parks, L. (2005). Personnel psychology: Performance evaluation and pay for performance. *Annual Review of Psychology*, 56, 571–600.

Salas, E., Stagl, K., and Burke, C. (2004). '25 years of team effectiveness in organizations.' In: C. Cooper, and I.T. Robertson (Eds), *International Review of Industrial and Organizational Psychology*. Chichester: Wiley, 47–93.

Salgado, J.F. (1997). The five factor model of personality and job performance in the European Community. *Journal of Applied Psychology*, 82, 30–43.

Salovey, P., and Mayer, J. (1990). Emotional intelligence. *Imagination, Cognition, and Personality*, 9, 185–211.

Saucier, G. (2003). An alternative multi-language structure for personality attributes. *European Journal of Personality*, 17, 179–205.

Schabracq, M. (2005). 'Well-being and health: What HRM can do about it.' In: R. Burke and C. Cooper (Eds), *Reinventing HRM: Challenges and New Directions*. London: Routledge, 187–206.

Schabracq, M.J., Winnubst, J.A.M., and Cooper, C.L. (2003). *The Handbook of Work and Health Psychology*. Chichester: Wiley.

Schaufeli, W.B., and Bakker, A.B. (2004). Job demands, job resources and their relationship with burnout and engagement: A multi-sample study. *Journal of Organizational Behavior*, 25, 293–315.

Schein, E.H. (1969). *Process Consultation*. Reading, MA: Addison Wesley, Volume 1.

Schein, E.H. (1980). *Organizational Psychology*, (3rd Ed.). Englewood Cliffs, NJ: Prentice Hall.

Schein, E.H. (1983). The role of the founder in creating an organizational culture. *Organizational Dynamics*, 12, 13–28.

Schein, E.H. (1985). *Organisation Culture and Leadership*. San Francisco, CA: Jossey-Bass.

Schein, E.H. (1990). Organizational Culture. *American Psychologist*, 45, 109–119.

Schein, E. (1996). Career anchors revisited. *Academy of Management Review*, 10, 80–88.

Schmidt, F.L., and Hunter, J.E. (1981). Employment testing: Old theories and new research findings. *American Psychologist*, 36, 1128–1137.

Schmidt, F.L., and Hunter, J.E. (1998). The validity and utility of selection methods in personnel psychology: Practical and theoretical implications of 85 years of research findings. *Psychological Bulletin*, 124, 262–274.

Schneider, B., Goldstein, H.W., and Smith, D.B. (1995). The ASA framework: An update. *Personnel Psychology*, 48, 747–773.

Schneider, K.T., Swan, S., and Fitzgerald, L.F. (1997). Job-related and psychological effects of sexual harassment in the workplace: Empirical evidence from two organizations. *Journal of Applied Psychology*, 82, 401–415.

Schwartz, S.H. (1994a). *Packet for Participation in Cross-Cultural Research on Values*. Department of Psychology, The Hebrew University.

Schwartz, S.H. (1994b). 'Beyond individualism/collectivism: New cultural dimensions of values.' In: U. Kim, H.C. Triandis, S.C. Kagiticibasi, G. Choi and G. Yoon (Eds), *Individualism and Collectivism: Theory, Method and Applications*. London: Sage, 85–119.

Schwartz, S.H. (1999). A theory of cultural values and some implications for work. *Applied Psychology: An International Review*, 48, 23–47.

Schutz, W.C. (1978). *FIRO awareness scales manual.* Palo Alto, CA: Consulting Psychologists Press.

Searle, S.J. (1997). 'Sickness absence: Facts and misconceptions.' In: H.A. Waldron and C. Edling (Eds), *Occupational Health Practice.* Oxford: Butterworth-Heinemann, 112–113.

Seligman, M.E.P. (2002). *Authentic Happiness: Using the New Positive Psychology to Realize Your Potential for Lasting Fulfillment.* London: Nicholas Brealey.

Seligman, M.E.P., and Csikszentmihalyi, M. (2000). Positive psychology: An introduction. *American Psychologist,* 55, 5–14.

Senge, P.M. (1990). *The Fifth Discipline: The Art and Practice of the Learning Organisation.* New York: Doubleday/Currencey.

Siu, O., Phillips, D.R., and Leung, T. (2004). Safety climate and performance among construction workers in Hong Kong: The role of psychological strain as mediators. *Accident Analysis and Prevention,* 36, 359–366.

Sizoo, S. (2006). A comparison of the effect of intercultural sensitivity on employee performance in cross-cultural service encounters: London vs. Florida. *Journal of Euromarketing,* 15, 77–100.

Smith, P., Fischer, R., and Sale, N. (2001). 'Cross-cultural industrial/organizational psychology.' In: C.L. Cooper and I.T. Robertson (Eds), *International Review of Industrial and Organisational Psychology.* Chichester, UK: Wiley, Volume 16, Chapter 5.

Smith, P.B., and Bond, M.H. (1993). *Social Psychology Across Cultures.* Cambridge, UK: Harvester Wheatsheaf, University Press.

Snyder, C.R., and Lopez, S.J. (2002). *Handbook of Positive Psychology.* Oxford, UK: Oxford University Press.

Snyman, J.R., and Sommers, De K. (1999). *Mims Disease Review.* Pretoria: MIMS.

Sonnentag, S., Niessen, C., and Ohly, S. (2004). 'Learning at work: Training and development.' In: C. Cooper and I. Robertson (Eds), *International Review of Industrial and Organizational Psychology.* Chichester, UK: Wiley, 249–289.

Spears, J.C., and Lawrence, M. (2004). *Practicing Servant Leadership: Succeeding Through Trust, Bravery, and Forgiveness.* San Francisco: Jossey-Bass.

Spector, P.E. (1986). Perceived control by employees: A meta-analysis of studies concerning autonomy and participation at work. *Human Relations,* 39, 1005–1016.

Spreitzer, G.M. (1995). Psychological empowerment in the workplace: Dimensions, measurement, and validation. *Academy of Management Journal,* 38, 1442–1465.

Staw, B.M., and Ross, J. (1985). Stability in the midst of change: A dispositional approach to job attitudes. *Journal of Applied Psychology,* 70, 469–480.

Steers, R.M., and Porter, L.W. (1991). *Motivation and Work Behaviour,* (5th Ed.). New York: McGraw-Hill.

Sternberg, R. (1994). *In Search of the Human Mind.* New York: Harcourt Brace.

Strümpfer, D.J.W. (1995). The origins of health and strength: From 'salutogenesis' to 'fortigenesis'. *South African Journal of Psychology,* 25, 81–89.

Strümpfer, D.J.W., Danana, N., Gouws, J.F., and Viviers, M.R. (1998). Personality dispositions and job satisfaction. *South African Journal of Psychology,* 28, 92–100.

Sue-Chan, C, and Latham, G.P. (2004). The relative effectiveness of external, peer, and self-coaches. *Applied Psychology: An International Review,* 53, 260–278.

Sundstrom, E., De Meuse, K.P., and Futrell, D. (1990). Work teams: Applications and effectiveness. *American Psychologist,* 45, 120–133.

Swanson, R.A., and Holton, E.F. (2001). *Foundations of Human Resource Development.* New York: Berrett-Koehler.

Szilagyi, A., and Wallace, M. (1987). *Organizational Behavior and Performance,* (4th Ed.). Glenview, IL: Scott, Foresman and Co.

Tannenbaum, R., and Schmidt, W.H. (1958). How to choose a leadership pattern. *Harvard Business Review,* 36, 95–101.

Tasho, W., Jordan, W., and Robertson, I. (2005). *Case study: Establishing the Business Case for Investing in Stress Prevention Activities and Evaluating Their Impact on Sickness Absence Levels.* London: Health and Safety Executive.

Tellegen, A., and Waller, N.G. (1995). 'Exploring personality through test construction: Development of the multidimensional personality questionnaire.' In: S.R. Briggs and J.M. Cheek (Eds), *Personality Measures, Development and Evaluation.* Greenwich, CT: JAI Press, Volume 1, 23–42.

Tett, R.P., Jackson, D.N., and Rothstein, M. (1991). Personality measures as predictors of job performance: A meta-analytic review. *Personnel Psychology,* 44, 703–742.

Theobald, T., and Cooper, C. (2004). *Shut Up and Listen: How to Communicate at Work*. London: Kogan Page.

Thomas, R.R. (1996). *Redefining Diversity*. New York: Amacom.

Tierney, L.M., Mcphee, S.J., and Papadakis, M.A. (1999). *Current Medical Diagnosis and Treatment*, (38th Ed.). Stamford, Connecticut: Appleton and Lange.

Tinsley, H.E.A. (2000). The congruence myth: An analysis of the efficacy of the person-environment fit model. *Journal of Vocational Behavior*, 56, 147–179.

Triandis, H.C. (1994). *Cultural and Social Behaviour*. New York: McGraw-Hill.

Trist, E.H., Murray, B.J., and Pollack, A. (1963). *Organizational Choice*. London: Tavistock.

Trist, E.L., and Bamforth, K.W. (1951). Some social and psychological consequences of the long-wall method of goal-setting. *Human Relations*, 4, 3–38.

Trower, P. (1990). Situational analysis of the components and processes of behavior in socially skilled and unskilled patients. *Journal of Consulting and Clinical Psychology*, 48, 327–339.

Turner, N., Barling, J., and Zacharatos, A. (2002). 'Positive psychology at work.' In: C.R. Snyder and S.J. Lopez (Eds), *Handbook of Positive Psychology*. Oxford, UK: Oxford University Press, 715–728.

Van der Molen, H., and Gramsbergen-Hoogland, Y.H. (2005). *Communication in Organization: Basic Skills and Conversation Models*. New York: Psychology Press.

Van Knippenberg, D., and Schippers, M.C. (2007). Work group diversity. *Annual Review of Psychology*, 58, 515–541.

Voskuijl, O., Evers, A., Anderson, N., and Smit-Voskuijl, O. (2005). *Blackwell Handbook of Personnel Selection*. Oxford: Blackwell Publishing.

Vroom, V.H. (1964). *Work and Motivation*. New York: Wiley.

Walumbwa, F.O., Lawler, J.J., and Avolio, B.J. (2007). Leadership, individual differences, and work-related attitudes. *Applied Psychology: An International Review*, 56, 212–230.

Warr, P. (2002). 'Learning and training.' In: P. Warr (Ed.), *Psychology at Work*, (5th Ed.). London: Penguin Books, 153–177.

Warr, P. (2007). *Work, Happiness, and Unhappiness*. London: Lawrence Erlbaum.

Warr, P., and Pearce, A. (2004). Preferences for careers and organisational cultures as a function of logically related personality traits. *Applied Psychology: An International Review*, 53, 423–435.

Watkins, M.L. (2001). Industrial psychology: An identity crises and future direction. *South African Journal of Industrial Psychology*, 27, 8–13.

Watson, D., Clark, L.A., and Tellegen, A. (1988). Development and validation of brief measures of positive and negative affect: The PANAS scales. *Journal of Personality and Social Psychology*, 54, 1063–1070.

Weick, K. (2000). 'Emergent change as a universal in organizations.' In: M. Beer, and N. Nohria (Eds), *Breaking the Code of Change*. Boston: HBS Press, 223–224.

Weick, K.E. (1985). 'The significance of corporate culture.' In: P.J. Frost, L.F. Moore, M.R. Louis, C.C. Lundberg and J. Martin (Eds), *Organizational Culture*. Beverly Hills, CA: Sage, 381–390.

Weinberg, A., and Cooper, C. (2007). *Surviving the Workplace: A Guide to Emotional Well-being*. London: Thomson.

Werner, J.M., and Bolino, M.C. (1997). Explaining US courts of appeals decisions involving performance appraisal: Accuracy, fairness, and validation. *Personnel Psychology*, 50, 1–24.

Wechsler, D. (1944). *The measurement of adult intelligence* (3rd Ed.). Baltimore: Williams & Wilkins.

Wexley, K.N., and Latham, G.P. (1991). *Developing and Training Human Resources in Organizations*, (2nd Ed.). New York: HarperCollins.

Whetzel, D.L., and Wheaton, G.R. (2007). *Applied Measurement: Industrial Psychology in Human Resources Management*. Mahwah, NJ: Lawrence Erlbaum.

Whyte, W.F. (1955). *Money and Motivation*. New York: Harper.

Wiggam, A.E. (1931). 'The biology of leadership.' In: H.C. Metcalf (Ed.), *Business Leadership*. New York: Pitman.

Wood, R.E., and Bandura, A. (1989). Impact of conceptions of ability on self-regulatory mechanisms and complex decision-making. *Journal of Personality and Social Psychology*, 56, 407–415.

Wright, G.E., and Multon, K.D. (1995). Employer's perceptions on nonverbal communication in job interviews for persons with disabilities. *Journal of Vocational Behavior*, 47, 214–227.

Wright, P.L. (1996). *Managerial Leadership*. London: Routledge.

Wright, T.A. (2003). Positive organizational behavior: An idea whose time has truly come. *Journal of Organizational Behavior*, 24, 437–442.

Wright, T.A., and Cropanzano, R. (2000). The role of organizational behaviour in occupational health psychology: A view as we approach the millennium. *Journal of Occupational Health Psychology*, 5, 5–10.

Wright, T.A., and Wright, V.P. (2002). Organizational researcher values, ethical responsibility, and the committed to participant perspective. *Journal of Management Inquiry*, 11, 173–185.

Yukl, G.A. (2006). *Leadership in Organizations*, (6th Ed.). Upper Saddle River, NJ: Prentice-Hall.

Zaleznik, A. (1993). 'Managers and leaders: Are they different.' In: W.E. Rosenbach and R.L. Taylor (Eds), *Contemporary Issues in Leadership*. Oxford: Westview Press, 36–56.

Index